# THE IMMIGRATION OF IDEAS

O. FRITIOF ANDER

# The Immigration of Ideas

*Studies in the North Atlantic Community*

Essays Presented to

O. FRITIOF ANDER

Edited by

J. IVERNE DOWIE

and

J. THOMAS TREDWAY

AUGUSTANA HISTORICAL SOCIETY

ROCK ISLAND, ILLINOIS

1968

AUGUSTANA HISTORICAL SOCIETY

*Publication No. 21*

---



Library of Congress Catalog Card Number: 68-28713

PRINTED IN U.S.A.



WAGNERS PRINTERS
DAVENPORT, IOWA

# *Foreword*

Augustana College is itself a product of the "immigration of ideas." At the outset the College sought to serve its people by preserving the traditions of the old world. However, pioneers from Scandinavia became part of a wider and more diverse community when they came to America. Their children and their children's children have moved again, not geographically so much as culturally, into the main stream of American life. The story of the College reflects this movement. Now the perimeter of influence of the College marks the wider world of contemporary American society.

Several of the essays in this volume focus upon persons who came to live in a new world intellectually as well geographically. Others are concerned directly with the movement of ideas across the Atlantic. Heretofore the Augustana Historical Society has devoted its publications almost exclusively to the Scandinavian-American milieu. This volume enlarges the field of the society's concern by including certain aspects of English and German intellectual history. The writers have responded to contemporary trends in immigration historiography with its emphasis upon the role of the immigrant in the intellectual as well as the social history of Europe and America.

The roster of contributors to this volume clearly indicates the esteem in which O. Fritiof Ander is held by historians. These forms of recognition seem most appropriate for a scholar whose teaching and research have been largely in the field to which this book is devoted. Now, four decades after Professor Ander began to teach and write history, his friends and colleagues present these essays to him with the hope that the happiness which comes from a productive life in the company of those who respect him may continue in the days and years to come.

C. W. SORENSEN, *President*
Augustana College

# *Introduction*

In the western tradition wondering and wandering have frequently arisen in company with one another. Whatever the cause-effect relationship between them, geographical and intellectual exploration and expansion seem to have been bound together, whether in Homeric Greece, the Renaissance, or the Space Age. Over the bodies of the Athenian dead, Pericles told his fellow citizens that "Our adventurous spirit has forced an entry into every land and sea," and it does no injustice to the other great cultural traditions of the world to inscribe that statement over the entire history of the West. It is one part of the restless movement of men and ideas in the Occident to which the Augustana Historical Society devotes this volume, the twenty-first in a series begun in 1931.

The title of the volume is perhaps pretentious, and the editors want to make it clear at the outset that this book makes no claim to being exhaustive; a glance at the Table of Contents will make that plain enough. These essays focus only upon facets, chosen by the contributors themselves, of the movement of people and thought from northern Europe to North America. Some are studies of individuals whose lives as well as their ideas witness to the relationship between the immigration of the body and that of the spirit. Others are concerned with those strands which bind intellectual movements in Europe and America together. But all are studies in the "Immigration of Ideas," and thus the title.

Few other themes would have been as appropriate to honor O. Fritiof Ander, we think. His own life represents that movement from Europe to America which we have asked our essayists to examine. His professional career has been spent in an institution whose life has been nourished by the transplantation of men and ideas. And at Augustana for thirty-five years Professor Ander's teaching and research were focused upon the areas of intellectual and immigration history. And so the theme.

In all frankness the editors of this volume must report that the intellectual concerns of the members of the Augustana Historical Society are more impressive than the modest resources of the organization. We are fortunate in having a roster of friends who have supported us in this publication, particularly the Swedish Pioneer Historical Society. We acknowledge with special appreciation the counsel and tangible support of President C. W. Sorensen and Augustana College. Ernest Espelie has assisted us in this enterprise at many important points. We recognize the careful preparation which Kathy Milton gave to manuscripts and galley proof on their way to the press. The editors wish to thank Ben Jasper for his design of the jacket for this book.

J. I. D. and J. T. T.

# *Table of Contents*

# *On the Meaning of Faith in the Great Awakening and the Methodist Revival*

Ross Paulson

The existence of a transatlantic triangle of influence among the leaders of the great pietistic revivals of the 1730s and 1740s has been noted frequently by historians interested in the development of American cultural and intellectual patterns.[1] From this fact has sprung the truism that the Great Awakening was not a unique colonial phenomenon but "merely one variant of a universal occurrence in Western culture." At the same time, the Great Awakening is viewed as a "turning point, a 'crisis,' in the history of American civilization" and the beginning of a new era in the evolution of the American Mind.[2] While attention has been focused on the role of transatlantic influences in determining the revivalistic *form* of the Great Awakening and of the Methodist movement, it is equally important to determine the contribution of transatlantic influences in shaping the evangelical *content* of revival theology.

On both sides of the Atlantic the initial spark that ignited the fires of revival was the proclamation of the doctrine of justification by faith in bold and dramatic new ways by key figures: Jonathan Edwards, George Whitefield, and John Wesley.[3] The phrase "justification by faith" is deceptively simple, however, and lends itself to various interpretations depending on the signification of the last term. Is faith the gift of God through grace or man's achievement? In the perspective of intellectual history, the crucial question is this: if the pietistic revivals of the early eighteenth century are to be regarded as great awakenings of *faith,* what did faith mean to them? A semantic analysis of the meaning of the term faith in its theological and psychological setting will provide a convenient microcosm for the larger problem of the acculturation.[4]

The New England Puritans, through their early contacts with the Rhineland Protestants, were familiar with the Lutheran formula: salvation by grace, justification by faith, and sanctification by the spirit. The thrust of this movement was from God to Man. Good works did not earn or merit salvation; but the just would do good works for the neighbor. This theological perspective drove them to confront a psychological problem: how did men know if they had faith.[5]

The seventeenth century Puritans had been limited in their ability to answer this question by their psychological theories. Elizabethan psychology posited a trichotomous nature of man: body, mind, and spirit (or soul). In the natural man, the body was subject to the passions, the mind to reason, and the soul to the will. When invaded by God's grace the natural man experienced the miracle of regeneration. Grace "calmed and assuaged the passions, rectified the will, opened the eye of reason to spiritual truths, and by cleansing the motives enabled men to practice true charity in their daily lives."[6] Grace was a total psychological revolution wrought by a supernatural act of God.

The possibility of a purely psychological understanding of faith was ruled out, however, by their theology and their understanding of reason. The humanistic logic of Petrus Ramus, which exercised so profound an influence on the Puritan mind, stressed the role of reason in achieving the security of faith. Though faith ultimately came from God, yet He respected man's humanity and worked through reasonable inducements. Faith was, therefore, reason elevated by grace; it was not an irrational intoxication of the spirit. The essence of faith was rational perception; it was *belief that* God was just and righteous. The hallmark of such faith was the absence of doubt.[7]

That men need have no doubt about the faithfulness of God was the inner meaning of Puritan covenant theology. God had promised in the covenant of grace to supply the means of faith. If a man could prove that he had faith, then he could rely on God's promise. The rhetoric of the early Puritan sermons was designed to convince men of the reasonableness and faithfulness of God. But an increasingly ritualistic invocation of the covenant robbed the believer of that radical sense of insecurity that had prompted the original inquiry into the mystery of redemption.[8]

In the intervening century between the Great Migration and the Great Awakening, the tensions inherent in this system of thought exerted a subtle pressure on Puritanism. Rather than being the gift of grace which freed men from sin and damnation, faith gradually came to be understood as the condition of a covenant which bound God to its terms. As the memory of persecution in England faded, as political events in England settled temporarily the question of the nature of English society, and as the task of accommodating to the New World environment became acute, something happened to Puritanism. The passions flared in sporadic social conflicts, the will to believe flagged and waned, the eye of reason no longer discerned spiritual truths as the heresies of Arminianism and Deism exalted reason unduly. The motives of men scrambling for wealth in a chaotic and shifting mercantile economy seemed no longer to turn toward true Christian charity. Whatever the causes, the symptoms all added up to one grand conclusion for Puritan preachers in the decades prior to the Great Awakening: declension of the faith.[9]

When the inherited ideas of a culture no longer correspond to its perceived realities, men are especially open to new intellectual influences. Such was the case in New England in the beginning of the eighteenth century. Yet men do not respond uniformly to new ideas. A Samuel Johnson might flee the aridity of Puritanism for the humane reasonableness of English letters, a Benjamin Franklin might find the deistic arguments in imported books more convincing than their "orthodox" refutations, a Timothy Cutler might embrace Anglicanism, but a Cotton Mather could bend imported ideas to support the shell of orthodoxy at the same time that he subtly changed its substance.[10]

By the first decade of the new century, Mather had resolved to rekindle the fires of Puritanism not with the fierce winds of doctrinal dispute but with the gentler breezes of pietism. Probably through the influence of Anthony William Boehme (1673-1722), a German tutor in England, Cotton Mather became acquainted with the works of such German pietists as Johann Arndt, Bartholomew Ziegenbalg, and August Herman Francke of Halle.[11] On December 9, 1709, Mather recorded in his diary: "My intention was, to lodge these Treatises [the *Heavenly Conversation* and *Dust and Ashes*] in ye Hands of many Ministers, throughout ye country. I represented ye methods of *piety* proposed in these Essayes, as being ye new American *pietism.* I shall also endeavor to send these things unto Dr. Franckius, in Saxony."[12]

Perry Miller's conclusion that Mather's pietism originated "entirely out of the exigencies of New England society, owing little (except for English examples of reforming societies) to extraneous influences," seems strained in the light of Mather's transatlantic contacts.[13] The *need* for the new theology emerging from the New England context does not rule out the possibility that transatlantic influences helped to shape the *content.* The pertinent questions for research are these: How did Cotton Mather see his relation to German pietism? Did he incorporate anything from German pietism into his own thought? In particular, what was Mather's concept of faith and how did it compare with Francke's view?

In his pamphlet of 1710 entitled *Heavenly Conversation,* Mather introduced his readers to the essence of the new theology:

> Reader, Behold an Essay, which may be Entitled, *American Pietism.* As there is a *Fanatick,* so there is an *Orthodox,* a *Reformed,* and Heavenly Pietism. It wrote [sic.], yea, and [has] *Wrought,* Wondrous Things in the midst of Europe formerly. By *Taulerus,* and *Besoldus,* and *John Arndt,* and others, the Spirit of God breathed excellent Things upon His Chosen in the World. It is now again *Doing Wondrously.* Go on, my dear *Franckius,* and thy coadjustors. The Lord is with you, ye mighty men of Piety! A people formed and filled by that SPIRIT OF CHRIST and REPENTENCE, will shortly do the part of the stone cut out of the Mountain. Oh! May the whole Earth be filled with it![14]

Moving quickly to the doctrine of justification by faith, Mather showed that it did not free men from the moral law and that "the same *Faith* which lays hold on the Righteousness of a Christ, that a sinner may be *justified,* will also fly to Him, for to be *Sanctified,* and for *Grace* and *Strength* to subdue corruption." This faith is no mere inference of reason, but a vital touch on the heart.[15] In laying the stress on sanctification, Mather broached the touchy subject of good works. Was he saying that good works could merit justification? No, for he asserted the orthodox view as a premise to his next study, *Bonifacius;* no good works could be done until a man had been justified. Then he moved on to his main point: "And then, Secondly, Tho' we are *Justified* by a *Precious Faith* in the *Righteousness of God our Savior;* yet Good Works are demanded of us, to *Justify* our *Faith;* to *Demonstrate,* that it is indeed that *Precious Faith . . .*"[16] Here was the slogan with which Mather *hoped* to revive New England Puritanism and to end the declension of faith: "A *Workless Faith* is a *Worthless Faith.*"[17] Henceforth, sanctification would be taken as evidence of justification. The true test of faith would be physical, not just psychological.

In spite of Mather's efforts the revival did not come to New England. In 1716 he recorded in his diary:

> April 19. Quaere, whether ye *Marvellous Footsteps of Ye Divine Providence* [an illusion to Francke's *Segensvolle Fusstapfen,* 1701] in what has been done in ye *Lower Saxony,* have not such a voice in ye World, that I may do well to think of some farther methods, to render it more sensible unto these American Colonists.[18]

It is clear from his correspondence with Boehme that Mather regarded American Puritanism and German pietism to be of one piece, yet one may wonder whether he fully understood Francke's concept of faith. Francke, influenced by the German mystical tradition, saw faith as union with God, participation in the fullness of His divinity which lifted men above fear into the perfect faith that could overcome all obstacles. In short, perfection was something given by God, not something achieved by man. Mather, for all his sentimental rhetoric and belief in particular faith (private emotional renewal of the elect), could not escape the rationalistic tradition of the covenant theology and make faith anything other than a personal and public committment to the inherited structure of Puritanism. In spite of these differences, in 1726, in one of his last great works, Mather was still invoking the authority of Francke to buttress his own system of pietism.[19]

While Cotton Mather attempted unsuccessfully to use German pietism as a goad for a revival of New England Puritanism, Jonathan Edwards made his own appropriation of transatlantic influences. Perry Miller has shown how as a young man Edwards grasped the essential logic of Lockean psychology and Newtonian naturalism and used them to restore Puritanism to its basic Reformation committment to the sovereignty of God and the dependency of man. In the process, he also redefined the nature of faith.

In his 1733-1734 sermons on justification by faith and the nature of grace, Edwards asserted that faith was not simply reason elevated by grace but a true perception of the reality of God's presence in the world. Faith existed in the total sequence of salvation but not as the "cause," in mechanistic terms, or the "occasion," in scholastic terms, of justification.[20] Rather, it was "a true sense of the divine excellency of the things revealed in the word of God, and a conviction of the truth and reality of them thence arising." The spiritually enlightened man, therefore, "does not merely rationally believe that God is glorious, but he has a sense of the gloriousness of God in his heart."[21] There was a difference, Edwards asserted, between having an opinion based on reasonable inference (belief that) and having a conviction based on sensible perception (belief in).

Edwards thus supplemented the trichotomous psychology of original Puritanism with the Lockean notion of sensation to create a new understanding of grace: that which was given, beyond man, but which worked within the economy of the human psyche. Henceforth, emotional sanctions, the beauty of holy affections, would warrant the reality of the religious experience. However vague it might be to talk about the head (reason) and the heart (will), the impact of Edward's innovation was clear enough: Instead of reaching notional assent of rational propositions, Edwards wanted men to achieve personal assurance through the perceived realities of experience.

Edwards was, however, no mere enthusiast bent on giving the emotions free play. The fruits of the spirit had to be tested to see which ones were genuine or "gracious." This was the problem that Edwards later explored at length in *The Distinguishing Marks of a Work of the Spirit of God* (1741) and *A Treatise Concerning Religious Affections* (1746). Edward's first opportunity to examine the question of the genuineness of conversion experiences had come in 1735-1736 when his letter to Benjamin

Colman on the Northampton revival was published in Boston and in London. This work was destined to have an influential, if somewhat obscure, role in the transatlantic triangle of influences that created the great evangelical revivals of the next decade in England and the New World.

At the same time that Jonathan Edwards had been viewing the doctrine of justification by faith under the light of Locke and Newton, the Wesley brothers and George Whitefield had discovered Francke's works on pietism. In 1734, when Whitefield was studying at Pembroke College, Oxford, he contrived to meet the Wesley brothers, whose reputation as leaders of the Holy Club had attracted his attention. Charles Wesley gave him a copy of Francke's *Nicodemus* along with some other works on pietism. These led, indirectly, to Whitefield's conversion experience in 1735. John Wesley also had discovered Francke's works and took a copy of *Nicodemus* with him on the voyage to his new duties in Georgia.[22] The reactions of the two men varied, but the encounter with Francke's pietism did have long-range effects on their conceptions of faith and, therefore, on the great revivals.

In Whitefield's case exposure to pietism provided the key phrase of his theological position, "new birth." His first published work in 1737 was entitled, *The New Nature, and the Necessity of our New Birth in Christ Jesus in Order to Salvation.* But the "boy preacher" had not yet developed his full theological position as he himself acknowledged in his Journal in 1737:

> The doctrine of the new birth and justification by faith in Jesus Christ (though I was not so clear in it as afterwards) made its way like lightening into the hearer's consciences . . .[23]

When two young men tried to argue with Whitefield about the doctrine of regeneration, he outwitted them by exposing their own confusions and countered with the "Methodist" doctrine of the indwelling of the Spirit.[24]

This latter doctrine not only opened Methodism to the charges of enthusiasm and mysticism but also raised the troubling problem of the genuineness of conversion experiences. If grace, which was necessary for sanctification, was the impress of the Holy Spirit upon the heart, how did one know that he had such saving grace? In his sermon, *The Marks of the new Birth,* Whitefield addressed himself to the issue:

> Acts XX.V Have ye received the Holy Ghost since ye believed?

> I shall shew who the Holy *Ghost* here spoken of is, and how we must all receive him before we can be styled[?] true Believers. Secondly, I shall lay down some Scripture Marks *whereby* we know, whether we have thus received the Holy Ghost or not. Thirdly, By the way of Conclusion, I shall address myself to several distinct classes of Professors, concerning the Doctrine that shall have been delivered.[25]

The scriptural marks recapitulated the perfectionist standard inherent in pietism: a spirit of prayer, avoidance of willful sin, conquest of worldliness, neighborly love, and love of the enemy. In spite of the emphasis on the Calvinist doctrine of election that Whitefield added to his theology, the Arminian implications of his concept of faith continued to crop up in his rhetoric. Faith was an act of will made possible by the gift of God's grace to those who yearned for it. "Repent therefore and be converted, that your Sins may be blotted out," he cried. "See that you receive the Holy Ghost before you go hence . . ."[26] This was the slogan that he carried to New England on his fateful voyage in 1739.

John Wesley's struggle with the pietistic conception of faith was neither so short lived nor so conclusive as that of his young disciple. Wesley had returned to England from Georgia in 1738. In his journal Wesley brooded over his failure in Georgia and confided:

> It is now two years and almost four months since I left my native country in order to teach the Georgian Indians the nature of Christianity. But what have I learned myself in the meantime? Why, what I the least of all suspected, that I, who went to America to convert others, was never myself converted to God . . .
>
> Does all I ever did or can *know, say, give, do* or *suffer,* justify me in his sight? Yea, or the "constant use of all the means of grace" (which, nevertheless, is "meet, right and our bounden duty")? Or that "I know nothing of myself [I Cor. 4:4]; that I am, as touching outward, moral righteousness, blameless? Or (to come closer yet) the having a "rational conviction" of all the truths of Christianity? Does all this give me a claim to the holy, heavenly, divine character of a Christian? By no means, if the oracles of God are true . . .[27]

In characteristic Anglican fashion Wesley had distinguished between the faith of adherence (faithfulness in the use of the sacraments) and the faith of assurance (psychological certitude), between rational conviction (belief that) and emotional sanction (belief in), between faith as trust and faith as hope.

Then came Aldersgate. Wesley's continuing dialogue with the Moravian Brethern and his hearing of the reading of Luther's preface to the epistle to the Romans led to the moving personal experience that has been described as his "tower experience." The profound conviction of sin as the total orientation of man toward God that preceded his conversion experience was a sobering insight for a man raised in the perfectionist tradition of sin as particular atomistic acts or faults to be corrected. He had discovered the theological and psychological dimensions of faith as a right relation with God and a sense of personal assurance resting on the sure promise of God. Yet he still lacked something. "I walked in peace but not in joy," he recorded in his journal. What still troubled him was the question of sanctification. If the faith which brought a *private* sense of assurance was a gift of God and not the achievement of man, was not the *public* dimension of that faith the responsibility and, hence, the achievement of man?[28]

On October 9, 1738, while walking from Hut to Oxford, John Wesley read Jonathan Edwards' narrative of the Northampton revivals. Wesley was so struck with the theme of the book that he sent an extract of it to a friend. In the letter Wesley raised the issue of "the state of those who are 'weak in faith.'" From his journal and his correspondence during this period, Wesley's concern with sanctification seems to have been the point that attracted him to Edwards' theology. After Aldersgate he had a sense of *personal* assurance (however much it might waiver in periods of self-doubt.) What he lacked was a sense of *public* consecration on his efforts. "I have not that joy in the Holy Ghost; no settled, lasting joy," he wrote. "Nor have I such a peace as excludes the possibility either of fear or doubt."[29] He had trust, but he did not yet have unbounded hope.

Jonathan Edward's *Narrative* may have helped Wesley to see the fruits of faith as a public sign or witness of the presence of the Holy Spirit. A conversion was essentially private; a revival was inherently public. Edwards' account stressed the reign of love in Northampton that accompanied the revival. "Surely 'this is the Lord's doing, and it is marvelous in our eyes,'" Wesley wrote.[30] Could it be that sanctification (or perfection in good works) was also a gift of God and not, as his Moravian friends seemed to imply, a necessary condition of repentance?

Like all genuine ecumenical encounters, Wesley's confrontation with Edwards' thought drove him to inquire more deeply into his tradition.[31] In November, 1738, Wesley "began more narrowly to inquire what the doctrine of the Church of England is concerning the much-controverted point of justification by faith."[32] Following a concise restatement of the Homilies of the Church of England on the doctrine of justification by faith as a gift of God's grace, Wesley elaborated the distinction between dead faith and lively faith to settle the issue of sanctification:

> For [true] Christian faith is not only [a belief of] all the things of God which are contained in Holy Scripture, but also an earnest trust and confidence in God that he is careful over us as the father is over the child whom he [loveth] . . . [And this true faith, when we consider] what God hath done for us, is also *moved through continual assistance of the Spirit of God* to serve and please him, to keep his favour, to fear his displeasure, to continue his obedient children, showing thankfulness by observing his commandments; considering how, clearly without [our] deservings, we have freely received his mercy and pardon.[33]

It was a matter more of tone and emphasis than of substance, but it completed the development of Wesley's theological system.

Shortly thereafter George Whitefield returned from New England, fresh from his triumphal tour, and persuaded Wesley to join him in outdoor preaching at Bristol. The Methodist revival began and Wesley was caught up in its dynamics. Fortunately the content of Wesley's theology had been fixed before its revivalistic form was thrust upon it.

The subsequent falling out between Whitefield and Wesley (ostensibly over Calvin's doctrine of election) and the ultimate disintegration of Whitefield's *Tabernacle* indicated that Whitefield's early pulpit success had stunted his theological maturity. His message was so intimately related to his oratorical methods that only his printed sermons revealed the paucity of his ideas.

What, then, was the role of transatlantic influences in shaping the evangelical content of revival theology? The relationship between the Old World and the New was not simply a case of an exported European theology impacting on a receptive American situation. Neither was it a case of similar circumstances producing similar results. Rather, the relationship was a complex interaction in which ideas introduced into diverse patterns of behavior produced "feed back" effects upon all the participants in the interchange.

Cotton Mather's attempt to utilize German pietism of the Franckean type to revive New England Puritanism helped to break down the inherited intellectual structure of Puritanism and to prepare the way for Great Awakening. At the same time, his emphasis on piety as practical charity (works justify faith) helped to secularize the Puritan work ethic. The revival emphasis on conversion experience threatened to reverse the dialectic of salvation and infer "backwards" from sanctification to justification and thus to exalt the role of man at the expense of the role of God. This danger was most evident in the preaching and ministry of George Whitefield and those who attempted to emulate him. James Davenport's claim "to be able to distinguish infallibly the elect from the damned" did as much to discredit the revival as his pulpit sensationalism. Whitefield's reworking of the pietistic conception of mystical union into an emotional conviction of new birth did as much to release the springs of anti-intellectualism as his attacks on the unconverted clergy.[34]

Jonathan Edwards' appropriation of Lockean psychology and Newtonian naturalism provided the checks that prevented his concept of faith from ending up in mere emotionalism. Emotional sanctions played a role in his theology but only within the tightly knit framework of grace as a new "simple idea" of perception. Faith as existential response could be expressed in revivalism or private conversion but it could never be accepted as genuine without reference to its source. John Wesley's confrontation with Edwards' ideas provided the impetus that brought his own theology to completion. The realization that sanctification was also the gift of God's grace freely given on behalf of the justification already wrought by Christ freed Wesley from the fear of self-righteousness that had always hindered his efforts. It allowed him to distinguish between the dead faith of formal adherence and the living faith of loving inherence; from such unbounded hope, all things, even the revival of religious purity, seemed possible.

*NOTES*

1. Michael Kraus, *The Atlantic Civilization: Eighteenth-Century Origins* (Ithaca, N. Y., 1949), chap. iii, Edwin Scott Gaustad, *The Great Awakening in New England* (Gloucester, Mass., 1965), 21-26; Perry Miller, *Jonathan Edwards* (New York, 1959), 133.
2. *The Great Awakening,* ed. by Alan Heimert and Perry Miller (Indianapolis, 1967), xiv-xv.
3. Miller, *Jonathan Edwards,* 74-78 and 102-105; Albert D. Belden, *George Whitefield-The Awakener* (New York, 1953), 33-36; and *John Wesley,* ed. by Albert C. Outler (New York, 1964), 16-17 and 121-122.
4. The problem of acculturation of intellectual influences between America and Europe was a topic that long occupied Fritiof Ander's thought and provided a recurrent theme for his treatment of American intellectual history, immigration, and American ideals in his popular courses at Augustana College.
5. Leonard J. Trinterud, "The Origins of Puritanism," *Church History, XX* (March, 1951), 37-57. Trinterud maintains that the English Puritans owed more to Rhineland Protestants such as Oecolampadius than to Calvin. In *Errand into the Wilderness,* Perry Miller belabors the same point and concludes that the New England Puritans were not Calvinist but shared certain "Calvanistic" assumptions with their European contemporaries.
6. Paul H. Kocker, *Science and Religion in Elizabethan England* (San Marino, Calif., 1953), 311.
7. Perry Miller, *The New England Mind: The Seventeenth Century* (Cambridge, Mass., 1954), chap. v.
8. *Ibid.,* chaps. xi and xiii.
9. Perry Miller, *The New England Mind: From Colony to Province* (Cambridge, Mass., 1953), Bk. I.
10. *Ibid.,* chap. xxiv.
11. Harold S. Jantz, "German Thought and Literature in New England, 1620-1820: A Preliminary Survey," *The Journal of English and German Philology,* XLI (1942), 19-24. For Mather's original letter to Francke, see Kuno Francke, "The Beginning of Cotton Mather's Correspondence with August Hermann Francke," *Philological Quarterly,* V (July, 1926), 193-195.
12. Kuno Francke, "Cotton Mather and August Hermann Francke," *Harvard Studies and Notes in Philology and Literature,* V (1896), 58.
13. Miller, *New England Mind: Colony to Province,* 417.
14. Cotton Mather, *Heavenly Conversation* (Boston, 1710), Preface.
15. *Ibid.,* 4 and 30.
16. Cotton Mather, *Bonifacius* (Boston, 1710), 36.
17. *Ibid.,* 37.
18. Kuno Francke, *Harvard Studies and Notes,* V, 62-63.
19. Gerald R. Craig, *The Church and the Age of Reason. 1648-1789* (New York, 1961), 101-102; Martin Schmidt, *John Wesley: A Theological Biography* (New York, 1962), I, 140-143; Miller, *New England Mind.* II, 417.

20. Miller, *Jonathan Edwards,* 64-68, 72-82, and 95-98.
21. Jonathan Edwards, "A Divine and Supernatural Light," reproduced in *Theology in America: The Major Protestant Voices from Puritanism to Neo-Orthodoxy,* ed. by Sydney E. Ahlstrom (Indianapolis, 1967), 181-182.
22. Maximin Piette, *John Wesley in the Evolution of Protestantism* (New York, 1957), 316-317; Belden, *Whitefield,* 19; Schmidt, *Wesley,* I, 140-143.
23. George Whitefield, *Journal of a Voyage from London to Savannah* (London, 1738), 34.
24. *Ibid.,* 141.
25. George Whitefield, *The Marks of the New Birth* (6th ed.; New York, 1739), 3-4.
26. *Ibid.,* 19.
27. *John Wesley,* ed. by Outler, 48.
28. *Ibid.,* 66-68; Schmidt, *Wesley,* I, 306.
29. *The Journal of the Reverend John Wesley,* ed. by Nehemiah Curnock (Standard ed.; London, 1938), II, 88-91.
30. *Ibid.,* 84.
31. *John Wesley,* ed. by Outler, 16.
32. *Journal of Wesley,* II, 101.
33. *John Wesley,* ed. by Outler, 130-131. Italics added.
34. Gausted, *Great Awakening,* 38.

# *Jacob Letterstedt and Nordic Cooperation*

Franklin Scott

The Danish editor of *Nordisk Tidskrift* worked late on New Year's Eve, 1881, and while writing to his Swedish senior-editor he must have dozed off. Before him appeared the vision of Consul General Jacob Letterstedt who had died about twenty years earlier. The awesome visitor demanded to know if Swedish and Danish were now one language — that was what he had left his money for![1]

He had indeed left much money in a variety of funds for the promotion of Scandinavian culture and cooperation. Letterstedt was an emigrant who made his fortune in South Africa and died in Paris, but he was imbued with his generation's ideal of pan-Scandinavianism. Because of the money that enabled him to embody his dreams in lasting projects the weight of this dead man's ideas has been felt for a century throughout the North, and one large fund is still untapped. He is one of the few visible links between the sentimental Scandinavianism of the mid-nineteenth century and the practical cooperation of the mid-twentieth century. The career of this Swedish Mycenas is an odd but necessary background to an appreciation of his significance.

The family name was Lallerstedt (earlier still Lallerman) and came from the ancestral farm Lalleryd near Jönköping.[2] Jacob's great grandfather had been district police officer, and men of the family appeared repeatedly in successive generations as regimental trumpeters in the Östergötland regiment; one was a minister, and one a district governor (*häradshövding*). The roots of the family were deeply intertwined with the history of Sweden. Jacob was born at Lalleryd on 15 December, 1796, and his father, stern and stubborn, early decided that this one of his four children should be a farmer. Since he thought a farmer did not need, and should not have, "superfluous knowledge," a school education was considered unnecessary, and it was only through the mother's manipulations that the boy got a summer in a private school when he was nine years old. When the lad was thirteen he was permitted to spend a year with an aunt in Norrköping, where the town's industries fascinated him. From the age of fourteen to eighteen he did a man's work on the farm, but his eagerness for forbidden knowledge led him to read behind his father's back from the family library — science, travel literature, history, and even Aristotle. At eighteen he spent a year with his mother's brother, who was priest and also farmer; at nineteen he enlarged his field of operations by going to his older brother, a county clerk. Here he helped to oversee his brother's distillery, and had an opportunity to experiment with technical improvements.

Both on the farm and with his brother, Jacob had indulged in "moonlighting," trying to earn extra money by trading. Usually he lost, but he would not give up. Instead, he wanted to stand on his own feet, and against the opposition of father and family he went to Stockholm at age twenty to go into the business of distilling *brännvin* by himself. He rented the Järfa bränneri, and within a year had lost the two thousand riksdaler his brother had lent him, plus some two or three thousand riksdaler in debts to others. He explained his plight as the result of inexperience, some unfortunate speculations, and especially his perpetual eager experimenting "without sufficient knowledge of mechanics and chemistry." Perhaps the simultaneous general failure of crops also affected the business. In all events the outlook was gloomy.

Wounded in pocket and in pride, but determined to build a new life, Jacob left Sweden at age twenty-two (in the fall of 1819) and headed for Lisbon. However, in London he was persuaded by the priest in the Swedish legation and others to take advantage of the English government's energetic push to find settlers for Cape Colony. A last hour illness almost made him miss the ship, but he got on, and in March of 1820 landed in Cape Town, South Africa, one of some five thousand who emigrated that year from England, with a ten pound subsidy for each. It was a three-month voyage, and it gave him a chance to learn a little English, as well as to change his name from Lallerstedt to Letterstedt. He would be a new man, but he had no capital and must start at the bottom.

At first Letterstedt did ordinary day labor, then helped a man to build a successful distillery, and for a couple of years worked as bookkeeper in a warehouse. He also manufactured small items for sale. But progress was slow and he considered moving on to Mauritius or the East Indies. At that juncture a woman entered the scene: the recently widowed Mrs. Dreyer, who had known Letterstedt first as a gardener and then as adviser in her complicated estate problems, and come to like him as well as to respect his talents. Presumably it was she who proposed marriage, against the opposition of her aristrocratic family connections. But Jacob accepted, and the wedding took place on 14 September, 1822.

Now Letterstedt's restless striving began to pay off. He built his wife's modest inheritance, a farm worth about £2000, into a major substance by careful planning and hard work. In his household he raised three stepchildren and three other children of his wife's relatives, one of whom eventually married his own nephew, Oskar Hedelius. Within seven years he had accumulated enough surplus that he could send his brother the money to pay off the debts that had driven him from Sweden. His brother made an occasion of this by inviting the other creditors to dinner and surprising them with a repayment they had not dared to expect.

In 1837 Letterstedt was able to return home in state, the failure who had made good. He took with him gifts of South African natural phenomena and was graciously received by Crown Princess Josephine. To the Academy of Science he gave a collection of gazelles and birds. He also held another banquet for his former creditors. All this was quite appropriate, for he had obviously retained a strong feeling for the home country. Both in England and in South Africa he had been aided in his difficult years by fellow Swedes, and as he became affluent he employed many Swedes in his operations. When Swedish ships came to Cape Town he entertained the officers and crews, evidently reveling in grand displays of hospitality. He was in turn rewarded by appointment as Swedish-Norwegian consul in Cape Town, 1841, and in 1857 was made consul-general. In this capacity he was influential in the rapid development of Scandinavian trade with the Cape (14,000 rkdr. in 1842 to 1,345,000 rkdr. in 1861). He was also made knight and later commander of the Order of Vasa.

Acquaintanceships that Letterstedt made at the Academy of Science, and especially Professor Anders A. Retzius, became lifelong friends. Retzius was just Letterstedt's age, and already a distinguished anatomist; he made pioneering discoveries with the microscope, but is perhaps best remembered for his classification of mankind as dolichocephalic and brachycephalic. It was on Letterstedt's initiative and with his help that young J. A. Wahlberg, Retzius' brother-in-law, went to South Africa to collect specimens of flora and fauna for the Academy. Letterstedt sent to Sweden many chests of material gathered by Wahlberg all the way north from Cape Town to the Limpopo. His second expedition alone produced 553 mammals, 2537 birds of over 400 varieties, 480 reptiles and amphibians, 5000 insects, plus fish preserved in spirit and many botanical specimens.[3] Though himself but an interested amateur, Letterstedt gave significant assistance to Swedish science even before his gifts of money.

Altogether Letterstedt made five trips back to Europe, not only for nostalgic satisfaction but also for business. It was on his second trip, in 1848, that his wife died and he had to hurry back to the Cape. But he took advantage of the trips to visit the wineries and distilleries of southern France and of Germany or Italy, gathering ideas for the improvement of his South African enterprises. Back at the Cape he built a steam flour mill and acquired a practical monopoly for providing both government needs and the ships that supplied themselves at this major way-station between Europe and the Far East. He built a brewery and improved both milling and brewing with his own inventions, for several of which he won prizes. In the field of finance he became a founder and director of the Cape of Good Hope Bank and of a fire insurance company. He was also a member of the municipal council, helped to found an agricultural society, and was a director of the South African Club. He was a leading citizen.

Letterstedt's association with the social and political élite, the "establishment" in the colony, finally landed him in trouble. In 1848 the British government decided to send some Irish and other prisoners from Bermuda to the Cape on tickets-of-leave. Reaction in Cape Town was strong. The idea of being used as a penal colony was abhorrent to the colonists, and at first Letterstedt as well as the governor himself protested the action. An "anti-convict association" was formed, and people took pledges to boycott the convicts and to boycott and destroy any fellow-citizen who hired them or even sold them provisions. Butchers must not sell them meat, nor bakers bread. This was going too far for Letterstedt's ideas of loyalty and legal process. It was also against his interests — he would be prevented from selling his produce. He made his opinions known and from then on he was regarded as a traitor to the populace.[4]

The temperature of rebellion-fever rose in the spring and summer of 1849, and after an all day mass meeting with twenty-three speeches on July fourth (a date deliberately chosen) the appointive legislative council lost several members and could function no longer. Government came to a standstill. The leader of the popular opposition declared that anyone who accepted appointment to the council would be subject to eternal damnation. But Sir Harry Smith, the governor, succeeded in persuading three eminent citizens to take seats on the council: Pieter Laurens Cloete, brother of the sheriff, Abraham de Smidt, owner of the mansion Groote Schuur, and Jacob Letterstedt. "Sir Harry Smith could scarcely have made more judicious appointments." But the mob was outraged and got ugly. On July 10, after the first meeting of the reorganized council, de Smidt was mauled and Cloete had to seek refuge in his brother's office. Letterstedt came out between two friends, but was hit with a rock and saved from injury only by his thick velvet collar. He escaped to the South African Club and later by hired cart to his out-of-town residence, Mariedahl. That evening the mob burned the three new councillors in effigy, then was diverted, and turned to vent its wrath on Letterstedt's nearby properties. They broke into his flour mill and houses for his employees, threw furniture into the street and did other damage; fortunately they were thwarted from breaking into his wine store or things might have become worse. Boatmen refused to handle goods addressed to Letterstedt and others. Shortly all three resigned and the excitement died down. The affair was of such wide and lasting scope that it led to the granting of representative government both to the Cape Colony and to Australia, and influenced the ending of penal transportation.[5]

For Letterstedt his gruesome experience was damaging economically and psychologically. He soon left for a European visit to help feelings to calm, and it was on this trip that he met Miss Lydia Meredyth-Boys in a German spa and married her in London (9 October, 1851). He then returned to Cape Town and in 1853 his daughter was born — which event decreased the amount of his first donation to the Academy of Science (Vetenskapsakademien). His eagerness for new ventures was soon whetted by reports of copper in Namaqualand and he took his family with him to inaugurate a new life. The mining attempt failed, however, and he was soon off again on a fourth trip to Europe — this time for almost three years, in Italy, Germany, and traveling through Sweden to Dalarna, Uppsala, Stockholm and his home community. When at last he returned to South Africa it was to build an enlarged and improved brewery and to put his affairs in order. It was then that he gave largely for the building of the Lutheran church at Wynkoop and also for an infant school on his estate, named for his wife "The Lydia Letterstedt School." By 1860 he was ready for his final return northward. He visited once more in Sweden but then retired to Paris, where he died 18 March, 1862. His remains were, by his wish, returned to his native soil and interred at Wallerstad church.[6]

For Sweden and for Scandinavia the importance of Jacob Letterstedt came from the long reach of his South African fortune, about half of which he bequeathed to his homeland (after providing about 20,000 riksdaler for his daughter and the South African relatives). His first major gift was an endowment of £5,000 for a travel fund for promising young Swedes (1852).[7] The careful stipulation about the use of the interest foreshadowed the precise planning with which he set up his later donations. The right to choose the grantee was to rotate in a six-year cycle between the Academy of Science (twice), Uppsala University, Lund University, the Academy of Literature and the Agricultural Academy. The Academy of Sciences should alternate its choices between a theoretician and a technician or engineer. The grantee must be a Swedish man, twenty-five to forty years of age, of good character and exceptional talent; on his stipend he should reside out of the country at least one year, and he was not eligible to hold the grant more than twice. In case he later gained sufficient wealth it was hoped he would repay an appropriate portion of his stipend. If savings in the fund grew to as much as 20,000 rkdr. a new endowment should be created for domestic travel, further savings should go into the foreign travel fund up to 100,000 rkdr., after which a new domestic fund should be established. The list of beneficiaries of this fund in its first twenty years (1862-1883) reads like a "who's who" of young Swedish intellectuals: Hans Hildebrand, the historian; Oscar Montelius, the archaeologist and later editor of *Nordisk Tidskrift;* Harald Hjärne, philosopher and historian; Gustaf Retzius, anatomist, ethnologist, editor, and himself donor of an important fund for science; Oskar Nylander, industrialist and politician — and others of similar caliber.[8]

In his wills of 3 May and 22 October, 1860, Letterstedt left an additional £5,000 sterling to the Academy of Science. Of this the interest on £1,000 was to be given annually as a prize for an original work in science, literature, or art, or for a practical invention useful to mankind; most of the early prizes were given for books in various fields, but one was given for the discovery of dynamite, to Alfred Nobel (and his father), another Swede who worked mostly abroad, who was to invent still more and who was to leave to Sweden and Norway a yet larger donation for more far-reaching cosmopolitan ends. There were prizes also for translations, for scientific investigations, and for support of schools and sick travelers — all of these to come out of interest only.

The biggest endowment of all was a carefully structured series of funds with the primary purpose of furthering Nordic unity. Details were spelled out in wills of 11 May, 1861, and 27 January and 26 February, 1862, just before the testator's death. A state councillor and two professors were named and given full powers, equal with Letterstedt's own, to state and modify the terms and purposes of the gift, and thus was set up the Letterstedt Society for Industry, Science and Art (Letterstedtska Föreningen för industri, vetenskap och konst). Letterstedt's friend and biographer, C. Annerstedt, thought that the donor may have had the Smithsonian Institution in Washington in mind as a model. On the basis of Letterstedt's testaments and instructions the committee of three stated the regulations for the Society (31 December, 1873): "to further community among the three Scandinavian kingdoms in respect to industry, science, and art and to encourage and support in these lands both practical and scientific development."[9] These purposes would be promoted by the publication of a journal, prizes, triennial conferences of Scandinavian intelligentsia, and exhibitions. Religious and political subjects were to be considered outside the scope of the society's concern. Three sections, one for each country, would be self-perpetuating after being first established through the Swedish nucleus, and the Swedish section would choose the executive board of twelve, headquartered in Stockholm. To start things the three named men chose twelve leading scientists and public figures, and these fifteen chose eighty-five more; then these one hundred Swedes chose seventeen Danes to be charter members from Denmark, and seventeen Norwegians for the Norwegian section. Monetary grants were immediately allocated to these affiliated societies.

The funds which came from South Africa at the end of the 1860s amounted to 316,781 Sw. kr., but had grown to 452,825 kr. by December 1873. The Academy of Science, of which Jacob Letterstedt had been made a member in 1860, has administered the funds from the beginning, for a prescribed fee of 2% of the annual income. Three separate funds were carefully defined. The first was a reserve fund of 26,000 kr. which, at 4% compound interest, would have to reach the amount of 500,000 kronor before the interest could be used. In the 1960s this fund matured and the interest was released for use. As of 1967 its book value was over 700,000 kr., and its market value over 1,000,000 kr. Second, a savings fund of 113,000 kr. should be allowed to accumulate at 4% compound interest until it reached 5,000,000 kr., when the interest might be used. In 1967 the book value of this fund was about 4,000,000 kr., and its market value already over 5,000,000 kr., but it was not yet freed for use. The third was a disposable fund of 313,825 kr., whose interest could be used at once, but whose capital should not be diminished — though it might be and has been increased.[10] Although Letterstedt donated to Sweden and Scandinavia £27,000 sterling, and the planned combination of spending and saving has maintained the significance of the grants into the second century after the testator's death. The cluster of funds is like a space ship launched into eternity, and boosted by two major refuelings.

The stimulating, pump-priming effects of grants and prizes and subsidies are impossible to measure with precision. Medical researchers, archaeologists, sculptors, painters, cartographers, geologists, jurists, philologists, zoologists and many others have been aided to travel and study. Journals in mathematics and several scientific fields have been aided, exhibitions for fisheries, and lectures of scholars from one Scandinavian country to others have been supported. The great triennial gatherings of Scandinavian intellectuals that Letterstedt envisioned have never been attempted — they did not fit with the practices of increasing specialization. But the Society has assisted and continues to assist a number of individual scholarly associations in their own all-Scandinavian congresses. Thus for conferences the developments of the past century indicate a modification rather than a failure of Letterstedt's purposes. One definite failure must be charged: community of language, which so worried Letterstedt's ghost (or the Danish editor!) is probably farther from realization in the 1960s than it was in the 1860s.

The most solid visible monument of the Letterstedt Society is the ninety-year file of the *Nordisk Tidskrift för Vetenskap, Konst och Industri,* available in every respectable library in northern Europe, and widely distributed around the world. Steadily it has published excellent articles under the editorship of a series of outstanding scholars, including Oscar Monteliue, Nils Herlitz, Ingvar Andersson, and the present Örjan Lindberger. In this journal the Swedes, the Danes and the Norwegians have cooperated effectively. The vast diversity of subject matter originally planned has been limited, and the limitation justified by the support given to other journals in scientific fields (among many are: *Nordiskt Medicinskt Arkiv, Tidskrift för Nordisk Filogi, Tidskrift för Retsvidenskab, Teknisk Tidskrift).* In turn, restrictions against religion and politics in *Nordisk Tidskrift* have been modified, the explanation being that scientific and nonpartisan discussion would not violate the principles of the benefactor. Writers from all Scandinavia contribute to *Nordisk Tidskrift,* each in his own language, authoritative articles on a vast variety of subjects especially in humanistic and social science fields: Kensington Rune Stone, the Spanish Middle Ages, literary biography and criticism, classic Greece, polar exploration, Norwegian iron, and so on and on. In brief, the periodical is a gold mine of information, a superb reference source, and Letterstedt could take great satisfaction in conceiving and establishing on a permanent basis such a high-level magazine of intellectual interchange for all the North.[11] Unfortunately, virtue must be its own reward, and this valuable journal is probably used more for reference a decade or more after publication than it is for current reading. It is less than exciting in format, its private circulation is small, and as one friendly critic put the matter, "Only angels read it."

What beyond the journal is tangible evidence of the munificence of this Swedish-South African business man-inventor-idealist? The high hopes of the nineteenth century political pan-Scandinavianism gasped and died dejected as the Danes were left alone in 1864 to be crushed under Prussian boots. Again and again the brutalities of external force, impinging on one or two countries at a time, have interrupted the progress of Nordic cooperation. Yet again and again the ideal has sprung back to life, inspired by deep-rooted traditions and common interest, and nourished by the perennial activities of Letterstedtska and similar continuing institutions. This cooperation was regularized and strengthened by the founding of the Norden societies (one in each country, and all linked in a federative organization), and the close cooperation between these societies and the Letterstedt Foundations. Since 1925 the *Nordisk Tidskrift* itself has been published cooperatively by the Letterstedt Fund and Norden and its circulation thus expanded. The Society has subsidized many such ventures as the Danish-Norwegian-Swedish dictionary.[12] In innumerable ways the Letterstedt and other funds have sparked action that has grown. Cultural cooperation, meetings of Nordic professional groups, youth gatherings and scores of similar activities originated by private impulse are increasingly made governmental projects. Personal acquaintanceships originating in intra-Nordic conferences and education in common values have led in many instances to common action; the idealistic has given birth to the practical, such as the common front of the Nordic countries in the 1967 Kennedy-Round negotiations. Many of the leaders of government, business and culture have been touched by the Letterstedt influence, through prizes or grants or conferences, though scientific measurement is lacking to judge the impact of these stimuli.

One of the most intriguing questions is: what motivated Letterstedt himself, this expatriate Swede in South Africa? The problem of psychological incentives of any man are delicate and difficult, and the difficulty is compounded for a man dead for over a hundred years. The surviving records and autobiographical notes are meager, and the biographical accounts left by acquaintances are factual but not explanatory. We can deduce probabilities, little more.

The boy Jacob had little schooling, and that he felt the lack is evident from his own testimony of the reading and book-buying he did on his own, and by his explanation for the failure of his new processes for the distillery — he lacked knowledge of chemistry and physics. His eager study later on in southern Europe of brewing and wine-making indicates a continuing desire for practical education. He also read widely and was reputed to be a learned man. His letters to Professor A. Retzius and Baron Berzelius indicate a wide range of interests — politics (especially in Sweden and France), economic affairs, flowers and animals and other natural phenomena, and art.[13] He was a "self-made man" — though the widow's nest-egg helped. In his wills, repeatedly, he showed a keen interest in schools, education, intellectual achievement. Did the restraints put upon him by an unsympathetic father enhance his appreciation for the things he lacked? Similarly, was it the memory of his own illness as a young man in London that led him to provide a fund for the care of sick travelers?

Despite his own childhood deprivations (perhaps exaggerated in memory?) Jacob retained a nostalgic fondness for his home and his country. This is a phenomenon found frequently among emigrants, who in the lonesomeness of their success ennoble the deficiencies of their background. Perhaps the love of the language he learned as a child enhanced his sense of continued belonging to a country he had long left. And it is noteworthy that he established a prize for superior translations into Swedish. "Absence made the heart grow fonder," and his lavish entertainment for visiting Scandinavian naval and merchant marine personnel at the Cape, his use of Swedes as workers and foremen in his South African enterprises, his effective promotion of trade between Sweden and Norway on the one hand

and South Africa on the other, plus his official activities as consul — all indicate an unusual interest in the fatherland, and help to explain why his money was sent "back home." All his testaments indicate a deep appreciation for the Swedish sense of values and their possible contributions to the world outside Sweden. In all probability the bitterness bred by the events of 1848 in Cape Town disinclined him to leave much of his money there, and perhaps that is partly why he did not want *Nordisk Tidskrift* to get involved in controversial subjects such as religion and politics. He dearly loved the estate he had made to bloom and prosper, at the foot of Table Mountain, and he felt a paternal fondness for his workers. But as he wrote to a good friend in 1859:

> Mariedahl is beautiful now, so it will be hard to leave it, but aside from this there is nothing here that interests me. All life's needs are unreasonably dear here. The colony has had many misfortunes, with severe drought in the interior, and loss of domestic animals . . . Costs are double those in Paris, so there is no advantage to live in South Africa.[14]

His special encouragement to science, both practical and theoretical, is probably the simplest thing to understand, for this was his own metier. To Vetenskapsakademien he gave not only money, and the administration of most of his estate, but also collections of scientific interest from South African bird and animal life. What little of Letterstedt's correspondence survives is largely letters to and from other members of that Academy.

Yet the bulk of Jacob Letterstedt's life accumulation was given not just to science, nor to Sweden, nor to schools and hospitals. It was given for these purposes *in a Scandinavian setting*. Partly this was doubtless due to the fact that Sweden and Norway were then united kingdoms, and that he had been consul-general for the united kingdoms. Some influence may be due to the fact that his teen years coincided with the "Policy of 1812," the war against Napoleon and the establishment of the union. Two other factors were presumably more important. One was the factor of his travels and experience in Europe and Africa, the cosmopolitanizing influence of a wider world and his two "foreign" marriages. He could no longer be parochially Swedish, and from the distant perspective of South Africa he thought of all Scandinavia as his home. And, more specifically, it was just the decade in which he was writing and revising his numerous wills, and during which he made his visits to Sweden, that there came that surge of sentiment among the youth of the North that promoted dreams of Scandinavian brotherhood. Norway and Sweden were united and dreams of Danish adhesion were rife. His own nephew was writing vigorously of the Russian threat and of an all-Scandinavian response to outside danger.[15] But Letterstedt's interest was in practical and intellectual achievement and cooperation rather than in the political. Clearly he considered the cultural aspects of unity as fundamental.

Nordic cooperation is a man-made thing, not an inevitable product of irresistible historical forces. Jacob Letterstedt was one among many men who was concerned for this broad-minded cause, one among very few who was ready and able to back his beliefs with a significant if not a spectacular amount of cash. He was, furthermore, not only a man of dreams but of practical good sense. Thus we have a "text-book example" of a popular cause (Scandinavianism) becoming institutionalized (through *Nordisk Tidskrift,* subsidies, conferences, etc.) and yet retaining enough adaptability to change with changing times (for example, through alliance in the twentieth century with the new Norden societies). Letterstedt provided some impetus and a few solid bricks for an edifice of mutual understanding in the North — an edifice still far from complete, but under construction, and thus he projected his own ideals effectively into future generations.

*NOTES*

1. Nils Herlitz, "Nordisk Tidskrift under femtio år," *Nordisk Tidskrift,* New series, No. 3 (1927), 558.
2. The following biographical details are dependent on several interrelated sources, similar but occasionally contradictory on small points: C. Annerstedt, "Jacob Letterstedt och hans Stiftelser," *Nordisk Tidskrift,* I (1878), 1-19; and a revision of this in *Lefnads anteckningar öfver Kunglig Svenska Vetenskapsakademiens aflidna Ledamöter,* II (1878-1885), 433-464. This is the most thorough account of Letterstedt's life and is based on the autobiography. Briefer sketches in *Svenska Män och Kvinnor, Svensk Uppslagsbok,* etc., are largely based on Annerstedt. A. A. Retzius left a very brief manuscript biography now in the library of Vetenskapsakademien.

3. *Svensk Uppslagsbok:* Wahlberg, Retzius. In the circle of friends and relatives were also Professor P. F. Wahlberg and Baron Jacob Berzelius, the chemist, who was also the vigorous and constructive secretary of the Academy of Sciences. J. A. Wahlberg earned part of the expenses for his expeditions by elephant hunting, and in 1856 was killed by an elephant in South West Africa. His sister, Mrs. Retzius, established a fund in his memory.
4. In addition to the Swedish accounts, which treat the South African phase sketchily, see Alan Hattersley, *The Convict Crisis and the Growth of Unity. Resistance to Transportation in South Africa and Australia, 1848-1853* (Pietermaritzburg, Union of South Africa, 1965), chaps. iii-v.
5. Hattersley, 42-55 and 127-136; Annerstedt, 446-450 and 453.
6. Annerstedt, 451-455.
7. Letterstedt's will of 1852 was elaborated in wills of 1857 and 1860, and he made several others. He seemed to have as much a penchant for writing and rewriting wills as did that later and greater South African, Cecil Rhodes.
8. Annerstedt, 457.
9. *Ibid.,* 460.
10. Annerstedt, 460-462; Vetenskapsakademien records; and conversations with the Treasurer and with the Director, Dr. Wilhelm Odelberg, Sept. 4, 1967.
11. See the files of *Nordisk Tidskrift* itself, and also the descriptive surveys appearing therein, especially Nils Herlitz in the 1924 volume, 1-9, and his longer "Nordisk Tidskrift under femtio år," cited in note 1 above.
12. Natanel Beckman, *Dansk-Norsk-Svensk Ordbok* (4th ed., Stockholm, 1923).
13. Twenty-two such personal letters are preserved in the library of Vetenskapsakademien in Stockholm, dated from 1838 to 1861.
14. To Professor A. Retzius (?), from Mariedahl, 20 September 1859, Vetenskapsakademien.
15. There must have been some lively discussions, when he was home, between Letterstedt and his nephew, Gustaf Lallerstedt — but we do not have the evidence. Lallerstedt was the son of that older brother with whom Jacob had lived and worked for a year, and who had lent Jacob the money with which to start his ill-fated distillery venture. And this boy Gustaf had become by the 1850s a prosperous and widely known publicist. He owned a double share of a publishing firm in Stockholm and he is remembered now for his book *La Scandinavie, ses craintes et ses espérances* issued first in Paris early in 1856, just at the end of the Crimean War. This sharp volume had two cutting edges — one was its violent anti-Russian propaganda, the other its appeal to a combined Scandinavian defense.

# *High Churchmen in a Hostile World*

THOMAS TREDWAY

A century ago few Protestant churchmen, on either side of the Atlantic, would have been angered by the allegation that their liturgical life was lean or that their appreciation of church history deficient. Indeed, it might have been taken by some as a commendation, for many nineteenth century Protestants shared a contempt for ceremony and tradition. Anyone too reverently concerned with liturgics or church history was likely to be accused of "popery" and watched with unconcealed suspicion. Simplicity characterized the public worship of Protestant congregations, partly, one supposes, because of a desire for clear distinction from the elaborate rites of Roman Catholicism. And most Protestants of one hundred years ago were somewhat nervous in the presence of church history, probably because they feared that such Catholic apologists as the French primate, Bishop Jacques Bossuet, were correct in asserting that Protestantism had no history before the sixteenth century and the church of history was the Church of Rome. In view of these attitudes, it is significant that in each of the main branches of Protestantism — Lutheran, Reformed, and Anglican — there arose movements which may be described as revivals of churchly, sacramental, and historical awareness, qualities usually taken as marks of "high churchmanship."

Certainly of these three movements, the one associated with John Henry Newman and Oxford University is the best known in the English-speaking world. Newman's lifelong struggle with "liberalism" culminated in his conversion to Roman Catholicism in 1845, after two decades spent in the unsuccessful effort to establish the Church of England as a *via media* between Rome and the Reformation.[1] Within the confessional revival in German Lutheranism, three figures were of special importance: A. F. C. Vilmar, Wilhelm Loehe, and Theodore Kliefoth. Each of these men combined an intense pastoral concern for the daily life of the church with an informed theological interest that resulted in significant contributions to theological scholarship of the last century.[2] Kliefoth's *Einleitung in die Dogmengeschichte* (1839) is concerned with the same problem which occupied Newman in his *Essay on the Development of Christian Doctrine* (1845): the continued existence of the underlying truths of Christianity in the midst of historical development and change. The third of these movements, the "Mercersburg Theology," sought to recall the Reformed or Calvinistic churches of the United States to their true heritage, and especially to John Calvin's doctrine of the Real Presence of Christ in the Eucharist. The most articulate expression of this movement was John Nevin's *The Mystical Presence* (1846). The work aroused such opposition in German Reformed circles in America that Nevin and his colleague, Philip Schaff, in the Reformed seminary at Mercersburg, Pennsylvania, were forced eventually to leave the school where they taught. Nevin became President of Franklin and Marshall College, and Schaff went on to a brilliant career in ecclesiastical history at Union Theological Seminary in New York.[3]

A treatment of this brevity cannot do justice to the rich diversity of nineteenth century churchly revival. The purpose of this essay is to seek the points of similarity between them, those basic assumptions about the Christian faith and those common conclusions about its needs in the mid-nineteenth century milieu which the three movements shared. It is tempting to seek to establish a definite historical connection between the Oxford Movement, the German Neo-Lutherans, and the Mercersburg Theology. And, in fact, there is evident an immigration of ideas between them. Wilhelm Loehe's view of Lutheranism as a *Mittelweg* between Romanism and Free Church Protestantism is, for example, reminiscent of Newman's defense of Anglicanism as a *via media.* By the same token, it is clear that

Nevin and Schaff were well acquainted with developments in German theology and with the Tractarian or Oxford Movement in Britain as well. But it would be a mistake to assume that because of their similarities these three movements must have had a common source. For every point of likeness, there is also one of difference. The most obvious is that while Newman went over to Rome, the Reformed and Lutheran high churchmen remained Protestants, in spite of their enemies' frequent cries of "popery." There are also significant differences in regard to the doctrines of the church, the ministry, and the sacraments which preclude a facile identification of the movements. Therefore, it would be misleading to posit a direct historical connection between the church revivals of the last century and to assume that this connection accounts for their almost simultaneous appearance. The fact that Germany, Britain, and America each spawned a "high church" movement is better explained by the general condition of Protestantism in the last century than it is by some alleged conspiracy of crypto-Romans or by some other historical relationship for which there is little evidence save the circumstantial. What then were the conditions which evoked these reassertions of churchly tradition?

For Newman, Nevin, Loehe, and the others, thought and practice, theology and liturgy, were opposite sides of the same coin. When they weighed contemporary Protestantism in the scales and found it wanting, it was in both respects. They were especially troubled by the state in which they found the worship of their church. In *The Anxious Bench* (1843), Nevin argued that "Puritanism" gripped the life of the American denominations.[4] With its emphasis upon emotion and its lack of concern for the traditional modes of Christian devotion, this tendency threatened totally to impoverish the life of American Protestantism, he felt. On the Continent traditional Lutheran worship had fallen upon hard times. For example, when the sacramental elements were distributed during Holy Communion, two formulae commonly recited by the minister were:

> Eat this bread; may the spirit of devotion rest upon you with all its blessings. Drink a little wine; moral power does not reside in this wine, but in you, in the teachings of God, and in God.

and:

> Use this bread in remembrance of Jesus Christ; he that hungereth after pure and noble virtue shall be filled. Drink a little wine; he

> that thirsteth after pure and noble virtue shall not long for it in vain.[5]

Reflected in these formulae was the common view that a reasonable religion found its true essence in morality. Along with dispensing with traditional liturgical and devotional forms, many Germans in the post-Kantian period were willing to jettison the Incarnation, the Trinity, and the Atonement, doctrines which had no place in a moral religion confined within the "limits of reason alone." It was in reaction to such views that Frederich Schleiermacher, in an effort to preserve for religion a domain of its own, independent of reason and morals, elaborated his understanding of religion as *Gefühl* or "feeling." In their student days many of the leaders of the German Lutheran confessional awakening had been attracted to Schleiermacher's thought. Subsequently, however, they discovered in his theology the same critical weaknesses that had brought about their dissatisfaction with the earlier moralistic rationalism which Schleiermacher had sought to correct: theological carelessness, misunderstanding of revelation, and indifference to the sacraments.

These were the same faults which the Oxford Tractarians detected in the British theology of the early nineteenth century. Newman spoke often of "the Religion of the Day," a creedless system which was quietly obliterating whatever it found alien to itself in orthodox Christianity and retaining only those elements which it could with ease adapt to its own assumptions and uses. By this process the true Gospel was being transformed into a comfortable sanction for the current English way of life, Newman held. In his sermon on "The Religion of the Day," he defined the views of its adherents:

> . . . they argue that it is our duty to solace ourselves here (in moderation, of course) with the goods of this life, — that we have only to be thankful while we use them, — that we need not alarm ourselves, — that God is a merciful God, — that amendment is quite sufficient to atone for our offences, — that though we have been irregular in our youth, yet that is a thing gone by, — that we forget it, and therefore God forgets it, — that the world is, on the whole, very well disposed towards religion, — that we should avoid enthusiasm, — that we should not be over serious, — that we should have large views on the subject of human nature, — and that we should love all men.[6]

Certainly a comparison of British latitudinarianism, American revivalism, and German rationalism reveals important differences. Nevertheless, they manifest significant similarities. Each viewed traditional theology as of secondary importance and looked upon confessional differentiation as hair-splitting. What mattered was good will and moral living, and so long as one attained these, whether at an American camp meeting or in a German university, he was, in the best sense of the word, "religious." The traditional forms of worship were seen as divisive and the sacramental concerns of the ancient church and the Reformation as concessions to paganism and supersition. The factors which divided the denominations were, in this view, largely dead limbs of the past, and once they had been pruned away, Christian unity would be attained. An American Lutheran, Samuel Simon Schmucker of Gettysburg Theological Seminary, spoke for many nineteenth century Protestants when he issued his *Fraternal Appeal to the American Church, with a Plan for Catholic Union, on Apostolic Principles* in 1838.[7] Included in the "Apostolic Principles" were none of the doctrines which had divided the sixteenth century Reformers, such as their views on the sacraments, church government, or patterns of worship. All these were the creations of men with no integral connection with the simple truths of apostolic Christianity. To object that denominational and confessional differences arose out of vital historical issues which must still be given weight was to be guilty of the same sin as that of the Roman Church: giving to historical tradition a weight which only Scripture deserved. By this enslavement to the dead past the Church of Rome had forfeited her claim to the attention of enlightened men. To the extent to which they retained vestiges of Romish error, the churches of Protestantism must be purified too. Beneath the differences between revivalism, rationalism, and latitudinarianism, were these shared assumptions.

It is, therefore, impossible to understand or evaluate the churchly movements of the last century without an awareness of the situation which called them forth. Pleasing or not, it can hardly be denied that in early nineteenth century Protestant Christianity, the voices of tradition were either stilled altogether or went unnoticed when they were raised. Thus, the biographies of the principals in the churchly movements under discussion here reveal a common quality: dissatisfaction with the state of Protestantism as they found it. It does not do justice to Newman, Nevin and Schaff, and the Lutheran confessionalists, however, to assume that their protests were merely reaction and their significance simply negative. While the conservative and traditional qualities in their thought and work are unmistakable, they alone do not explain the force of nineteenth century churchly revival. At the heart of each of these movements were views of positive theological significance. James H. Nichols points out that in crucial ways the Mercersburg Theology anticipated the theological development of the twentieth century.[8] This is certainly true of the Oxford Movement and of Neo-Lutheranism as well, as a discussion of key doctrinal and liturgical issues makes clear.

Quite obviously, the "churchly" revival was concerned with the doctrine of the Church. A. F. C. Vilmar, for example, divided all history into seven periods, the last of which, his own, was the Age of the Church. In it the true understanding of the Church, the Body of Christ, had emerged. Vilmar agreed with Loehe and Kliefoth that a serious weakness of Protestantism had been its tendency to separate the ideal Church from the actual one and to assume that the biblical metaphors for the Church — "Body of Christ," "Bride of Christ," "Chosen People," — referred only to the ideal Church or, in the language of the Protestant Reformers, to the "Invisible Church." Loehe and his colleagues carried on extensive charitable and educational activities in their parishes, and this activity arose from their concern to create a situation in which the ideal and the real Church would be closer to identification. John Henry Newman was equally concerned with the visible Church. He was able to remain in the Church of England only so long as he believed it to be a true branch of the one Church catholic. When he became convinced that by her errors and insularity the Anglican Church had forfeited that claim, Newman submitted to Rome.

The particular issue upon which the English Tractarians centered their efforts was the relation of Church and State; indeed, it was the attempt of the British Parliament to reduce the number of Anglican bishoprics in Ireland which provoked the first of the *Tracts for the Times* which became the means by which Newman and his fellows spread their views. The German confessionalists were concerned with the same matter. Erastianism reached new heights in early nineteenth century Germany, finding expression in the refusal of the Elector of Hesse to ratify Vilmar's overwhelming election by his fellow pastors to be Superintendent of the Hessian church in 1855, among other episodes. What seem on the surface to have been simple struggles over Church-State relations are on closer inspection even more important than this. Beneath the political issue, significant enough, was the larger question of the very nature of the Church itself. Was it to become a sort of sanctification of nineteenth century culture, waiting obediently to do the bidding of the spirit of the age? Or was it rather to stand apart from, and in some cases in judgment upon, the actions and creations of men, free to fulfill a prophetic function? The twentieth century German scholar, Emanuel Hirsch, is sharply critical of German Neo-Lutheranism because of its failure to support the movement for German unification and its stubborn insistence on confessional distinctions.[9] But his indictment would have been accepted as a compliment by Loehe, Vilmar, and Kliefoth. As they saw it, kingdoms would rise and fall, while Christ's Church remained. For the Church to have offered her services to German nationalism would have been a denial of her very essence. The fact that they failed in their efforts to recall German Lutheranism to a role independent of state control in the last century has bearing on the failure of the German state churches to resist Nazism in this century.

Seen in this light, the Mercersburg Theology shares the qualities of the German and English movements. While the problem of Church-State relations seemed to be solved in America by the end of government support for religion, the question of the relationship of Protestant Christianity to American culture was far from settled. And when it was decided, as Winthrop Hudson points out in *The Great Tradition of the American Churches,* it was not in the direction of affirming the independence of American religion in its relation to national culture. Nevin and Schaff sensed the impending fusion of biblical Christianity with the American dream and warned the churches against it for the same reasons that moved the Tractarians and the Neo-Lutherans to protest British and German Erastianism.

One of the major reasons for these objections to the easy identification of Christ with culture was that such an identification was based upon a perverted reading of Christian history. It was no accident that each of the movements being discussed made significant contributions to the study of Church history. Newman's is best known. In the months just preceding his conversion, Newman composed the *Essay on the Development of Christian Doctrine,* his effort to reconcile the idea of doctrinal development with the eternal and changeless essence of Catholic truth. He argued that in spite of seemingly radical changes, certain central characteristics had governed the growth of the theology of the Church.[10] By this means Newman hoped to make room in his theology for history and dogma, being and becoming, existence and essence. His concern for history accounts for Newman's unhappiness with the ultramontanist faction at the Vatican Council of 1870: it ignored historical growth for the sake of allegedly static dogma and threatened to choke the continued unfolding of Catholic truth.

In a different form, the Lutheran confessionalists struggled with the same problem. If, as they never wearied of insisting, the Lutheran creedal statements contained a complete and adequate statement of biblical truth, what was the meaning of the long history of doctrinal development? In the effort to harmonize history and dogma, Vilmar and Kliefoth elaborated schematic views of Church history strongly dependent upon Hegel. Through a series of necessary dialectical movements, Christianity had now arrived at the Age of the Church, a period, they maintained, in which ecclesiology had come into its own. The true understanding of the Church which this ecclesiology presented had from the beginning been implicit in Christian thought, of course. With these concepts Vilmar was able to justify his concern for the Church Fathers while maintaining at the same time that his own age was in a unique sense the era of ecclesiology.

A special aspect of the problem of history was the question of the status and meaning of the Reformation of the sixteenth century. The usual view held by Protestants in the last century might be labeled a "tunnel theory" of Church history, according to which, true Christianity had gone underground sometime in the first Christian centuries (a popular date for this being the reign of Constantine), not to emerge until the Reformation. In the long centuries between, Romish supersition had ripened into the decay that finally resulted in reformation. From this perspective, one reminiscent of what A. O. Lovejoy calls the "primitivism" of the sixteenth century Ana-baptists, the meaning of the Reformation was clear: it was the rebirth of true biblical Christianity. But if, as the proponents of churchly revival held, the *entire* history of the Church was of positive significance, such a view of the sixteenth century was impossible. One finds, therefore, a somewhat ambiguous attitude toward the Reformation among them. It is viewed by Loehe and Nevin, for example, as a necessary correction of certain excesses and abuses in the late medieval Church, but hardly as a complete reversal of direction in Christendom. Indeed, one of the least fortunate results of the Reformers' work in the minds of the churchly revivalists was that their work had itself led to abuses, directly opposite to those of the medieval Church, but dolorous nonetheless. Both Nevin and Schaff and the German confessionalists were concerned to show the important connections between the Church Fathers and the Reformers, and the Oxford Anglicans were equally occupied with validating their position with supporting evidence from the Patristic Church. Newman himself took a very dim view of the Reformation; to him it had been an unmitigated disaster, an almost fatal blow at catholicity and apostolicity. His *Lectures on Justification* (1838) are a vehement attack upon a central doctrine of the Reformation, justification by faith alone.

One of the mournful effects of the Reformation in Newman's mind was the eclipsing of the sacraments. In his *Apologia Pro Vita Sua* he recalls that at a very early age he espoused the doctrine of the Real Presence in the Eucharist and that his faith never waivered thereafter. Nevin's major work, *The Mystical Presence,* was devoted to Communion, and the Neo-Lutherans made the reassertion of Luther's sacramental theology a central concern of the German confessional revival. It is therefore possible to treat these three churchly movements as being essentially eucharistic revivals and to seek their basic meaning in the revitalization of the doctrine of the Real Presence in the nineteenth century theological world, where a "Zwinglian" or memorialistic view of Holy Communion did prevail. But this would be a mistake. Each of these movements interpreted the sacraments in the light of a still more vital doctrine: the Incarnation. This dogma was the heart of the churchly revival of the last century. It informed the views held by the high churchmen of all other doctrines. The understanding of the Church as the Body of Christ anticipated the twentieth century view of the Church as the extension in human society of Christ's Incarnation and recalled at the same time strands in biblical and patristic thought. With such a doctrine of the Church, the opposition to Erastianism that characterized the movements was inevitable, as was their concern for Church history. In Germany there arose a re-emphasis upon the *kenosis* Christology of the second chapter of Philippians, in which St. Paul refers to Christ's having emptied himself in becoming man and taking on "the form of a servant." As this emptying of himself *(kenosis)* began the world's salvation, so must the sacrifice of itself in service to others by the Church bring its redemption to completion. These ideas were the motive force behind Loehe's charitable work at Neuendettelsau in Bavaria, where as a result of his ministry there sprang up orphanages, hospitals, and asylums. John Nevin prefaced his *Mystical Presence* with a translation of an essay by the German theologian Karl Ullman in which Ullman maintained that the person of the Incarnate Christ himself was the foundation of all true theology. And, according to Ullman, the Incarnation was to be understood not merely as a formal doctrine, but as a living reality. Thus, for Nevin the significance of Holy Communion was that it was the supreme means of effecting the union of the individual Christian with Christ. This union was for Nevin the continuation of the Incarnation, and it was "emphatically concentrated in the mystery of the Lord's Supper."[11] Newman's adherence to the centrality of the Incarnation is less rigid, since he tended to see flexibility as one of the great virtues of Roman Catholicism and could hardly turn around and declare any one doctrine as *the* crucial one in Christian theology. But his own sentiments are clear: "I should myself call the Incarnation the central aspect of Christianity, out of which . . . the main aspects of its teaching take their rise."[12] Newman held too that the very principle of dogma itself followed from the Incarnation: "supernatural truths irrevocably committed to human language, imperfect because it is human, but definitive and necessary because given from above."[13] For Newman, therefore, the whole body of Christian thought depended in a sense upon the Incarnation.

None of the churchly revivals was a "success" if judged by its failure to change the nature or direction of the life of the church in which it occurred. Of all of the men mentioned in this essay, only Newman and

Schaff attained any great recognition in their own time, and even they shared with the others a feeling of frustration and disappointment at the emerging shape of "modern" life. The optimism of the nineteenth century world was, for its part, impatient with what seemed to be a gloomy medieval insistence upon outmoded and cumbersome forms and ideas, a denial of the meaning of "progress" itself. This was the same mood which prompted C. G. Coulton's outburst against the eulogizers of the Middle Ages in his work, *The Medieval Village,* published in 1925. But Coulton's protests to the contrary, the century which has elapsed since the churchly revivals waxed and waned has vindicated many of their judgments upon the age in which they lived. Charles Kingsley, whose accusations concerning the truthfulness of the Roman clergy provoked Newman's brilliant *Apologia,* or the self-important ministers of the German Reformed Synod of Pennsylvania, whose efforts hounded Nevin out of their seminary, have not worn nearly so well as have the recipients of their scorn. Certainly the twentieth century is no more "religious" than the nineteenth, and it may well be, as often claimed, that western man has finally and irrevocably entered upon his post-Christian maturity (or senescence). But the churches of our own time may enjoy one small advantage over their ancestors of a hundred years ago: they seem no longer to confuse the advance of civilization with the advent of the Kingdom of Heaven. It is no accident that in their efforts to redefine their faith and work, the churches have been driven to re-examine the questions which occupied the proponents of churchly revival — the nature of the Church, its sacraments and worship, as understood in the light of the doctrine of the Incarnation.

Professor Jaroslav Pelikan has noted that, like most historians, the historian of the Church is likely to concern himself more with change than with continuity, and that, because of this, the history of theology is apt to be written in terms of novelty and controversy rather than stability and steady development.[14] It is because they represent an underlying continuity between medieval and reformed Christianity on the one hand and twentieth century religion on the other that the movements discussed in this essay have recently been subject to the re-examination of church historians. But beyond this, they remind any intellectual historian, if only because of their continued protests against it, of the growth on both sides of the North

Atlantic of a cultural Protestantism whose implications for social, political, and economic history are enormous. It is noteworthy that, along with such perceptive critics of this culture-religion as Charles Dickens, Herman Melville, and Jacob Burckhardt, there were men in the churches themselves who sensed the uneasiness of the alliance between Christianity and nineteenth century western civilization and called for a re-examination of the terms upon which it had been concluded. There has been no dearth of such criticism in our own time, and much of it, especially that stemming from the thought of Karl Barth, has gone in another direction from that taken by the high churchmen treated here. But in the last century these voices were among the few raised from within the Church in warning prophecy against the facile identification of the kingdoms of heaven and earth. As such these men represent the first waves of a strong tide in twentieth century religious thought, and their lives as well as their ideas are significant evidence of the existence of the cultural Protestantism they so protested.

*NOTES*

1. The most thorough and readable biography of Newman remains Wilfrid Ward, *Life of Cardinal Newman* (2 vols.; London, 1912), although newer studies, notably Muriol Trevor, *Newman. The Pillar of the Cloud* (Garden City, N. Y., 1962) and *Newman. Light in Winter* (Garden City, N. Y., 1963), have appeared. R. W. Church, *The Oxford Movement* (London, 1897) is still the standard study of the Oxford Movement.
2. There is a lack of English language material on nineteenth century German Neo-Lutheranism. Brief biographical sketches of the principals may be found in *The New Schaff-Herzog Encyclopedia of Religious Knowledge,* ed. by Samuel Maculey Jackson (New ed.; 1951-1957). Short treatments of their theology appear in F. Lichtenberger, *History of German Theology in the Nineteenth Century* (Edinburg, 1889) and in O. Pfleiderer, *Development of Theology in Germany since Kant* (3d ed.; London, 1909).
3. Since its publication the basic work on Nevin and Schaff has been James Hastings Nichols, *Romanticism in American Theology* (Chicago, 1961).
4. Nichols notes that what Nevin called "Puritanism" might now be called "Evangelicalism."
5. Quoted in J. F. Ohl, "The Liturgical Deterioration of the Seventeenth and Eighteenth Centuries," *Memoirs of the Lutheran Liturgical Association,* IV (1902), 77.
6. John Henry Newman, *Parochial and Plain Sermons,* I (New ed.; London, 1877), 319.
7. The original title of the work, which went through several editions, was simply *Appeal to the American Churches.*
8. Nichols, *Romanticism,* 4.

9. Emanuel Hirsch, *Geschichte der neuern evangelischen Theologie,* V (Gütersloh, 1960), 207 ff.
10. The seven characteristics are: preservation of type, continuity of principles, power of assimilation, logical sequence, early anticipation, preservative additions, and chronic continuance.
11. John Williamson Nevin, *The Mystical Presence* (Philadelphia, 1867), 51.
12. John Henry Newman, *An Essay on the Development of Christian Doctrine* (Image Books ed.; Garden City, N. Y., 1960), 59.
13. *Ibid.,* 311.
14. Jaroslav Pelikan, "An Essay on the Development of Christian Doctrine," *Church History,* XXXV, No. 1 (March, 1966), 8.

# O. E. Hagen, A Pioneer Norwegian-American Scholar

THEODORE C. BLEGEN

Ole Eriksson Hagen (1854-1927) is little known in American educational history and all but forgotten by Norwegian-Americans. Yet he was one of the relatively early group of American scholars trained to the Ph.D. level in Germany; he held a chair in Scandinavian and other languages for a decade in the University of South Dakota; he published several books and numerous articles in German, Norwegian, and English; he was a linguist, a writer of history, and a poet; and he made independent studies of such puzzles as the Dighton Rock and the Kensington rune stone.

That Hagen's story has been neglected is understandable. After a decade of university teaching, he abandoned his academic career and spent the remaining twenty-six years of his life on a farm in Wisconsin. Nearly all his books, manuscripts, and correspondence were destroyed when his house burned down a year before his death. And to some he seemed enigmatic because of his formalized English writing, his addiction to Latin phrases, and perhaps the unconventionality of a trained scholar turning aside from the academic paths of his time.

It is not surprising that Hagen had a zeal for learning, for he had gifted parents. His father, Erik O. Hagen, was a lay preacher of the Haugean school who won no little fame in his native land, especially his home valley of Gudbrandsdal, before he emigrated with his family from Norway in 1869. Like Hans Nielsen Hauge, the founder of his school of religious thought, the elder Hagen linked spiritual interests with a liking for practical affairs and the outdoors. In his youth he was a hunter and mountain climber, in his later years a hard worker on his farm. The mother of O. E. Hagen came of a family that gave Norway a nineteenth-century poet of some distinction.

Hagen's father took up farming in Dunn County, Wisconsin, not far from the city of Eau Claire, after his emigration, but he continued as a lay preacher, working among the Norwegian immigrants through a long life; and he was active as a church member who, as the years went by, affiliated with groups which, in his judgment, seemed closest to the Haugean pietistic movement. It is impossible to say where the influence of one parent began with the young Hagen, and where that of the other left off. Certainly the force of the father's intellect influenced the son, as did his mother's poetic heritage. In his mature years, O. E. Hagen wrote a biography of his father and also a booklet about his mother's near relative, the poet Sylvester Sivertsson.[1] The son himself chose the path of linguistic and historical scholarship, but his writings cite verses and ballads, and he wrote several poems.

We know little about O. E. Hagen's years in Norway. He was fifteen when the family left for America. He was born at Skiaker (now Skjåk) on September 28, 1854.[2] It may be assumed that in Norway he had an elementary education or its equivalent in private instruction, perhaps more. His interest in reading and study had deep roots; from some of his writings we know that he took an early interest in folklore and in tales out of the Norwegian past. In the United States he did preparatory work in an academy at Galesville, Wisconsin, in 1875 and 1876, but these dates leave the period 1869-75 unaccounted for. It seems certain that in those years he helped his father on the farm, and he also worked in sawmills on the Chippewa River. In one of his essays he tells of hearing an old ballad recited by a Norwegian immigrant for a group of lumber workers in the summer of 1873, when he was a laborer in a sawmill.[3] Whatever his preparation for a higher education, he seems to have been a common-school teacher for a short time, and then he enrolled at the University of Wisconsin in 1878.

In 1882, at the age of twenty-eight, he received the degree of bachelor of arts and also that of bachelor of literature from the University of Wisconsin. His four-year undergraduate record shows that he excelled in the study of languages, and it is almost startling to realize what a formidable array of languages his "classical" course included. There were Greek, Latin, Anglo-Saxon, Icelandic, French, and German; and in his language classes he usually received grades in the 90s (sometimes as high as 98). Despite the predominance of languages, Hagen's program also records courses in history, mathematics, physics, zoology, botany, astronomy, English literature, philosophy, even political economy and constitutional law. His highest marks were won in Greek, Anglo-Saxon, Icelandic, and literature, his lowest in astronomy. His Wisconsin studies were carried on during the presidency of John Bascom, and the university faculty had such notable teachers as William F. Allen in Latin and history, Lucius Hermitage also in Latin, Alexander Kerr in Greek, and Rasmus B. Anderson in Scandinavian studies. Among Anderson's achievements was that of building a nucleus for a library in the Norwegian field, and Hagen helped him to list the holdings in that area.[4]

After completing his work for the bachelor's degrees, Hagen taught Greek and Latin for a year at Galesville. In 1884 he was awarded two more degrees by the University of Wisconsin, those of master of arts and of literature, perhaps on the basis of informal studies and continued academic interest.[5] Then, with four degrees, he returned to Galesville as a professor of classical languages and literature (1884-86). Not much is known about his experiences at Galesville, but an address he delivered there on Washington's birthday in 1883 under the auspices of a student society was printed as a pamphlet. It was called *Our Country, Origin and Growth of Its Liberty, and Our Possibilities as a People.* If the subtitle seems a trifle grandiose to modern ears, the speech was thoughtfully composed and contained ideas unusual for their time and place.

Historical studies, Hagen said, "must necessarily be comparative." They must deal with cause and effect. A "historical event is not a simple isolated fact." Seeing it as the culmination of "an aggregate of conditions and circumstances," he argued that it had taken all the ages of time to make possible the doings of an individual. By similar reasoning, the "influence of our actions, good or evil," he said, "extends to all eternity." If mankind could understand this idea, as a "law of responsible moral beings," there would be "no need of any hell to frighten, or any heaven to stimulate man to righteousness."

Another arresting part of this address was a passage on tolerance. This, to Hagen, was what made life "agreeable, promising and possible." Without it, life, he said, is a dungeon, a hell. National and religious prejudice he described as "the direct offspring of ignorance and a base heart."

A clue to an important turn in Hagen's career was his comment that the United States did not possess a single true university. He added that about six hundred American students were currently studying in German universities and that almost every distinguished American scientist was "equipped with European learning." This situation, he declared, must be changed before America could take its place "among the scientific nations of the world." And he was ahead of his time when he said that the "fickle and impatient American mind must accustom itself to the slow plodding of the honest investigator." Near the end of his address, he suggested that "the government must be more liberal in behalf of science and learning." It "must relieve the patient searcher from his petty cares, so that he can devote himself entirely to his chosen specialty. It must encourage the higher grades of learning, not only indirectly, but also directly." If this should come about, Hagen thought that we could then take "our proper place upon the arena of modern civilization." He spoke in the early 1880s, but his language bore the accents of more than a half century later.[6]

In 1886 Hagen took a step which he may have had in mind three years earlier when he spoke of American students in Germany. In that year, aided by a loan, he went to the University of Leipzig. There, for four years, he studied languages and history, especially under the distinguished Assyriologist, Friedrich Delitzch. In his *Vita,* presented at the end of his Ph.D. work, he also mentioned, among his teachers, Professors G. Voigt, B. Lindner, and W. Maurenbrecher.

Hagen supplemented his formal studies at Leipzig with research in the British Museum, the Louvre, and the Royal Museum in Berlin. As in earlier years, he was an avid student of languages. On the later evidence of his son, he ultimately was competent in thirty languages and dialects.[7] He wrote a series of monographs and articles in German, including *Keilschrifturkunden zur Geschichte des Königs Cyrus,* his Leipzig doctoral dissertation.[8] His research for these and other studies took him into archaeology, philology, history, epigraphy, ethnology, and geography, and he drew upon his knowledge of Assyrian, Persian, Greek, Latin, and Hebrew. Those who knew him mentioned many years later, not only the range of his knowledge of languages and dialects, but also his general information. In conversation he moved easily from mythology to history (ancient and modern) and to literature; and from the church fathers to runology, history, and folklore.[9]

His studies in Germany came to an end when, in 1890, he received from the University of Leipzig the degrees of master of arts and doctor of philosophy. Thus equipped with specialized education and the highest degrees attainable, he seemed destined for an academic career in America. After some months he returned to the United States, and in 1891 he accepted an appointment as professor of modern languages in the University of South Dakota at Vermillion. One report suggests that President Harper of the University of Chicago knew about Hagen and called his name to the attention of the University of South Dakota officials.[10]

The South Dakota appointment was announced in June, 1891, and Hagen took up his teaching duties when the university opened in the fall of that year.[11] The catalogue listed his courses as German, French, Italian, and Scandinavian, with an explanation that the last-named field meant "Norse and Swedish and Old Norse with Gothic." For some years, it seems certain, more courses were offered than taught. In 1897-98 the catalogue listed Spanish and separate courses in modern German and modern French literature, plus Old German Philology and Old Scandinavian Philology. The giving of a course obviously hinged upon the number of students who enrolled for it, as indeed the catalogue occasionally stated. The university paper, the *Volante,* noted as early as November 5, 1891, that Professor Hagen had arranged for a class in Icelandic, an elective which the editor of the paper hoped would be "required in the regular courses in the near future." A change in Hagen's teaching field took place in 1898, when he was shifted from "modern languages" to Greek, Hebrew, and the Scandinavian languages. The latter included modern Norwegian, Danish, and Swedish, but also Old Norse. And the college paper reported in the winter of 1899 that Hagen had "another class in Norse" which met four times a week.[12]

It is curious how difficult it is to piece together the story of a teacher through a decade distant in the past by more than fifteen college generations. One does find casual notes here and there, however. For instance, the University of South Dakota sent an exhibit in 1893 to the World's Fair in Chicago consisting of a series of hand-written papers by students, one volume of which came from modern languages, presumably Hagen's classes. Another item is a report that Hagen in 1894-95 taught a class in Biblical literature at the Y.M.C.A., attested by a note in the college paper stating that he had been chosen by "unanimous vote" on an "informal ballot." Early in 1895 he was meeting this class three times a week. Still another mention is that of a lecture that he gave in 1895 at a Congregational church in Vermillion on baptism. It occasioned an editorial in the *Volante* which spoke of his "exposition" as deep, thorough, and logical.[13]

These surface items may suggest a placid, gentle academic existence, but if so, they are misleading. Actually the decade of the 1890s was a period of turbulence in the history of the University of South Dakota; of faculty dissension and dismissals of professors; and, before its end, the resignation in October, 1897, of the president, Joseph W. Mauck, followed by the appointment of a new president in 1899 after an interim acting president. Hagen was in the thick of the controversies. He was disengaged from his professorship in 1896, reappointed in 1897, and finally asked to resign in 1901.

A friend of Hagen suggested, many years later, that religious cleavages in the faculty were involved in his resignation. Hagen was a Lutheran; many of his colleagues were of other denominations; and there is some evidence that Hagen's interest in the Y.M.C.A. was not unconnected with a feeling that it and the Y.W.C.A. were influencing Scandinavian Lutheran students to join other churches than Lutheran. One student many years later wrote that in the spring of 1895 Hagen publicly declared that the Y organizations should be abolished. The same student said that for ten years the university campus was "on fire" with controversy about Darwinism, with Hagen one of the leaders of the anti-Darwinists.[14] Yet another student remembered controversy about the "modernizing" of courses, with several professors taking the position that "a man was not educated unless he was what they called a classical scholar."[15] The implication seemed to be that Hagen was one of the professors who held such a view. There can be no doubt that Hagen and the administration were mutually hostile. Hagen clearly had no regard or respect for the president; it seems equally certain that the president could not work with Hagen. It should be added that, although students thought Hagen was an excellent teacher, he was also regarded as an "individualist" and a "very odd" personality.[16] He did not lack support, for in 1897, after a year's absence, he was reappointed; Mauck stepped out as president; and an acting president came in for a couple of years. The troubles were by no means at an end, however. Finally, in 1901, the South Dakota "Regents for Education" investigated the faculty dissension, heard witnesses, and then, "in the best interest of the University," requested the resignations of Hagen and Woodford D. Anderson, the principal of the College of Commerce.[17]

No details of the charges against Hagen and Anderson, or of the evidence given by witnesses, have been found. There seems to be only the allegation of dissension in the faculty. A newspaper commented that the session of the regents "was not the least bit sensational."[18] Both men promptly resigned. A hint of the divergence of opinion between Anderson and Hagen is afforded by an address that Anderson gave in 1900 to the National Education Association. He argued vigorously for business education, but said that "it would be a farce" if planned or directed by classicists and scientists.[19]

It does not seem possible, more than sixty years after these events and with almost no specific evidence, to disentangle and weigh the factors that led to Hagen's resignation. The institution was only nine years old when Hagen appeared on the scene and it was struggling to find itself. It had no system of professorial tenure, but its board held hearings before requesting resignations. It had little experience with the problems of academic freedom and of faculty dissidence. Perhaps universities cannot mature without undergoing ordeal by conflict of ideas. The German-trained classicist was as fully disillusioned with the university as its administration was with him. We know what some of the issues were, but we do not know what relative importance Dr. Hagen attached to them. His subsequent career reveals scars left by his academic experience, but except for a single derogatory allusion to the university in his later years, he wrote no account of his South Dakota experience, as far as is known. It must be added that, unless the evidence from South Dakota is misleading, Dr. Hagen's attitudes do not seem consistent with the views he voiced in 1883 on toleration and prejudice.[20]

The troubles in South Dakota, climaxed by Hagen's severance from his professorship, marked a decisive turn in his career. After leaving Vermillion, he went back to the farming community in Dunn County, Wisconsin, where his father had settled more than thirty years earlier. There he bought a small farm and soon built a house adapted to his needs, including space for his books and papers. In 1898 he had married Constance E. Johnson, a native of Minneapolis, who is described by L. M. Gimmestad as an unusually gifted woman; and they had two sons, one of whom died at an early age. The other, Odin, survived his father. Some years after the first land purchase, Hagen bought another piece of farm land; and thus established, he spent the remaining years of his life (to 1927) as a farmer or, more accurately, a scholar-farmer.

He lived in what seems to have been, in part at least, a self-imposed exile. By education he was prepared for research, writing, and advanced teaching, but he never served in another academic position. Apparently he made no effort to secure a new appointment; and his frame of mind seemed to be that if any institution desired his services, it would know where to find him. Notwithstanding the unhappy termination of his professional career, there is no evidence that he would not have accepted a chair in some other university if it had been tendered him. As far as is known, no Norwegian-American college sought his services, and nothing has been found to indicate that he himself desired an appointment in a church-related college.

If the turn in Hagen's life seems puzzling, the picture of his later years is by no means one of scholarly passivity. Hagen was busy with his pen on his farm, especially after the first few years of separation from the academic world. Through books and articles he reached out to an audience of readers; now and then he gave lectures; he won the friendship of his neighbors; and he may have written much more than is known on the basis of his published work. One cannot escape the impression, however, that he was hemmed in intellectually. He was handicapped by lack of funds for travel to research centers in the United States and Europe; and there was an air of frustration about his career. Long before his withdrawal from academic life, he had spoken of the need for governmental subsidies to encourage productive scholars; and he reverted to this theme in later years. After he died, his friend, Gimmestad, reviewing his career, lamented the failure of wealthy persons of Norwegian backgrounds to provide funds that might have assured the publication of Hagen's writings.[21] What was at stake, however, was not alone publication, but something more important: a richer and more productive life than was within his reach during his last quarter century.

Notwithstanding the lack of a professorship or of research grants, Hagen continued with his writing. We have no reliable information as to how many manuscripts were destroyed when fire consumed his Wisconsin house in 1926; and the compilation of a dependable Hagen bibliography offers difficulties, for he may have contributed articles to newspapers and magazines to which we have no clues. If he kept reprints or clippings, they presumably were lost in the fire. Even so, however, he left an impressive record of known publication.

In addition to his Galesville address of 1883, as well as his doctoral dissertation and other works in German, he published book-length studies of his father's life and of the Norwegian poet Sivertsson; an essay on Vinland; several studies of the Kensington rune stone; and more than a score of articles relating to his interests in folklore, history, and poetry (including some poems of his own composition). Telling of the burning of his house, he mentioned the destruction of an Assyrian dictionary which he had prepared in manuscript.[22] Possibly his most deeply felt loss, however, was a manuscript article, or monograph (we do not know of what length), on the Kensington inscription, a study which he seems to have worked on for many years and for which, in 1924, he had promised publication. What other manuscripts, including correspondence, were burned, we do not know.

In 1908, before Hagen (as far as is known) published anything about the Kensington stone, he wrote an essay, in Norwegian, entitled (in translation) "Some Words about Research on Vinland." This appeared in Rasmus B. Anderson's newspaper *Amerika* and was thereafter reprinted as a pamphlet.[23]

In *Amerika* Hagen had read an article on Vinland by a certain P. P. Iverslie and had taken note, among other things, of Iverslie's allusions to the Dighton Rock and the Newport Tower. He had also seen in print a lecture by Professor Julius Olson, and he had been tempted to reply to it. He did not do so, and in explaining his reason he commented on the state of literary criticism in America. He pointed to what he called "a false conception of what constitutes criticism." Appraisals of literary works were customarily complimentary, often little more than advertisements, whereas genuine criticism was considered offensive to the author.

Hagen drew a distinction between what he called negative and positive criticism. He instanced Professor Gustav Storm of Norway as one who practiced negative criticism — Storm was a distinguished scholar whose views on Vinland had occasioned sharp controversy with Rasmus B. Anderson and others. The negative school of criticism, Hagen conceded, had its values. It counteracted rashness and exposed unscientific work and "irresponsibility." Generally, its unbending conservatism weakened its power of judgment and its effectiveness in utilizing evidence. The true historical scholar, Hagen believed, must take both negative and positive approaches in his gathering and arranging of evidence and in orienting himself to the spirit of the times with which he deals. He must put aside tendentious influences; he must view the past in the light of its own conditions.

The sources on the Vinland voyages — Hagen referred to the sagas — seemed basically trustworthy to him, yet Storm, he thought, dealt with them in a spirit of such excessive caution that it bordered upon hostility. Hagen gave several illustrations of historical problems which, if subjected to Storm's method, would lose all continuity and be reduced to masses of unrelated episodes. The sagas offered firm ground, but he also believed that in due time sources would be found to confirm the saga accounts — he mentioned the possibility of finding pertinent materials in the Vatican and in various cloisters.

His reference to further researches in European manuscript collections led him to comment on an idea he had touched upon in 1883. One could not do research and at the same time conduct a profitable business. He suggested that scholarship — and he had in mind especially the Vinland problems — would prove a rewarding field for wealthy Norwegian-Americans to cultivate with funds and encouragement.

Hagen next considered the question why Norway, after the earlier Vinland voyages, did not maintain its earlier connections with the New World. The answer, he indicated, was obvious. The chronology of the saga accounts ran from 986 to 1347 A.D.; and at the end of that period it stopped. The reason was the devastating pandemic, the Black Death, which swept across Europe, scourging one country after another. He then wrote a brilliantly concise account of the origin and spread of the dreadful disease, its fearful effects, and especially its impact upon Norway.

Hagen's essay included a discussion of the petroglyph known as Dighton Rock, in Massachusetts.[24] Unlike Iverslie, he could find in its weird markings nothing that had relevance to Vinland. He had made a first-hand inspection of the famous rock in 1886, while on his way to Leipzig. He spent two days studying its inscriptions; and he had prepared himself with such transcripts as had been made by others, with photographs, records of all known forms of runes, alphabets of various languages, and even syllabaries. He chalked the Dighton inscriptions and copied them with care. Later, he said, he showed his copies to eminent European paleographers, and they merely laughed at them.

Hagen was not content summarily to dismiss the matter, and on his return to America, after finishing his studies at Leipzig, he again visited Dighton Rock. This time he had the advantage of paleographic knowledge gained from his German studies. Once again, however, he found the inscriptions to be, in his own words, an "epigraphic impossibility." He detailed his reasons — in general the inscriptions were without form or system — a miscellany of unrelated markings.

He then went into a lengthy discussion of runes, in which he took note of linguistic changes in this form of writing through centuries in the several Scandinavian countries. He admired runic writing and emphasized its beauty, compactness, and adaptability to "epigraphic combinations." Toward the end of the essay, he gave attention to the much-discussed Newport Tower in Rhode Island. He had not personally visited it, he said, and his observations were therefore based on what he had heard and read. The structure was one that called for specialized study by a historian of architecture, but on the basis of his information, he thought that scholars were not likely to reach early judgments about it in "chronological or ethnological terms."[25]

Hagen's first known contribution to Kensington literature was not made until 1910. On March 10 of that year he signed an article on the Kensington problem which Rasmus B. Anderson published under Hagen's Latin title, "Ad Utrumque Parati Simus," in the newspaper *Amerika.*[26]

Hagen had known about the Kensington stone, but he had not previously given it much time or thought. He was aware of the fact, however, that the museum committee of the Minnesota Historical Society was preparing a report on it. The occasion for his article was primarily a couple of pieces that R. B. Anderson had written for *Amerika.*[27] Scoffing at the inscription, Anderson had urged the museum committee "to go slow" about endorsing it. In one article he wrote about a petrified man excavated in northwestern Minnesota in the middle 1890s. It had been found somewhere between Warren and Argyle and had been exhibited in both villages. Anderson's information was that a man named "Ohman" had had something to do with this "fossil man," and he implied that this Ohman was none other than Olof Ohman, the finder of the rune stone.

No one named Ohman was involved in any way with the alleged petrified man. But there was such a hoax in 1896. A "fossil" man was dug up — a ditch operation — in the township of Bloomer, between Warren and Argyle (Marshall County), on June 8, 1896, and was exhibited shortly afterwards. There were several claimants; the supposed "body" was sold several times at enlarged prices; it was taken to Crookston and

Winnipeg; and a law case developed over its ownership. It was a palpable, an absurd, fraud; in fact the molds used in making the "petrified" man were later found in Argyle. Two judges in the case, Andrew Grindeland of Warren and William Watts of Crookston, informed Upham in 1910 that the name of Ohman presumably had been confused with that of one O'Brien (Lucius), the perpetrator of the fraud, who had long since left the state.[28]

The episode is of interest for two different reasons. One is that such a hoax actually occurred in northwestern Minnesota only two years before the Kensington stone was dug up. For those who believe the Kensington inscription to be fraudulent, the incident is a curious one. For others, skeptical or not about the Kensington stone, it is noteworthy that the counterfeit "fossil man" induced Hagen to break his silence on the Kensington puzzle.

Hagen's Latin title meant "Let us be prepared for either [contingency]." Obviously he implied that one should be ready for a verdict either against or for the genuineness of the Kensington inscription. Because of the title and the somewhat stiff English that Hagen used, some writers thought he was cryptic and confusing. But he liked and often employed Latin phrases, and his English style of 1910 was not much unlike that of his published address in English in 1883. It was his own, and if he spoke guardedly, he did so because he had not reached a conclusion about the rune stone. What was significant was that the article signalized publicly the beginning of an interest in the Kensington stone which he cultivated for more than a decade and a half.

If the stone was a fake, Hagen said, "the deception should be relentlessly exposed." If it proved to be genuine, it should be guarded as the "most extraordinary and valuable find" relating to pre-Columbian history that American soil had yielded. He advised the Minnesota Historical Society to "move slowly and carefully but resolutely." Until recently, he said, he had not given much attention to the Kensington stone, and all he now ventured to do was to "help a little in clearing the track" and to "point out a few sidelights." He scoffed at the idea that popular interest, as exhibited in a public meeting, had any significance as a test of the stone, adding that "ostentatious moves and pretentious claims" had surrounded the stone with a "shroud of suspicion."

The deciphering of the inscription, Hagen wrote, "ought to present no difficulties worth mentioning." The "inscription is alphabetic with very few and easily controlled variants, the phonetic values are well established, and the vocables all fall within a thoroughly surveyed dialectic range." The only criticism he had to offer was that the inscription contained "words and phrases of a decidedly suspicious nature both as to form and use." He insisted that the stone *"bears its own evidence, — its own vindication or condemnation,"* and he underlined these words.

Geographically Hagen could discern no valid reason for thinking it improbable that the Norsemen "navigated the sounds and seas to the west and south of Baffins Bay." Fishing, sealing, hunting, and exploring new lands were attractive and tempting, and he cited the "Kergistorsoak" cairn inscription from 1135, as he thought, found on an island in Baffin Bay, in support of his ideas.[30] Hagen, suggested that if early voyagers made their way westward from either Vinland or Greenland, a northern route (he meant Hudson Bay) seemed the most probable to assume. Hudson Bay was a "pocket of the northern seas," and its shores and islands "may contain many records and relics of early mariners." All this, however, was "mere hypothesis" and a "useless speculation" as long as the "genuineness of the inscription" was not established.

Hagen then rejected the assumption, advanced by some, that Scandinavia did not possess "rune scribes" in the 18th and 19th centuries. A runic *calendarium,* with a description of runic letters, had been kept at Uppsala from 1690 to 1840. And Hagen called attention to C. J. Ljungström's *Runa-List,* a booklet on the art of reading runes, which was published in Sweden in 1866, with a second edition in 1875 of which the government distributed 2,000 copies to teachers' seminaries and among public school teachers. The runic symbols were "both well known and used in Sweden at the close of the nineteenth century," and they were also known in many places in Norway. Such evidences brought runology "very close to our days" and "not confined to the learned classes, but including the lay people as well." This, in Hagen's opinion, was a fact to be taken into account in discussions of the rune stone. He closed, as he had begun, with a Latin phrase, "Benavide igitur ingrediamur."

One of the strange byways of the rune-stone controversy is the fact that a well known professor in the University of Wisconsin believed that it was Hagen himself who devised the Kensington inscription! The professor in the case was none other than Julius E. Olson, who taught Scandinavian languages and literature for many years at the University of Wisconsin and who was deeply interested in Vinland.

Dr. Warren Upham of the Minnesota Historical Society spent some days in Madison in the spring of 1910, when he was trying to gather up information about the Kensington stone. He talked with Olson and recorded his conversation in his notebook. He heard Olson allege that Hagen, after his Leipzig studies, "forged" the Kensington inscription. Olson noted that Hagen, while a student at Wisconsin, had examined and arranged the Scandinavian books in the University library as a service to Professor R. B. Anderson. In doing so, he had come upon certain books dealing with runes. The incident was presumably a minor one — and Olson may not have known that Hagen took a great interest in the Vikings and also studied Icelandic for two academic years while an undergraduate. Professor Olson believed that he had the "requisite learning" to concoct the Kensington inscription.[31] Having the "requisite learning" to forge an inscription and actually doing it are, of course, two different things. Professor Olson voiced a suspicion, a theory — and he clung to his ideas for many years, making no secret of them.

Not a shred of evidence has turned up, however, to link Hagen with Kensington or with the Ohman farm on which the stone was found. Nor, if the Kensington inscription was a hoax, can one postulate a convincing motive for Hagen to have committed it. Professor Olson said that the deception had been done in 1891. If, as some have supposed, the motive had been to trap other scholars who were less prepared but perhaps more successful than Hagen, the period Olson had in mind was unrealistic. For 1891 was just after Hagen returned from Germany in triumph upon completing his doctoral studies. And it was before he left home for South Dakota to begin his teaching. The year 1896-97 is an open year in Hagen's life and nothing is known about it, but again, there is no hint of a motive and no connection with Kensington. The South Dakota troubles did not come to a final head until about two and a half years after the Kensington stone was unearthed. It may be added that Olson possibly attributed Hagen's supposed authorship of the inscription to jealousy because, in 1884, Olson was appointed as R. B. Anderson's successor at the University of Wisconsin. But this was before Hagen's German studies for the doctorate, and even if one assumed that Hagen was a better student at Wisconsin than Olson — they were fellow students — the hypothesis of a jealousy taking such a subtle form as the devising of an inscription that might not be found and made public for years strains the imagination.

Hagen returned to the subject of the Kensington inscription later in 1910, this time with an article in Norwegian entitled (in translation) "The Kensington Stone."[32] He now wrote with firsthand information, for he had been in St. Paul in August, 1910, after an earlier summer trip to Saskatchewan, and he had examined the Kensington stone in the rooms of the Minnesota Historical Society, then housed in the State Capitol. With good lighting he made a copy of the inscription for himself; and in his article he gave special attention to certain words, including *from* and *se efter* (look after), about which there had been sharp controversy. In his discussion he drew upon his knowledge of dialectal as well as regular linguistic forms.

Hagen was not ready to take a stand on the question of authenticity. He pointed out that those who purportedly carved the runes were not experts, like the trained Egyptian and Babylonian scribes who followed hard and fast rules in their writing. They were, instead, travelers who knew little about grammar and orthography. In studying an inscription such as that on the Kensington stone, one should keep the door open, he suggested, for recognition of dialect words and dialect ways of speech. He had not made up his mind, but his consideration of a few special linguistic problems suggested that he may have been beginning to lean toward accepting the inscription as genuine.

Like George T. Flom of Illinois, however, the scholar-farmer spurned any notion that scholars should be swayed by nationalistic feelings or should consider any personal wishes that they might entertain with respect to the truth or falsity of the document. To do so was to invite charges of charlatanism.

Epigraphic considerations were of first importance, he believed, in dealing with the Kensington inscription, philological considerations next, but both should proceed together. It is characteristic of Hagen's caution that he closed with a warning that the archaeological field had witnessed many frauds. Numerous alleged artifacts, supposedly found at Pompeii and other Roman sites, were fraudulent; hundreds of Babylonian cylinders, sold as genuine to tourists, were only replicas, usually made from originals at Baghdad. He himself had been offered some in London, and he recalled, somewhat ruefully, one which he had refused to buy; and later he had never been able to find its original, a valuable historical record. Tourists were often victimized, he said, by fraudulent Egyptian papyri.

Hagen's article testifies to a deepening interest in the Kensington stone, but without more study he would not offer a judgment. His closing words of warning meant that scholars should consider all possibilities of fraud at Kensington.

In 1911 Hagen commented on the text of a ballad transmitted orally from the time of the Black Death (a period of great interest to him). He had heard it sung by a mill worker in Wisconsin as early as 1873. Its text had appeared in a *bydelag* publication (*Telesoga*) in 1909, and the editor explained that he had received it from a man who remembered many traditional ballads of Norway (a certain Olav Tortveit).

Hagen reprinted the ballad in *Samband,* another *bydelag* publication, with explanatory notes.[33] He seems to have done this, not so much because a phrase in the ballad resembled a disputed passage in the Kensington inscription, but because the ballad was intrinsically interesting to him. As a Norwegian folklorist had said, it was "first hand," that is, from the approximate time of the Black Death in Norway.

The possible relevance of the ballad to the Kensington text centers in a couple of lines that appear in the very first stanza and are in part repeated in some of those that follow:

Hjelpe os Gud å Maria møy,
Å frels os alle av illi!
[Help us, God and Virgin Mary,
And save us all from evil!]

The lines call to mind a phrase in the Kensington inscription:

"AVM fräelse af illy."

Hagen refers to the Kensington inscription in an explanatory note and says that the occurrence of the phrase, as quoted, should render unnecessary any rejection of it in the runic inscription.

Arguments can go two ways, however. Dr. Erik Wahlgren, dealing with what he views as a hoax, writes that if Hagen heard the words of the ballad in 1873, they might have been familiar among Norwegian immigrants twenty or more years later, when, as he believes, the Kensington inscription was carved. He also wonders if it is a coincidence that Olof Ohman's immediate neighbor, Nils Flaten, had emigrated from Telemarken, the Norwegian source of the ballad.[34]

The files of *Samband,* in which the ballad appeared, disclose the little known fact that in its pages, from 1911 to 1915, Hagen published more than twenty articles. He wrote about the Black Death in Norway and an abandoned church hidden for centuries in a wooded spot. He commented on poetic interpretations of Norway's nature, comparing the works of Bjørnson and of Sivertsson. He discussed the origins of the Norwegian people; ancient folk tales from the valley of his ancestors; even Assyrian letters and dispatches; a study of David's 139th psalm in the light of research in the Veda; and sundry other subjects. Now and then he contributed long narrative poems, two of which afterwards appeared as pamphlets.[35] He wrote poems in memory of his mother and his father.[36] Some of his articles were long, some short. All bore the marks of careful preparation; and the author's sensitive feeling revealed itself most fully in his writings about his homeland, especially the valley he had known in his youth.[37]

On Hagen's birthday in 1924, some of his friends held a celebration in his honor in a local church. Following speeches of greeting and the presentation of a gift, he responded with a talk in which he said, among other things, that he intended soon to publish his findings with respect to the Kensington stone and its inscription.

It was two years after this birthday celebration that a furious fire destroyed his house near Meridean, and all, or nearly all, its contents. Hagen told of this event in a letter to a friend and Waldemar Ager printed it in his newspaper *Reform,* (April 29, 1926) in Eau Claire.[38] The fire had consumed Hagen's pictures, photographs, furniture — just about everything he had in the house. Most irreparable was its "literary and scientific" destruction. His books, many of them rarities in Assyrian and other linguistic fields, works in Oriental and Biblical archaeology, and the greatly prized writings of the German scholars, Franz and Friedrich Delitzsch — all these were lost. In a moving passage Hagen said that he had begun to understand the feelings of scholars in a distant past when great libraries such as that at Alexandria were destroyed.

Most of all, he regretted the loss of his research materials on Oriental sources related to the cosmogony and prehistory of Gothic forefathers, his own manuscript dictionary of Assyrian, and his papers on the Kensington inscription.

That the Kensington manuscripts had been destroyed was the more painful, he wrote, because some time ago he had promised publication of his findings on that subject. As things now stood, he could not fulfill that pledge. For the present, all he could do, he felt, was to make a "categorical" statement.

Hagen had not been able, he said, to find tenable epigraphic evidence that the Kensington inscription was anything except what it purported to be. He had spent a full day examining the stone, with all possible kinds of lighting, and he found the runes to be "on the whole, what I expected to find from the time and the people named in the inscription." On the linguistic side there were peculiarities, perhaps some "graphical" errors, but he had not found any "actual philological proof" that the inscription was fraudulent.

In the controversies, the negative side, he believed, had "often utilized assertions and an argumentation" which, to his mind, constituted "scientific irresponsibility." His view was that the inscription was an "intelligible document." The negative side, in order to make its case, must present evidence of forgery. Such evidence, he said, had not yet been forthcoming. He then referred to reported and extraordinary finds in the Kensington community which seemed to corroborate the record of the stone. His final counsel was that a depository should be found for the Kensington rune stone so that it could be preserved as an important epigraphic document relating to American history. This statement has usually been interpreted as an unqualified endorsement of the Kensington inscription, and if this is a correct interpretation, it places Hagen in conflict with the runologists, whose findings point to a nineteenth-century hoax.

It should be noted, however, that Hagen phrased his statement with due caution. Nearly every phrase is put guardedly, with a hint of reservation: "failed to discover;" "on the whole;" what he "expected to find;" and "intelligible document" — that is, comprehensible; failure to find "actual philological proof;" evidence of forgery "not yet" forthcoming; and "important epigraphic document." Nowhere does he say explicitly that the inscription is authentic, that it is of fourteenth-century origin. In a word, the statement seems somewhat less than categorical. Though he leans toward acceptance of the inscription as genuine, one can scarcely avoid the impression that he did not regard the question as settled unequivocally.

The letter of 1926 was Hagen's final public comment on the Kensington stone. A year later he died. It is not yet wholly clear what papers of his survived the fire of 1926. An obituary noted that he had emerged from the burning house "with his arms full of manuscripts and documents" and there is reason to believe that some of his papers may have been in a second house that he owned, a house that was not burned.

*NOTES*

1. For background, see O. E. Hagen, *Erik O. Hagen. Kort Omrids af Hans Liv og Virksomhed i Norge og Amerika. Et Haugiansk Livsbillede* (Madison, 1909). In a foreword Hagen indicated that he was preparing a fuller work about his father, who lived from 1822 to 1908. A copy of the 1909 biography is in the St. Olaf College Library. Hagen's *Sylvester Sivertsson* was published in 1908 at Eau Claire, Wis. He tells about his father's exploits as a hunter and mountain climber in "En haugianers oplevelser i høifjeldene," *Samband,* No. 62 (June, 1913), 388-402. The fullest and best informed newspaper sketch of O. E. Hagen is by L. M. Gimmestad. It was printed in *Skandinaven* (Chicago), Mar. 25, 1927, *Reform* (Eau Claire), April 28, 1927, and *Minneapolis Tidende,* May 5, 1927.

2. The early newspaper obituaries record Hagen as born in 1850, but Gimmestad gives the date as 1854. The date is confirmed by Hagen himself in the "Vita" at the end of his doctoral dissertation.

3. Gimmestad's sketch (see note 1) reports that Hagen worked in Eau Claire sawmills; Hagen himself referred to this in *Samband,* No. 42 (Oct., 1911), 363.

4. Merle Curti of the University of Wisconsin arranged to have a facsimile of Hagen's scholastic record as an undergraduate sent to me. The original is in the archives of the University of Wisconsin.

5. Curti writes (April 13, 1965) that there is no formal record of Hagen's work for the master's degrees, but that they were probably awarded

on the basis of informal study and continuing interest. The additional work was seemingly done in 1883-1884. See a sketch in R. G. Thwaites, *University of Wisconsin* (Madison, 1900), 472.

6. O. E. Hagen, *Our Country, Origin and Growth of Its Liberty, and Our Possibilities as a People—An Address Delivered on Washington's Birthday before the Utile Cum Dulci Society, Galesville University, Wis. (Galesville, 1883)*. A copy of this rare 36 page pamphlet, with a page of "Errata," is in the library of the State Historical Society of Wisconsin and was made available to me through interlibrary loan to the Minnesota Historical Society.
7. Earl Chapin interviewed Odin Hagen, a son of O. E. Hagen, and printed a story in the *St. Paul Pioneer Press,* June 26, 1955.
8. A copy of Hagen's dissertation (Leipzig, 1891) is in the Center for Research Studies at the University of Chicago and was made available to me through the courtesy of E. B. Stanford of the University of Minnesota Library.
9. Gimmestad, *Skandinaven,* March 25, 1927.
10. *Ibid.*
11. For information about Hagen's career at the University of South Dakota I am indebted to Professors Herbert S. Schell and Cedric Cummins of that university and to Donald N. Meeks, a graduate student at the university, who checked catalogues, checked the files of *Volante,* the campus newspaper, and consulted other sources. His notes are filed with my Kensington materials. Through Meeks, Cummins also made available to me copies of two letters written to him in 1954 by former students of Hagen. Meeks also had a valuable letter from a former student of Hagen.
12. *Volante,* Jan. 30, 1899, cited by Meeks.
13. *Ibid.,* Oct. 8, 1894, Jan. 14, Oct. 28, 1895.
14. See Gimmestad, *Skandinaven,* March 25, 1927; also W. A. Knox of Toledo, Ohio, to Cedric Cummins, Aug. 20, 1954 (Xerox copy in my possession). Mr. Knox was a member of the class of 1900. He admired Hagen but felt that he carried "some things too far," and in fact seemed to feel that it was "his right and duty to run the university."
15. See William Williamson to Meeks, May 4, 1965. Mr. Williamson of Rapid City, South Dakota, described Hagen as "a rather slender man with long thin fingers. He walked with a slight bend of the shoulders. He spoke in a rather low voice with very good enunciation, so that he was easily understood." Letter in my Kensington file.
16. O. E. Hagen, *Nogle Ord om Vinlandsforskningen* (Madison, 1908), 16.
17. *Seventh Biennial Report of the Regents of Education of the State of South Dakota (1900-1902),* 104, 107, 108, cited in notes from Meeks.
18. *Dakota Republican,* April 4, 1901 (Note from Meeks.)
19. The text of Anderson's speech is in *Addresses and Proceedings of the National Education Association, Charleston, S. C.* (Chicago, 1900), 549-555.
20. *Volante,* April 13, 1901; George T. Flom, "Norwegian Language and Literature in American Universities," *Studies and Records,* II (1927), 91; and Lewis E. Akeley, *This Is What We Had in Mind: Early Memories of the University of South Dakota* (Vermillion, 1959).

21. *Skandinaven,* March 25, 1927.
22. Hagen's letter (in Norwegian), telling of the destruction of his house, was written on April 10, 1926, to John Ovren of Eau Claire, and is in *Reform,* April 29, 1926.
23. The essay on Vinland first appeared in *Amerika,* June 26, 1908. The pamphlet, with the title *Nogle Ord om Vinlandsforskningen,* was published as a reprint from *Amerika* (Madison, 1908) and a copy is in the library of the State Historical Society of Wisconsin.
24. Dighton Rock is on the Taunton River, some eight miles from Taunton, Mass. Most of the marks on it seem to have been made by Indians in colonial times, but E. B. Delabarre, who has made careful studies of the inscriptions, suggests that underneath the meaningless scribbles is a message left by one Miguel Cortereal, a "lost" Portugese explorer. Delabarre, *Dighton Rock: A Study of the Written Rocks of New England* (New York, 1928); see also Delabarre's brief account in *Dictionary of American History,* II (New York, 1940), 146.
25. Hagen, *Nogle Ord,* 13-16.
26. *Amerika,* April 1, 1910.
27. *Ibid.,* Feb. 25, March 11, 1910.
28. *Ibid.,* March 12, 1910; see also *Minnesota Historical Collections,* XV (1915), 237.
29. Hagen wrote his article, or at any rate dated it, on March 15, 1910. The museum committee of the Minnesota Historical Society adopted a favorable report on the Kensington inscription on April 21, 1910. The society, through its executive council, did not endorse the committee's conclusion, but reserved for itself and for the society a conclusion as to the genuineness of the stone. *Minnesota Historical Collections,* XV, 267.
30. The "Kingiktorsauk" or "Kinggiktorsoak" inscription — the spellings vary — is pictured in H. R. Holand, *Westward from Vinland* (New York, 1940), 74. Magnus Olsen dates the inscription 1333, Holand 1291, Wahlgren "from about 1328-33." The dating from the fourteenth century seems to be accepted by modern scholars. There is a discussion of the inscription and of the cairns in Helge Ingstad, *Land under the Pole Star* (New York, 1966), 88.
31. Upham's notebooks are in the manuscripts division of the Minnesota Historical Society; see notebook No. 5, especially the entry for April 29, 1910. George T. Flom wrote to A. A. Veblen, Dec. 3, 1928, that Olson believed Hagen "did it." Veblen Papers, Minnesota Historical Society.
32. The article by Hagen, dated Dec. 20, 1910, was reprinted from *Skandinaven* in *Amerika,* Jan. 6, 1911.
33. *Samband,* No. 42 (Oct., 1911), 363-369.
34. Erik Wahlgren, *The Kensington Stone* (Madison, 1958), 162-163. The museum committee of the Minnesota Historical Society in its report on the rune stone called attention to the same ballad. *Minnesota Historical Collections,* XV, 252-253.
35. One was "Det fortryllede fjeldvand — En ungdomserindring," *Samband,* No. 59 (March, 1913), 194-224; the other was "Stenspranget," printed under the more general title "Fra Skiakers sagnverden," *ibid.,* No. 85 (May, 1915), 371-400. St. Olaf College has a copy of the rare pamphlet reprint of *Stenspranget.*
36. *Samband,* No. 73 (May, 1914), 382-387.

37. *Samband* was a monthly magazine dealing especially with the folklore, traditions, and history of Norway and the Norwegian immigrants in America, published in Minneapolis. Its editor was A. A. Veblen, a brother of Thorstein Veblen. See Jacob Hodnefield, "Norwegian-American Bydelags and Their Publications," *Norwegian-American Studies and Records,* XVIII (1954), 163-222.

38. *Reform,* April 29, 1926. Mr. Odin Hagen of Rock Falls, Wisconsin, was kind enough to make available to me his copies of his father's life of Erik O. Hagen, also the book *Sylvester Sivertsson,* and the two pamphlets, *Stenspranget* and *Det Fortryllede Fjeldvand.* He also gave me some information about other materials left by his father. I wish to record my thanks to Mr. Hagen.

# *The Role of Augustana in the Transplanting of a Culture Across the Atlantic*

CONRAD BERGENDOFF

The small trickle of Swedish emigration to the United States in the 1840s grew to a mighty stream before the end of the century, so that by 1900 over a half million Swedish people were incorporated in the American population. While considerable concentration of the newcomers occurred in Illinois and Minnesota these immigrant bands scattered over the entire country, notably in New England, New York City, Pennsylvania, Texas, Missouri, Michigan, Iowa, Nebraska, Kansas, Colorado, Utah, California and the Northwest. In a great number of cases, probably in the majority, the individuals and families merged with the local community and soon lost their identity. Some wanted to forget the past, the foreign manners, the Swedish language. They shunned distinctions from the American environment and even concealed their European ancestry. In places where anti-foreign sentiment prevailed the process was quickened. It is conceivable that the flood of Americanization could have swallowed up the entire Swedish immigrant stream, submerging the culture brought from Sweden and leaving only fading memories of what had been the motherland.

Indeed there was precedent for such an outcome. For in the seventeenth century there had been an immigration from Sweden to the banks of the Delaware. In Pennsylvania, New Jersey, and Delaware, over a thousand Swedes had made their homes. They built churches in what is now Philadelphia, Wilmington, and environs. They engaged in farming, trade and industry. But by the time of the Revolution they had forgotten their Swedish language. Their Lutheran churches had become Episcopalian parishes. Their children had married English or German partners. Only family names and "Old Swedes" churches reminded them of the origin of the Delaware colony.

That the immigration of the nineteenth century did not follow a similar course was due to a number of causes, such as larger numbers, wider distribution, and better communication. But most important was the emergence of an idea of "Swedish-America," the notion that in this new world a kind of replica of the "old country" could be created. While not interfering with the duties of American citizenship Swedish-America *(Svensk-Amerika)* would enable the immigrant to find a home in this country where he could retain his mother-tongue, observe age-old traditions, maintain his religious heritage and receive spiritual encouragement. The idea could become an illusion, fostering the hope that this community of mind and spirit would have permanence, and some spoke of *svenskhetens bevarande* — the preservation of Swedish culture. But the idea became a reality in the period between the Civil War and the First World War. The Great War shattered the illusion. But students both of immigration and of American history have missed the significance of the idea and its influence on the thousands of people who for a couple of generations thought of themselves as citizens of two worlds, the old and the new, of Sweden and of the United States. The purpose of this essay is to recall that era, before it is altogether lost in the past, and to discern some of the leading forces and personalities in the movement.

Foremost of the instruments in the creation of "Swedish-America" was the press. In almost every community of Swedish settlers an organ of public opinion soon sprang up. Chicago became the center where journals suddenly appeared and as suddenly died. A few gained a foothold and by mergers attained national circulation. Among these were *Hemlandet, Det Gamla och Det Nya; Svenska Amerikanaren, Svenska Tribunen, Svenska Kuriren.* Minneapolis was the home of *Skaffaren* and *Minnesota Stats tidning.* Worcester, Massachusetts, had its *Svea* and *Skandinavia.* New York was noted for *Nordstjernan. Vestkusten* came out of San Francisco, *Svenska Journalen* out of Omaha. Jamestown, New York; Duluth, Minnesota; Ironwood and Ishpeming, Michigan; Marinette, Wisconsin; Galva, Rockford, Moline, Illinois; Lindsborg, Kansas — these were the homes of minor Swedish publications, but they joined in the grand symphony of a Swedish journalism which covered the whole country.

Wherever these papers reached they proclaimed a solidarity of the Swedish population. The music was not always harmonious. Some of the papers were in constant warfare against each other. First, and for a long time foremost in the field, was the paper begun by the leader of the Augustana churches, T. N. Hasselquist. This was *Hemlandet, Det Gamla och Det Nya,* which started in Galesburg in 1855 and transferred to Chicago in 1859. It originated as a paper for Swedish Lutherans and was edited by Augustana pastors until 1869, when a layman, Johan Alfred Enander, took over. Its churchly position was considered too rigid by the liberal *Svenska-Amerikanaren,* and it came under attack by the still more radical *Svenska Kuriren.* Politics played a large part in most of the papers, which at election time could become propaganda sheets. In general the Republicans won over the Swedish papers — a tradition begun by Hasselquist and rooted to some extent in the Swedish hatred of slavery which was defended by the Democrats. *Hemlandet* had to endure not only the stings and arrows of the secularist journals but the opposition of the non-Lutherans. For each of the denominations gradually acquired its own spokesman. *Frihetsvännen,* (Galesburg) was Baptist and *Sändebudet* (Rockford) was Methodist. Later the Mission Friends joined the fray in *Förbundets Veckotidning* and *Missions Vännen.*

But whatever the political or religious platform of the paper, one note was sounded throughout all: "We are a Swedish people." A good deal of space was given to news from Sweden, and the reader was given the impression that events in that country still concerned him. The weather with its consequences for crops, the labor situation, the economic and political crises, the military program, the royal house, unusual happenings in city and countryside — such gave grist for the printing press. Swedish-Americans followed with eagerness the relations of Finland and Sweden as well as Sweden and Norway, and the papers gathered funds for the relief of hard times in northern Sweden. The visits of prominent Swedes to America created headlines; for instance the triumphal course of Christina Nilsson, the "Swedish nightingale." Letters of Swedish Americans visiting in Sweden found ready space. Clippings from Swedish magazines filled empty columns in the weeklies.

Along with the appearance of the Swedish papers in America went the national cry, "Don't forget the Swedish language" — natural because the existence of this press depended on the retention of the language. Yet this was not the ultimate reason. One cannot deny the pathos on the part of those who struggled to preserve the tongue of the fathers, "the language of honor and of heroes" *(ärans och hjältarnes språk)*. In an essay on "Language in Exile" Nils Hasselmo has shown how "the language represents history and traditions, home, parents, and childhood, religious and aesthetic ideals." It is a reminder of the homeland to the exile. It is a faithful friend in lonely moments, a travel companion and an escape. It is the tool whereby Swedish culture is spread and identified. It is the symbol of unity and joins the people scattered over the new continent. To preserve the mother tongue and keep it pure becomes a moral duty. Hasselmo quotes and translates these lines of Johan Enander:

> The Spirit of the Norseman, honest and faithful,
> Never can die in the tongue of the forefathers.
> Wherever in the world its voice is heard,
> There also his spiritual realm reaches.

In the effort to keep the Swedish language alive in America the Swedish press was more or less consciously attempting to combat the temptation experienced by the immigrant to discard the faith, the ideals, and the traditions of the land he had left. The proponents of Swedish argued that this meant a spiritual loss to the immigrant and was of no benefit to the land he had now "adopted." The Swedish-American best served America by contributing his spiritual treasures to the new world. But to conserve them he must be conscious of what these treasures were. Honesty, integrity, good workmanship, moral behaviour, and love of truth, beauty, and freedom — these were interpreted as Swedish characteristics. The man who sought to conceal or ignore his ancestry was not only foolish but a little less than sincere and patriotic. At least for the time being a Swedish man and woman were at their best in loving both the mother Sweden and the bride America.

How widespread this sentiment was is manifest by the number of publications proclaiming this policy. Gustav Andreen made a study of the Swedish-American press in the early years of this century. He found that in the half-century prior to 1904 there had been started fifty-nine weeklies, six biweeklies, fifteen monthlies, one quarterly, fourteen annuals — a total of ninety-five publications. Even congregations had attempted their own papers in Swedish and of the larger ones Andreen identified forty-six. They were usually written by the pastor of the congregation. But who were the journalists that were responsible for the national weeklies and monthlies, especially of the Chicago papers which by 1914 had attained a circulation of over 65,000 each?

Two names stand out in the history of *Hemlandet* and of the Swedish-American press as a whole. The first is that of T. N. Hasselquist, the remarkable figure who dominated the Swedish-Lutheran Augustana Synod from its foundation in 1860 until his death in 1891. His little paper printed in 1855 spread all over the country and in a few years had 1,000 subscribers. The name *Hemlandet, Det Gamla och Det Nya* (the Homeland, the Old and the New) breathed the spirit of the paper. Freedom for the citizen in this new land, freedom for the church to govern itself, but a freedom that entails responsibility, was the tone of the paper. His opposition to slavery (Hasselquist was on the platform for the Douglas-Lincoln debate in Galesburg, where he was pastor, 1858) led him into the Republican party, and much of Swedish-America followed him. But his interests were fundamentally religious. In 1856 he started another paper, *Det Rätta Hemlandet,* which in 1869 was combined with a missionary paper, *Missionären.* The combined papers became *Augustana,* the official organ of the Augustana Synod. *Hemlandet* had been edited by A. R. Cervine, Eric Norelius, and P. A. Sundelius — all having some connection with the Augustana people. In 1869 the editorship was given to John Alfred Enander.

Thus the second illustrious name is that of Enander, editor for most of the next forty years. He was universally regarded as the ablest and most representative leader of Swedish America. As a child in Sweden, where he was born in 1842, he early revealed interest in reading, writing and printing. He enjoyed a good education in Vänersborg high school, and came to America in 1869, enrolling in the Swedish-American school at Paxton, Illinois. There he planned to prepare for the ministry. But before the year was out, P. A. Sundelius, who had been editor of *Hemlandet,* suddenly went over to its rival, *Svenska-Amerikanaren.* Erland Carlsson and T. N. Hasselquist recognized the unusual qualities of young Enander. They persuaded him to fill the vacancy left by Sundelius.

At a dinner in his honor thirty years later, Enander expressed what had been his goal throughout the years. His words cast light on what he had encountered. "The goal which I have desired but also for which I have striven all my life, though often misunderstood, is this: to awaken to life the feeling of Swedish nationality, slumbering as if dead, to kindle in hearts that are lukewarm or cold a warm love to a common language, common historical memories, common song, and a common spiritual nurture in general, and to mold this into a harmonious whole with all the beautiful, the noble, the true, which the culture of the new fatherland has so freely offered the immigrant. I have wanted our nationality to be not only a receiving people, but likewise a people able to give."

With him it was not a mere wish. In addition to the editorship of the leading Swedish weekly, Enander was active in writing, in speaking, and in representing his people. In 1890 he became professor of Swedish language and Literature at Augustana College. Inspiration more than academic discipline was his gift to his students, for he awakened in them a passion for the great qualities in Swedish literature. After a brief period as editor of *Svenska Journalen* in Omaha he returned to *Hemlandet* in 1896. A heart attack weakened him in 1903. He died in 1910. Grateful countryman raised a large runestone monument on his grave in Chicago.

His writings included a *Förenta Staternas Historia* in several volumes (2d ed., 1882), essays on *Nordmännen i Amerika eller Amerikas upptäckt* (1893), *Våra Fäders Sinnelag* (printed in Stockholm, 1894), *Den Svenska Sången under det nittonde seklet* (1901). A collection of his writings appeared in 1892. He was orator at Swedish days at the expositions in Philadelphia, (1876), Chicago, (1893), and in Norrköping, Sweden, (1906).

His aid in Republican campaigns brought him the offer of the ambassadorship to Denmark in 1889, but he was unable to accept. Anders Schön, a competent critic of Swedish-American literature, called him "probably the most remarkable protagonist in Swedish-American history."

Enander was associated with another journalistic venture of a quality beyond that of the average weekly. In 1874 he headed a staff that produced *När och Fjärran.* This was an illustrated literary magazine striving for elegance in form and content. Its essays, biographies, short stories, serials, travel sketches, original poems, and translations offered the Swedish-American reader a magazine comparable to the best in Sweden. There were translations from American poets and verses from poets in Sweden — Tegner, Geijer, Runeberg. It was a laudable attempt, but its cost and literary level were probably above the capacity of the average immigrant. The result was a short life of only three years.

But the literary monthly had set a standard and awakened interest. In 1879 a group of faculty members and graduates of Augustana embarked on a bi-monthly, *Ungdomsvännen.* J. A. Enander and Olof Olsson were editors, and were followed by recognized church leaders such as C. A. Swensson, Eric Norelius, and C. M. Esbjorn. It became a monthly in 1886. The following year it was absorbed by a weekly *Hem Vännen,* enjoying contributions by A. Rodell, C. A. Bäckman, N. Forsander, S. P. A. Lindahl, A. O. Bersell, and J. A. Udden. Though of high quality the contents were too religious for general appeal. In 1889 this paper for young people was incorporated into the new *Augustana.*

A group of Augustana teachers and pastors had deplored the sale of *Hemlandet* in 1872 to private interests. They urged a distinctively religious church organ. Hasselquist's *Det Rätta Hemlandet* och *Missionären* had served as such until 1868. Then the Synod authorized a paper in Swedish, called *Augustana,* which absorbed the prior papers. Almost to his death Hasselquist bore the burden of editor. Eric Norelius served for a few years, then was followed by S. P. A. Lindahl who fashioned the paper as a popular synodical organ for almost two decades, 1890 to 1908. An even longer record was achieved by L. G. Abrahamson, editor-in-chief from 1908 to 1939. *Augustana* not only united the national synodical body but became an interpreter of the Lutheran church in the United States to the

Church of Sweden and to other branches of Christendom. Lindahl and Abrahamson realized the trend toward English but the columns of *Augustana* supported the prevailing Swedish character of the church until the World War undermined the language. Nowhere better than in this publication will we find revealed the spirit of a free Lutheran church operating in a democracy to create and revise its constitution and hold together the many diverse educational, charitable, evangelistic, missionary interests at home and on foreign fields. At its height *Augustana* had around 20,000 subscribers. Four thousand subscribers received the final number in December, 1956.

A second *Ungdomsvännen* made its appearance in 1895. A group of Minnesota pastors, led by Joel Hoff, started a literary monthly. It was soon transferred to Rock Island and published under the auspices of the Augustana Book Concern. Organized under Lindahl's leadership in 1889, the Book Concern was the publisher of *Augustana* and of the official literature of the Synod. More successful than its namesake, this *Ungdomsvännen* survived till 1918, and its program resembled that of the de luxe *När och Fjärran.* For many years it was edited by S. G. Youngert, the erudite professor at Augustana Seminary. It was profusely illustrated, often with reproductions of the best Swedish-American art. Translations of Swedish poets and original verse of Swedish-American writers were a prominent part of the monthly. G. N. Swan, the finest of Swedish-American collectors and critics, was a frequent contributor and his historical articles were of lasting value. Higher education was stressed, particularly the institutions of the church. It would be no exaggeration to claim that this journal represented the highest level achieved by the community we have called "Swedish America."

In 1909, midway through its course, *Ungdomsvännen* absorbed a quality publication that had striven for a similar goal and clientele on the East Coast, namely *Valkyrian,* begun in 1897. C. K. Johansen and Vilhelm Berger, both mainstays of New York's *Nordstjernan,* had made *Valkyrian* a distinguished periodical, but financial support was insufficient. How precarious such ventures were may be seen from the mortality rates of *Skandia* (New York) April to June, 1886; *Vega* (Boston) May, 1889 to July, 1890. *Freja,* the first literary monthly in the Northwest, survived only ten issues in 1893-1894. Chicago had even witnessed a futile attempt to put together a "Scandinavian" monthly, but Swedes and Norwegians failed to agree, though *Scandinavia,* November, 1883 to June, 1886, had gathered much valuable material.

Several annuals deserve more than mention. Foremost is *Korsbaneret* which began in 1880, under the editorship of Olof Olsson and C.A. Swensson, and continued through 1950. Devotional in character, these little volumes often contained original poems and historical articles. The annual obituaries remain the sole source of information on many of the pastors and laymen of the Augustana churches. Broader in scope and of high literary quality was *Prärieblomman* (1900 to 1913), an annual edited by Anders Schön. Some of the best of Swedish-American poetry is to be found in its pages. There are translations of English verse and articles of biographical, literary, and historical interest. Its obituaries, too, are invaluable records of men and women who helped create Swedish-America.

Strewn through the many pages of weeklies, monthlies, and annuals are the works of numerous persons who sought to transplant some of the treasures of Swedish literature to America and to acquaint fellow immigrants with masters of English verse. Ernst Skarstedt, one of the ablest of Swedish journalists, who spent most of his life in his beloved far Northwest, found some 300 *pennfäktare* (pen-pushers) in Swedish-America and claimed this list of fellow-authors was incomplete. In 1890 he published an anthology of Swedish-American poets, along with pictures and biographical notes of each. His selections, although not including some later figures, may serve as a contemporary judgment on the best of the versifiers.

One finds considerable unanimity in rating high such names as Jacob Bonggren, Magnus Elmblad, J. A. Enander, Ludwig Holmes, C. F. Peterson, C. H. Stockenstrom, M. Stolpe, Edward Sundell, A. Swärd, and Ninian Waerner. Stolpe confined himself to religious themes, Holmes and Swärd less so — all were ordained clergymen, graduates of Augustana. All had a deep-seated longing for the country they had left. Remembering that most of them left because of economic circumstances, one is inclined to consider this longing rather idealistic. But there is love for Swedish nature — for the waterfall, for the dark forest, for the Sabbath stillness.

There is pride in the great names of the past, and characteristically the Viking heritage is traced back to Edda days. Immigrant experiences are also reflected — the new language, the new neighbors, and a budding pride in Washington and Lincoln, as well as in the new freedom. They show pity for the poor, and sympathy for the laboring class. Swedish verse and Swedish song are celebrated, along with an ideal of Swedish peasant integrity. Whatever may be the critic's evaluation of these verses, we can find in them the love and hope and disillusionments of the Swedish immigrant.

Later than the men in Skarstedt's anthology came one of the most able of the literary representatives of Swedish-America, Ernst W. Olson. During his student days at Augustana he contributed (1890 and 1891) to the student publication "Balder" both original poems and a study of the Swedish poet Stagnelius and of the American Edgar Allen Poe. The *Lyceum Annual* (1893) contained his translation of Malmstrom's "Angelica." The following annual included his tribute to a fellow student, Oscar M. Benzon, whose early death as a graduate student at Stanford was a loss to a host of friends and admirers. Swan claims that Olson's "Angelica" and Benzon's rendering of Stagnelius' "Martyrerna" are the finest examples we have of translation from Swedish into English. Other translations, both from Swedish and English, were printed in *The Augustana Journal* and the *Alumnus.* In 1892 Olson won a prize in the contest for a college song. As editor of *The Young Observer,* also a publication backed by college people, Olson translated opening parts of Esaias Tegner's *Fritiof's Saga,* as well as some of his own poems. Skarstedt gave Olson first place as translator of these and other poems. In *Prärieblomman* we find his translations of Eugene Fields and Gustaf Fröding, as well as his own verse. He was often called on for state occasions and his tributes included odes to people as diverse as Oscar Montelius, Olof Olsson, Hjalmar Edgren, Johan Enander and the wife of Bishop von Scheele. O. A. Linder, the highly respected editor of *Svenska-Amerikanaren* after 1908, declared that Olson's *Cantata* for the Augustana Jubilee of 1910 "will undoubtedly be considered as the finest production written in Swedish in America."

Olson gave his whole life to literary labors. He went from the editorship of *The Young Observer* to a Moline enterprise *Nya Pressen* and followed it in 1896 to Chicago where it soon merged with *Fosterlandet,* which in 1900 was bought by *Svenska Tribunen.* Olson thus became chief of one of the most influential of the Swedish papers in America. He later became a literary secretary of the Augustana Book Concern, which more than any other publication house has supported the printing of literature in Swedish. As historian, Olson distinguished himself by joining with Anders Schön and Martin Engberg in producing the *History of the Swedes of Illinois,* one of the best of the chronicles of Swedish-America.

The contribution of Eric Norelius was unique. He had come to America in 1850 and been associated with Esbjörn in the founding of the Augustana Synod — in fact it was he who proposed that the church body be called "Augustana" in commemoration of the Confession of Augsburg (Latin = Augustana). Minnesota had become his field of labor and he ventured into the publication world when he started *Minnesota Posten* in 1857. This, however, merged with *Hemlandet* in 1858 and Norelius served briefly as editor, as later he had a stint with *Augustana.* For many years he was president of the Synod. From the first he had an instinct for historical material. In 1890 he was able to publish the first part of his monumental volume, *De Svenska-Lutherska Församlingarnas och Svenskanas Historia i Amerika,* the most complete work on the beginnings of the Swedish congregations in America and the more valuable because of the author's own participation in those beginnings. Norelius published a life of T. N. Hasselquist in 1900 and completed his history by a second volume in 1914.

While Chicago was sometimes described as the capital of the Swedish press, Rock Island could justly be called the literary capital. *Augustana,* which went to all corners of the land and even to Sweden, was printed in Rock Island. *Korsbaneret* came annually from the press there after 1880, and *Prärieblomman* after 1901. *Ungdomsvännen* was closely associated with the college and seminary. Literature for worship and Sunday School included reprintings of the Swedish Psalm-book, the collection of *Hemlandssånger,* translations of Catechism and Bible history, and texts for Swedish classes in congregations and in colleges. Both religious and secular books from Sweden could be secured in this literary center.

A focal point was the Department of Swedish at Augustana College.

In Paxton instruction was mainly in Swedish in all subjects except that of English literature and language. But after the removal of the institution to Rock Island, English gained, and soon a choice was possible between the Swedish classical and the English-Scientific course. Instruction in Swedish was combined with the chair in Christianity — so closely allied were these subjects. C. M. Esbjörn held this professorship from 1883 to 1890. "The most Swedish Swede in America," he was dubbed, and this son of the founder, L. P. Esbjörn, worthily represented the religious culture which had come to this country in Swedish form. Clear, logical and positive, he inspired respect in colleagues and students; but in 1890 he turned to parish work. Esbjörn, a member of the first graduating class in 1877, had gone on to study theology at Philadelphia. He was one of the group of "Ungdomsvänner" who urged Swedish letters, and until his death in 1911 he advocated affection for the culture imbedded in the language.

When the Swedish chair became vacant in 1890 it was separated from the Christianity department, and the college board succeeded in bringing to the campus Swedish-America's most celebrated exponent, J. A. Enander, editor of *Hemlandet.* No one with a greater knowledge or deeper love for Swedish literature could have been secured, and we can believe that his instruction was an inspiration to the students. But academic routine and discipline were not to Enander's liking. After three years he resigned, but his name and influence lived on in the college. Throughout his career Enander was a faithful member of the Augustana Synod, taking active part in his home parish and being held in high regard by leaders of the church.

G. N. Swan related long after the event that he had been at the commencement of Augustana College in 1887, where he had been impressed by the oration of one of the graduates, Ernst Zetterstrand. This student, a son of a teacher and organist in Sweden, had come to America after secondary education in Linköping to enter Augustana in 1874. The graduation speaker took a theme from Tegnér,

> "Eternal is beauty, though with eager hand
> We dip in the waves of time for its golden sand."

Zetterstrand had the love of beauty, and introduced a new emphasis when in 1895 he became Enander's successor at Augustana. His insistence on grammar and syntax was in opposition to Enander's emphasis, and he himself compiled a manual on rhetoric. His theoretical treatises on language and art were unique in America. For his M.A. degree at Augustana in 1898 he had written on "The fundamental quality of Swedish poetry." In 1901 he considered the question, "Has art a legitimate place in the Christian cult?" His forte was in the interpretation of particular poets. He turned his attention also to St. Birgitta and Carl von Linné. He was interested in "The influence of English on the Swedish language in America." Both before and after his academic career (1895-1901) Zetterstrand served faithfully in parishes, both in the Middle West and Connecticut, where he died in 1911.

Zetterstrand was not himself a poet. But the Augustana ministerium furnished some of the brightest stars in the Swedish-American firmanent. Axel August Swärd, who emigrated in 1883 and was a student at Augustana until his ordination in 1887, proved himself one of the most lyrical of Swedish writers. He met an early death in 1891. *Vilda blommor från prairien* was printed while he was still in college. *Från Västanskog* (1889) reflected his experiences in the Far West.

Ludwig Holmes, Mauritz Stolpe and C. A. Lonnquist were names known and respected wherever they appeared. Although graduates of Augustana, all were born in Sweden and ever expressed a longing for the land of their forefathers. Stolpe moved in a more restricted circle of religious verse. Holmes could write on high and lowly subjects but always with a flavor of gentility. Stolpe spent forty-five years as pastor in New York City, while Lonnquist directed a home for epileptics and mentally retarded in Nebraska; yet a common note of compassion and hope united them. They all represented a spiritual culture combining a love of God with a love of nature and man that rang true to the proclamation of Esbjorn, Hasselquist and Olsson.

As the younger colleges of the synod developed, the same kind of aesthetic environment was created in varying degrees. Carl Swensson of the Augustana class of 1877 carried it to the prairies of Kansas, and at Bethany College he established a love of music and art. His two accounts of trips to Sweden gave substance to a Swedish spirit in Lindsborg, and his oratorical ability in both Swedish and English became proverbial. A Lindsborg author, G. N. Malm, made *Charli Johnson* a portrait of the Swedish immigrant. A Bethany graduate, P. H. Pearson, sought to transmit something of the enthusiasm for Swedish letters to Drake University in Iowa, where he was head of the German department. At St. Peter, where Swensson's classmate, Mathias Wahlstrom, became president in 1881, Swedish found a strong champion in Prof. J. S. Carlson. Both he and his successor, A. A. Stomberg, brought an interest in Swedish to the State University of Minnesota. A strong Swedish influence was present at Upsala College from its inception in 1893, as well as at North Park College founded by the Mission Covenant about the same time. While the relationship of the colleges to Swedish was different from that of the press, each aided the other in the preservation of the language and Swedish culture in the new homeland. Together they fashioned a world of idea and sentiment that made them different from "American" colleges.

Even the Augustana students served the cause of Swedish by a custom that went back to the origin of the school. They needed income during the summers. The congregations needed students to teach "Swedish" school and to assist the pastor. Throughout the closing decades of the nineteenth century and almost to the First World War students responded to calls from the parishes. In earlier years they spent both mornings and afternoons, five days a week, teaching pre-confirmation children Catechism and Bible History in Swedish. There were also text-books in the Swedish language and literature, "Första" and "Andra" Läseboken, sometimes in "German" print. One may question the pedagogical methods and facilities. But there was often good instruction, music, games and parties, and enough was learned to make church boards feel that the program was worth the expense. Generations of Augustana students looked tenderly back on these vacation experiences — and not a few found in the parish a future wife. Few were the larger congregations that did not have a succession of students. Occasionally one would be rewarded with a call to become the pastor of the church. At the end of the summer, there was usually the "surprise party" which added to the remuneration of the vacation and made easier the return to another year of school. Thus the demands of summer contributed to their interest in the Swedish classes.

To the very large part of Swedish-America that read the Swedish papers, but had little or no interest in the churches, there were other means available of keeping alive the old culture. Fraternal organizations — Vasa Order, Svithiod, the Viking Order — combined social activities with insurance and aid provisions. In larger cities dramatic, gymnastic (the Ling system) or purely social interests were unifying factors. "Provincial" societies gathered persons from the same locale in the old country. Above all song was a group-building force. Almost every Swedish community had its singing society where music of Sweden was rehearsed and concertized. At first it was thought that Scandinavian clubs could unite Swedes, Norwegians, and Danes, and well attended "unions" were realized at the Exposition in Philadelphia in 1876, at Chicago in 1885, and at Minneapolis in 1889. Partisanship, however, soon outweighed the unity. In 1892, on the initiative of the "Lyran Club" of New York, a national union of Swedish singers was organized in the quarters of the Swedish Glee Club of Chicago, making possible a gala concert at the Chicago Exposition of 1893. A victorious trip to Sweden in 1897 lifted the aspirations of all clubs. A second trip in 1910 followed the fifth national "Sångfest" in Carnegie Hall, New York, and for the trip forty-five singers were chosen from Providence, Hartford, New York, Brooklyn, Jamestown, Pittsburg, Chicago, Moline, Rockford, Minneapolis, Duluth, Denver — all centers of Swedish-American song. Long after Swedish ceased to be the language of conversation it lived on in the programs of the glee clubs.

The desire to associate experiences in daily life with an invisible domain, somehow Swedish in character, extended even to professional groups. A Swedish Engineers' Society in Brooklyn dates from 1888, and a Chicago Society was formed in 1908. Detroit and Pittsburg followed the example. Several national exhibits were held by Swedish-American artists. Birger Sandzen at Bethany and Olof Grafstrom at Augustana ranked high in these circles. The Swedish population remained largely Republican until the Franklin Roosevelt era, and a national pride was exhibited when a Swedish-American attained high office. Gustavus Adolphus College counted John Johnson and A. B. Eberhardt among its former students and these governors of Minnesota added to the prestige of all Swedish voters. In Illinois Carl Chindblom, an Augustana alumnus (1890) not only represented his district in Congress but served as a spokesman for Swedish interests across the nation.

One characteristic of Swedish-America was a common exaltation of Swedish names that gained honor in America. The careers of Jenny Lind and Christina Nilsson were repeatedly celebrated, as was the achievement of John Ericson of *Monitor* fame. Chicago Swedes placed a statue of Carl von Linné in Lincoln Park. John Ericson was honored similarly in New York and Gunnar Wennerberg in St. Paul. Visitors from Sweden stimulated the immigrants' imagination. Especially in church life the bond was strengthened by visits such as those of Bishop von Scheele to Augustana, of P. P. Waldenström to the Mission Friends, and of Archbishop Nathan Söderblom whom all welcomed.

Church life especially was oriented to Sweden more than to America in the nineteenth century. The Bibles and hymn books and devotional literature used in the various communions were imported from Sweden. By the turn of the century Augustana was producing an English hymnal. The American and Anglican material came largely through the *Church Book* of the General Council, but many of the hymns were translations by persons mentioned above — C. W. Foss, Albert Rodell, E. W. Olson, A. O. Bersell, E. K. Zetterstrand, Olof Olsson. Especially Augustana congregations attempted to retain elements of Swedish architecture in their building projects. Olof Cervin, an Augustana alumnus who pursued graduate work at Columbia in architecture, was sometimes designated synod architect. Scandinavian influence can be traced in some of his work. Everywhere the canvasses of Grafstrom were found in Augustana sanctuaries. The ambitious church at New Britain reflected the Swedish traits of S. G. Ohman, and even its name, "Maria" kyrkan, was hardly American Protestant. No less able champions of Swedish were found in the Mission Covenant, the Baptist, and the Methodist churches, namely E. August Skogsbergh and David Nyvall, C. G. Lagergren and Olof Hedeen, W. Henschen and C. G. Wallenius.

Was Swedish-America a reality, a dream, or an illusion? It did not exist before the Civil War and its existence did not survive the First World War. But in that half century over a million Swedish immigrants sought homes in America. Leaving childhood scenes and often members of their families, they were homesick. They idealized what they had left, for most came from peasant villages. But what they had learned in school and church became precious to them here. They welcomed whatever could relieve their loneliness, and the weekly paper or meeting went far in creating the thought world in which the mind lived when the hands were not too occupied. They relived the woodlands and meadows and lakes of the old country. The poetry of Christmas and Midsummer shaped new pictures and quickened deep feeling. Only gradually did they learn the new language and read the history of the new nation. They realized that their children had different feelings, were acquiring new friends and manners, entering a world where parents could follow only stumblingly. So their own world seemed surer. Sometimes they would return to Sweden for a visit, a Sweden they had known little of beyond their childhood locale, and even that was changed.

But Swedish-America was real, although some would say it was neither Swedish nor American. Yet it had its idiom, its own ways, its songs, its churches, its hopes. In a world designed by prose and poetry with deep roots in the past the immigrant of the nineteenth century had his being. Fondly some thought there might be a Sweden in America as there was a Sweden in Finland. Whatever the future might be, Swedish-America was a state of thinking and feeling that bridged the Atlantic. For though the impressionable youth — and most of the immigrants were young — realized the vastness of the ocean he had crossed to come here, the fact that a Swedish-America existed gave him the consolation that there was a highway of the mind and soul on which he could go back and forth between the Old and New Worlds.

We have seen how many of the builders of the bridge were somehow associated with Augustana College and Seminary, the Augustana Synod, the Augustana Book Concern. We cannot understand the history of Augustana in the time of Hasselquist and Olsson unless we see it in the light of a realm that hovered over the lives of the immigrants among whom they ministered. May we change the imagery and say that the role of Augustana was that of a midwife, easing the travail of an older generation in a strange world, in giving birth to a new generation, in a fateful century?

# *Ernst Skarstedt: A Unique and Free Spirit*

Emory Lindquist

Seven decades ago, Oliver A. Linder, an editor of the Chicago weekly *Svenska Amerikanaren,* wrote in the fine New York literary monthly *Valkyrian,* "If the question should be asked 'Who is the outstanding person in Swedish-American literature?' nine out of ten would answer immediately: Ernst Skarstedt."[1] This was indeed a tribute to the Swedish immigrant who came to the United States in 1878 at the age of twenty-one. He had come from the university city of Lund to begin a varied career which ended with his death in Seattle, Washington, in 1929. The literary stature of Skarstedt has increased mightily since Linder's enthusiastic observation in 1897. Professor O. Fritiof Ander, writing in 1963, described Skarstedt's volume *Svenska-Amerikanska folket i helg och söcken* (1917), as the best of the accounts of the life of Swedish immigrants in America.[2] Many literary critics and historians have identified Ernst Skarstedt as the leading author among Swedish-Americans.

The distinctive personal qualities of this unusual man developed significantly as he shared the fine creative resources of his unique and free spirit in the American scene. There is something truly symbolic about him in the title, *Vagabond and Editor,* which he gave to the fascinating personal account of his first ten years in America. But Skarstedt was much more than a vagabond and editor, although his experiences in those capacities would have been more than enough for lesser spirits.

The family background of Ernst Skarstedt and his boyhood environment gave no suggestion that this son of Dr. C. W. Skarstedt, a rather austere and formal Professor of Theology at Lund University, would at the age of eighteen share in an adventure-filled but highly dangerous experience as a seaman. On June 14, 1875, he sailed on the "William" from Göteborg through the Arctic Ocean. Later that summer, during this same voyage, he was the key figure in helping three Czarist political prisoners escape from Mezen along the White Sea.[3] Nor could there have been any valid forecast that four years later, at the age of twenty-two, he would be breaking sod and plowing the good earth on the plains of Kansas, participating in the rugged life of Swedish pioneer immigrants. That same year, 1879, he was editing and publishing briefly at Lindsborg, Kansas, a weekly newspaper with the impressive name, *Kansas Statstidning*. But this was only the beginning of a career which included the severe demands on life in his voluntary choice of a home in isolated forest areas of Washington and alternate service as editor of leading Swedish language newspapers in Chicago, San Francisco, and New York. Moreover, several volumes of prose and poetry and many hundreds of articles and poems in newspapers and periodicals came from his pen.

In the interim of the years with their variety and contrasts, Ernst Skarstedt knew the desperate poverty of pioneer life in Kansas and the uncertainties of a precarious economic existence during his stay in distant forest areas. But he was later to receive from King Gustav V of Sweden, in 1916, the highly deserved medal, *Literis et Artibus* for excellence in literary achievement.

When reflecting in mature years about his boyhood life and after consulting the diary which he kept faithfully from 1871, Ernst Skarstedt described his remembrances about his youthful years when he wrote: "Ever since childhood my thoughts had gone obviously in another direction from those of my schoolmates. When they played, or frolicked, or threw snowballs, or fought, I sat by myself in some remote, hidden corner and read about plants or animals or foreign countries, or strolled alone around the countryside or in parks, imagining myself living on some distant, unknown coast, where I could examine new conditions, new plant life, and new animals." As he continued the chronicle of this period, he observed that

"The older I grew the more deeply rooted became this peculiar manner of thinking, this longing after something new, adventuresome, and unknown, all the more so since I began to read accounts and travel descriptions about foreign countries."[4]

Young Skarstedt describes in considerable detail this inner urge for freedom. He dreamed of the time when he might escape to a distant and beautiful land where he "could like Robinson Crusoe, live a simple, innocent life in nature, uninfected by civilization." This was a constantly growing interest for him. Further evidence of the boy's longing for the freedom which he felt resided in nature is found in the inscription written by him and dated August 13, 1871, on the title-page of his detested school textbook, *History of the Middle Ages,* by Jakob Edlund. There the fourteen year old dreamer copied four lines from the verses of *Talis Qualis,* the pseudonym of August Strandberg (1818-1877), who was the intellectual leader of the liberal Lund University students in that era. These lines describe Strandberg's and Skarstedt's burning desire "to experience life on the surging sea, on the smiling, green-covered, flowering island, where there would be quiet, and dreams, and finally death."[5] At intervals Skarstedt did realize some of his boyhood longings for the blessings of life in nature, intervals which punctuated his career as an editor and journalist.

The career of Ernst Skarstedt as a seaman referred to earlier was episodic. Moreover, his restless life of dissent in the family and in the society of the university town of Lund as well as his brief period of study at the Technical High School at Stockholm yielded to a new, if at times an uncertain, destiny in "the great land in the West," as Swedes referred to America. He arrived at Halifax, Nova Scotia, shortly after Christmas Day in 1878.

Many factors brought more than one million Swedes to the United States in the century after 1850. The motives of Ernst Skarstedt were described by him in 1914 in *Vagabond och redaktör* as follows: "I had absolutely no other purpose in my journey to America than to go away from the detestable European emphasis upon formal propriety, and, if possible, to realize an ambition from my earliest youth, namely, to find an unpretentious home in the bosom of nature. Nothing in the world was farther from my thoughts than the desire to gain wealth or to win a reputation for greatness."[6]

This description is characteristic of the man as his *vita* shows so clearly. Looming large in his view of life and how it could be lived was his commitment to resources available in nature. After serving with distinction as an editor of *Svenska Amerikanaren* in Chicago from June, 1880, to March, 1884, and later with *Svenska Tribunen* in the same city from July, 1884, to March, 1885, he was a pioneer in Clark County, Washington Territory, until March, 1888, except for about a year in Sweden in 1885-1886. There followed varied activities until he became editor of *Vestkusten,* San Francisco, August, 1891, to March, 1896, when again the call to return to nature brought him to Cowlitz County, Washington, where he was a farmer from September, 1896, to December, 1901. After brief periods of time in Oakland and Berkeley, he was again on the land at Laton, California, February, 1903, to February, 1906. He lost a magnificent collection of books and manuscripts in a fire at San Francisco in April, 1906. Then there were successive periods in Columbia City, near Seattle, December, 1906, to April, 1912, on Orcas Island on Puget Sound, May, 1912, to June, 1919, and several months in 1919 to 1920 in Friday Harbor on San Juan Island. Once again he returned to the life of a city dweller, serving as editor of *Nordstjernan* in New York City from June, 1920, until March, 1926. Thereafter, except for brief intervals, Skarstedt lived on a farm in the beautiful area of Friday Harbor, near Seattle, until his death in March, 1929.[7]

The delightful companionship of husband and wife, Ernst and Anna Skarstedt, brought immense joy during the years that life was theirs together prior to Anna's death in 1888. Almost indescribable hardship and sacrifice in their pioneer situation in Washington failed to dim their spirits. When sheer necessity forced the Skarstedts to leave their primitive home on Mount Bell near Battle Ground in Washington for residence in Vancouver, there was sadness and almost despair. Ernst and Anna Skarstedt's feeling about nature on that occasion is described by the former in *Vagabond och redaktör* in these words: "It was not our intention to become city dwellers. We agreed to do everything possible to get enough money to buy a farm sometime, and Anna received my promise that we were going to exert all our strength to be certain at least that our children would grow up in the country. She shuddered at the thought of being forced to see them grow up in the self-indulgence of city life with daily examples of ostentation and futility before their eyes."[8]

The deeper recesses of Ernst Skarstedt's sensitive thought are revealed in his book of poems, *Under Vestliga Skyar* published in 1907. The title, *Under Western Skies,* is symbolic of his response to nature. In the "Ode to Oregon and Washington," he recalls that although at times his pioneer life made heavy his steps, he loved the forest and the flowers, the silence and the sunsets, more than he should have loved them. When he was absent from the Great West, where unspoiled nature spoke eloquently to the best in man, he felt an intense longing, whenever the names of Oregon and Washington were mentioned, to return to these blessed sanctuaries of nature. In another poem, he glowed with joy over the fact that he had followed a path and built a house under the blue heavens and the bright sun, and although the sky was gray at times, nature's diversity and unpretentiousness enriched so immeasurably his life.[9]

The sensitivity of Skarstedt's feeling for nature was based upon keen observation, but it resulted occasionally in comments filled with delightful fantasy. He was convinced that all animals, and possibly plants, had means of communication, although this capability seemed incomprehensible to human beings. He had observed for several weeks one spring the animated daily dialogue between two small birds. As he watched and listened, the bird located in a bush made a comment, which the bird in the tree answered so rapidly that there was not even the interval of one-tenth of a second between the question and the reply. This exchange was followed by a quiet time for half a minute, when the conversation was resumed. He observed that "What these small beings had to say to one another was more than he could grasp, but they were saying something, perhaps sharing the joyous expression of being together . . . The whole life of birds, their movements, their activity, their songs, all are an unending hymn to the glory of life, a song of jubilation, the heart's gratitude for the gift of life." Moreover, in the world of birds, "no sullenness or gloominess is to be found."[10]

In 1910, while visiting in Chicago, Skarstedt clearly shared his feelings about city life as he wrote: "During the first days of my visit in Chicago I experienced a feeling of suffocation and agony amidst the noise of the streets each time that I elbowed myself forward through a mass of people, overwhelmed as I was by the unbearable, unending racket of the onrushing trolley cars above me and by the counterbalancing noise from the street cars, all this magnified by the echo from the walls of houses, iron pillars, stone pavements, etc. There was such a crowding of people at the street crossings that it could drive one crazy."[11] Small wonder then that Ernst Skarstedt wrote so jubilantly about the peace and quiet of life in nature.

The relationship of Skarstedt's restlessness and his devotion to life in nature has been interpreted by his close friend, Oliver A. Linder, who visited the Skarstedts in 1888 in their remote forest home near Battle Ground, Washington: "But for the individual who bothers to look more closely the restlessness in Skarstedt appeared as a completely logical consequence of seeking something: freedom. Freedom from the petty and false; freedom from hypocrisy and lies. Nature never makes use of pretense; she appears only as she is." Then he continued: "Only with nature, in nature has Skarstedt found what he sought. Thus has he been drawn irresistibly to nature, therefore has he abandoned again and again a good position and a promising future in order to become a farmer."[12] There was indeed something of Thoreau in Ernst Skarstedt.

The pattern of Ernst Skarstedt's life has many of the qualities that are typical of Henry David Thoreau, and it is not surprising that Skarstedt expressed formally his admiration for the Walden philosopher. The first essay of six studies in Skarstedt's volume *Amerikanska typer och karaktärer* (1919) recounts main aspects of the thought of Thoreau and presents an enthusiastic endorsement of his ideas. Skarstedt writes that "His (Thoreau's) first and greatest love was nature and independence and he had a greater and greater longing for the opportunity to devote himself more fully to that feeling." He agrees with Thoreau's sentiment, "In the same measure that life is simplified, so also do the problems of the world seem less unintelligible and loneliness ceases to appear as loneliness." Skarstedt points out that in Thoreau there was "no haughtiness, no pride, nothing of a feeling of superiority. All he asked for was freedom . . . He was interested in everything except in those things that carried the stamp of greediness or baseness." The basic factor in Thoreau's philosophy, as Skarstedt interpreted it, was to make man's style of life and needs more simple. "Thoreau believed that the civilized world was full of deceit and hypocrisy, injustice and suffering, selfishness and restlessness . . . His remedy for all that oppresses and pains the world was 'Simplicity'."[13]

Skarstedt, like Thoreau, loved nature and the simple life. It is understandable that he found deep meaning in what he refers to as Thoreau's "gospel of simplicity," which he points out "began as a philosophical ideal and became an art of living . . ." Skarstedt cited enthusiastically Robert Louis Stevenson's observation that Thoreau had "made his little cabin by the side of Walden pond, a station along mankind's railroad from slavery to freedom." Ernst Skarstedt, a unique and free spirit, who had developed across the years his own distinctive way of life, believed that Thoreau's *Walden* "with its many thought-provoking truths can never be read too often nor reflected on too seriously, and it should be found in every home, where it should be elevated to the rank of a family bible, since it is the messenger of salvation to everyone who seeks freedom."[14]

Although the career of Skarstedt manifests restlessness and change, there was nevertheless, throughout the years, a continuously constructive quality and great productivity. The facts are more convincing than the bare chronology suggests and certainly far more impressive than the deprecatory attitude that this overly modest and humble man recorded about himself for posterity. In 1914, after a literary and journalistic career that had already brought distinction, Skarstedt wrote as follows: "It isn't enough to set a goal, however inadequate it may be. In order to attain that goal, one must possess the necessary conditions in the form of will-power, efficiency, self-confidence, and tenacity. But these qualifications for success I never possessed. Already during my adolescent years, I constantly received reproaches from my father and others for a lack of ambition."[15]

Although there is no need to attempt in this survey of Ernst Skarstedt's career an *apologia pro sua vita,* it seems appropriate nevertheless to identify some of the principal achievements of this free and independent spirit. The preceding pages record the salient points in his career as editor of leading Swedish-American newspapers including *Svenska Amerikanaren,*

Chicago, *Vestkusten,* San Francisco, and *Nordstjernan,* New York. In addition, he served at times as a regular correspondent for a half-dozen Swedish-American newspapers. *Valkyrian,* published in New York, and perhaps the finest literary journal in the Swedish language in America, and *Prärieblomman,* an excellent annual publication, contained many of Skarstedt's historical, biographical, and travel accounts.

Skarstedt's full-length volumes are impressive in number, scope, and quality. *Våra pennfäktare* (1897) and the enlarged and revised edition, *Pennfäktare* (1930) published posthumously in Sweden, are excellent Swedish-American literary histories, containing invaluable biographies and materials related to the principal authors in the Swedish language in America. These volumes make available sources of information that are indispensable for understanding the Swedish-American literary tradition. The comprehensive description of Swedish-American life, *Svenska-amerikanska folket i helg och söcken* (1917), published in Sweden, testifies to Skarstedt's intimate knowledge of the economic, religious, literary, and other meaningful aspects of the achievement of an immigrant people in the American scene. Four historical volumes, *Oregon and Washington* (1890), *Washington och dess svenska befolkning* (1908), *California och dess svenska befolkning* (1910), and *Oregon och dess svenska befolkning* (1911), provide splendid resources for knowledge of these states and show the scholarly interests of the author.

Biographical studies of great Americans constitute the subject matter of Skarstedt's volumes, *Abraham Lincoln* (1918), *Amerikanska typer och karaktärer* (1919), and *Theodore Roosevelt* (1919). A unique and intimate volume in hectograph form, illustrated by the famous Swedish-American artist, Olof Grafström, *Vid hennes sida* (1889), presents a great tribute to his wife Anna. The volume of poetry, *Under vestliga skyar* (1907), portrays in delightful lyric form the author's sensitivity to nature. In addition to his own works, Skarstedt edited a number of books, including an anthology of eighteen Swedish-American poets, *Svensk amerikanska poeter i ord och bild* (1890), *Andra delen av M. Elmblads Dikter* (1890), and *Enskilda skrifter av A. A. Swärd* (1895). Skarstedt's detailed and fascinating description of his first ten years in America, *Vagabond och redaktör* (1914), has already been referred to on several occasions. Many articles were translated by him from Swedish and German into English. Hundreds of his poems, feature articles, and travel accounts appeared in a variety of Swedish-American newspapers and periodicals.

Alex Olsson, who was closely associated with Skarstedt in journalistic activities in San Francisco, writes that "Skarstedt possessed great capacity for work and could sit up and write night after night . . . But he always lived a simple life and that reveals his secret." Skarstedt recorded in an autobiographical article in 1898 that for a period of five years there was scarcely a night that he went to bed prior to 3 a. m. and often he wrote during the entire night.[16] Hard work and self-discipline included a unique pattern of keeping records that is not often associated with the poetic nature and free spirit of a man like Ernst Skarstedt. His own words describe this activity as "a regular passion to record everything." He points out that he carried on no physical activity without some kind of counting. If he chopped wood, he counted each piece of wood; if he plowed a field, he counted the furrows and kept track of their length. He had recorded evidence that during one day in Kansas he had cut with a corn knife 11,760 corn hills, each one containing up to six stalks and that he had walked fifteen to eighteen miles a day in following a horse-drawn plow in Washington and Oregon. Skarstedt has written "I can almost state exactly how many miles I have covered by foot on roads and also how many miles I have ridden on horseback, how many miles I have travelled by railroad and on boats, how many pounds of butter my wife has churned, how many cows, hogs, chickens, etc., that I have owned, how many photographs I have developed and much besides, yes, even how many drinks I have consumed." Skarstedt continued by observing that "It's a mania with me to want everything to be correct. Most people have a tendency to regard this as an absurd pedantry in being so exact in gathering data about trivial things, but this mania has given me both joy and utility and not infrequently has it been a means for deciding debatable questions."[17]

This preoccupation with detail also makes available interesting information about another aspect of Ernst Skarstedt's activities, namely, the amazing extent of his personal correspondence. In a letter to Karl Hellberg, a literary associate, Skarstedt pointed out that he carried on regular correspondence, year in and year out, with at least fifty persons. There were additional exchanges of letters on an interim basis. Moreover, he recounted the details for Hellberg. In 1914, Skarstedt wrote 940 letters. In the six-year period from 1911 to 1916, his correspondence totalled 4,484 letters. These letters were all hand-written by him.[18]

Although contemporary evaluations of individuals must be judged in the context of many personal and other factors, some containing unfair hostility and others unwarranted praise, the emergence of a distinctive consensus lends validity to the portrait which other evidence has already sketched in basic outline. There is more than a consensus among Skarstedt's contemporaries as to the unique traits of the man; there is decisive unanimity. Alex Olsson, who knew Ernst Skarstedt well, has written: "Skarstedt was an individualist. Personal freedom was dearer to him than anything else and he hated with the heartiest feeling all humbug, affectation, and duplicity. He was quite conservative in some aspects but radical when it came to uprooting of old customs and dogmas of sophistry."[19] Oliver A. Linder, who also knew Skarstedt intimately, wrote that "Ernst Skarstedt is not one who has a private and also an official opinion. No one who knows him distrusts him . . . He is an unusually honest person. He has attacked like one who attacks an enemy but he has never been insulting. Derison is a completely foreign element with Skarstedt; instead of it, indignation is found." Linder, using the pseudonym "Olavus," emphasized that "Skarstedt did not understand compromise. It could turn into a kind of stubbornness, but as a newspaper man, it can be said about him that he saved his soul."[20]

More significant than the testimony of contemporaries is Ernst Skarstedt's response to it and the evidence of the man himself. When Theodore Hessel wrote about Skarstedt, accusing him of "eccentricity and bizarre views about the life of a hermit and the corruption of civilization," the latter agreed that the criticism was accurate. Moreover, when Per Lärka observed that Skarstedt was "a queer fellow, full of a lot of eccentric ideas, but also a man with his heart in the right place," there was no objection from Skarstedt.[21]

In the context of the above statements, Skarstedt replied in a unique commentary describing himself by using the third person. He emphasized that "his eccentric ideas consist principally in that he loves solitude and freedom and will detest until death everything that is called propriety and etiquette, and all snobbery and extravagance of civilization." He opposed all kinds of tyranny, not only that of sea captains and others who are guilty of bullying and mercilessness towards subordinates, but he also opposed "the refined kind of tyranny, which under the name of socialism and the temperance movement and the like, seek with overpowering words to reshape people according to certain bigoted and narrow-minded patterns." Skarstedt was especially critical of "these small-minded reformers . . . who brag about liberal-mindedness, but who are in his eyes, collectively and individually, either humbugs or fools." Then he proceeded to describe what he meant by liberal-minded: "One who within his heart is a friend of man; one who is independent and gives reasons for what he asserts, but grants equally to his neighbor the right to think and believe in his own way, and concedes, too, that the other person may be right; one who will never press his belief on others, but allows tolerance to dwell in his heart."[22]

There is no great mystery nor are there any unusual secret places in the life of Ernst Skarstedt. He was forthright and outspoken. Skarstedt condemned unreservedly over a long period of time the prohibition movement and laws prohibiting the sale of alcoholic beverages as a serious invasion of personal freedom.[23] He lamented attempts to pass and enforce blue sky laws, designed as he contended, to force a Puritan Sunday upon twentieth century America.[24] Henry L. Mencken, the vitriolic critic of American life in the 1920s, was read appreciatively by Ernst Skarstedt. In *Nordstjernan* in June 1920, Skarstedt wrote a rather bitter editorial, "Hypocritical America," approving Mencken's statement that "We [Americans] are the most hypocritical nation in the world." "Why?" asked Skarstedt, and he answered: "Because hypocrisy's place of origin on earth is here."[25] As editor of *Nordstjernan* in the 1920s, Skarstedt commented editorially upon national and international issues. He was a constant and severe critic of Russian communism. Again, the issue was one that was central in Skarstedt's thinking — freedom. He emphasized that "Communism places the workers in a condition of industrial slavery."[26]

Ernst Skarstedt was a severe critic of the historic and contemporary church, but his criticism distinguished between the actual and the ideal. The church carried too much "dead-weight" in the form of "false and irrational doctrines." As a result of this "ballast" and under its influence, people became narrow-minded and lost perspective. The gap between profession and practice was wide. The results were consequently serious: "Do I find Christians more honest and conscientious, more simple and humble, more good-hearted and helpful than those outside the church? Not at all. In far too many cases I have found the complete opposite to be true."

In contrast to the church and the attitude of many of its members, Skarstedt wrote beautifully and sensitively about the Nazarene, the Master, "the representative of the simple life." It was the Master who "asked if life was not more than food and the body more than raiment." But those who claim to be followers of him "are in dress and manner, in deeds and action, just as vain, just as superficial, just as full of ostentation as if they had never heard the Master's life history and had never listened to a sermon about him." Moreover, as Skarstedt sat in church he reported that "it always seems to me that the Nazarene would not feel at home among the fashion plates and snobs and that the latter would not tolerate him." There was a solution according to Skarstedt: "Cast overboard the ballast of old-fashioned and irrational doctrines and train the members of the church in a more valid gospel — the gospel of simplicity and brotherhood."[27]

There are episodes in Skarstedt's travels that gave an acute accent to the man and his interests. He loved to play the violin. Even during his early years in America, when traveling by any possible means, his instrument hung from his shoulders. His fellow passengers, while bumming a ride with him in a box car on a freight train through western Kansas, were rather startled to have a companion with a violin. He played it on public occasions to appreciative listeners. He records, however, that among his audiences were the inhabitants of a prairie dog village near Wallace, Kansas, when one day in 1880, his spirit moved him to play the violin under the clear skies of the Kansas plains.[28] He played his violin on the ocean liner that brought him to California from New York in 1926. This was the trip during which he visited Havana, Cuba, and with great formality he went to a seaman's saloon to drink a toast to the memory of his grandfather Skarstedt, who had died in Havana from the yellow fever in 1820 when his ship was in port.[29]

A man's life consists of a wide range of hope and disappointment, of success and failure, but in the chronicle, there is often a kind of distillation that results from the essential view which gives life its orientation and direction. Ernst Skarstedt's varied life provided rewarding experiences that had been caused by, and at the same time, resulted from, his unique and free spirit. Although not a formally religious man, he had his own gospel of life, and one day in 1891, as if he were viewing the past and assessing the future, he placed it in verse form and called it simply, "My Philosophy.[30]

*My Philosophy*

To be content and cheerful, glad and free;
To yield to human power no forced contrition, —
That is the height of true philosophy,
The charmed goal that meets my approbation.
To do the duty, that may nearest lie,
As conscience and one's native talents guide,
And not what is not understood deny, —
Such is the faith, by which I would abide.

And then to shun as yellow fever pest
All snobbery, all sham and hollow glitter;
To honor Art, yet honor Nature best,
Toward humbug only to be hard and bitter;
To judge not him, who crushed by care and grief,
Has fallen 'neath the burden that he bore;
To love both man and beast, see, this in brief
Of homely wisdom is my cherished store.

Translation by Mrs. Aub. Woodward Moore, 1897

The chronicle of Ernst Skarstedt's life has many interesting chapters. The school boy at Lund dreamed of far away places, and he lived out his years under the western skies of far away America. The young seaman made possible freedom for three Czarist political prisoners whom he met along the White Sea; he continued across the years to seek for the minds of men freedom from social, political, and religious tyranny. He was a Swedish immigrant, writing almost exclusively in the language of his mother tongue, but he was a keen and sensitive student of American life and thought. There is a feeling of great regret in a succeeding generation that his unique and creative genius did not have a larger arena in American life.

The perspective also of a later generation, verified by Ernst Skarstedt's contemporaries, views him as an eccentric, and that, properly understood, is a compliment; some may lament, and others may applaud, his non-conformity, a non-conformity that was a natural and a genuine reaction to stifling, repressive conformity. Perhaps it is more appropriate to say about Ernst Skarstedt, in the words he quoted from Henry David Thoreau's *Walden,* "If a man does not keep pace with his companions, perhaps it is because he hears a different drummer."[31]

### *NOTES*

1. Oliver A. Linder, "Ernst Skarstedt. En porträttstudie," *Valkyrian,* I (June, 1897), 13.
2. O. Fritiof Ander, "An Immigrant Community during the Progressive Era," *The Swedish Immigrant Community in Transition,* ed. by Iverne Dowie and Ernest M. Espelie (Rock Island, 1963), 147.
3. Ernst Skarstedt, "Sjömans-Lif. Verklighets Bilder," *Valkyrian,* IV (1900). A series of articles in *Valkyrian,* beginning in May, 1900, describe this phase of Skarstedt's early life.
4. *Ibid.,* 219-220.
5. *Ibid.,* 220.
6. Ernst Skarstedt, *Vagabond och redaktör* (Seattle, 1914), 8.
7. Ernst Skarstedt, *Pennfäktare* (Stockholm, 1930), 169-170.
8. *Vagabond och redaktör,* 355-357.
9. Ernst Skarstedt, *Under vestliga skyar. Diktforsök* (Tacoma, 1907), 29-31. A copy of this volume was presented by the author to people who had contributed about $1,000 in a surprise observance of the author's fiftieth birthday at Seattle, April 14, 1907.
10. *Svenska Amerikanska Posten* (Minneapolis), May 2, 1928.
11. Ernst Skarstedt, "Intryck och Minnen Från en Sommarresa Till Östern," *Prärieblomman,* XI (1910), 61.
12. Linder, "Ernst Skarstedt," 14.
13. Ernst Skarstedt, *Amerikanska typer och karaktärer. Sex lefnads-och kar-aktärs teckningar* (San Francisco, 1919), 6-12.
14. *Ibid.,* 8.
15. *Vagabond och redaktör,* 8.
16. Alex Olsson, *Vestkusten,* March 21, 1929.
17. *Vagabond och redaktör,* 9-10.
18. Karl Hellberg, *Svenska Amerikanska Posten,* March 21, 1929.
19. *Vestkusten,* Mar. 21, 1929.
20. Linder, "Ernst Skarstedt," 4; and *Svenska Amerikanaren,* March 21, 1929.
21. Ernst Skarstedt, *Våra Pennfäktare* (San Francisco, 1897), 155.
22. *Ibid.*

23. Skarstedt wrote extensively on this subject at various times in *Vagabond och redaktör* in 1879 and 1880 (49-51) and as late as 1928 in *Svenska Amerikanska Posten* (August 8).
24. Ernst Skarstedt, *Nordstjernan,* Dec. 17, 1920.
25. *Ibid.,* June 4, 1920.
26. *Ibid.,* June 18, 1920.
27. Ernst Skarstedt, *"Kristendoms Svaga Punkter," Forskaren* (Minneapolis), Jan. 1910, 16-25.
28. *Vagabond och redaktör,* 97-99.
29. *Svenska Amerikanska Posten,* May 16, 1928.
30. *Under Vestliga Skyar,* 9-10.
31. *Amerikanska Typer och Karaktärer,* 11. The quotation from *Walden* is found in the "Conclusion."

# *Edward Price Bell--Anglo-American Spokesman, 1914-1917*

BENEDICT KARL ZOBRIST

The American Press was, for the most part, caught unprepared by the swiftness with which war engulfed Europe in July and August, 1914.[1] An exception to the predicament of most American publications, the *Chicago Daily News* was immediately able to supplement the Associated Press releases with informative special dispatches from its Foreign News Service. Established in 1898 primarily for gathering "sidelight" news supplementing the barren factual dispatches of the Associated Press, the Foreign News Service soon became one of the major organizations of its kind breaking a path toward comprehensive and interpretative world coverage oriented to the American readers.[2] A large share of the recognition ultimately won by the Middle Western intruder at the news capital of the world must be attributed to its London director. Edward Price Bell not only effectively administered the paper's European staff for twenty-two years, but also performed a number of journalistic feats which gained for him personal acclaim.

During the early months of the First World War, Bell's activities were varied. He devoted much of his time to directing the functions of the European staff, covering the London scene, and aiding stranded American travelers. But more than this, Bell now stood as dean of the foreign correspondents in London.[3] A decade and a half in the largest city of the world had made for him a wide selection of acquaintances, many persons of influence. The proven dependability and accuracy of his reporting had gained prestige not only for himself, but also for the *Chicago Daily News*. As a result, it was only natural that Bell would take a deep interest in the British struggle, and oftentimes become an active participant in British policies bearing on news-gathering and in affairs relating to Anglo-American relations.

Repeated British violations of American neutral rights on the high seas caused Anglo-American relations to become strained in January, 1915, and prompted Bell to make the first of many efforts to interpret the English position to Americans, to inform the English of American opinion, and to set forth his own considered and honest judgment as to where America's best interests lay. The occasion was a note sent by the American State Department to London on December 26, 1914, protesting British interference with American shipping.[4] In describing European reaction in general toward America, Bell cabled a dispatch to the *Chicago Daily News* on January 11 indicating that his conversations with persons speaking from both Allied and German viewpoints revealed the conviction that "the United States is making no real friends in this war. . . . it is impossible not to see that the American name is suffering and that conceivably the republic is laying up grave trouble for itself in the future."

More specifically, according to Bell, the Allied Powers charged the United States with "displaying a shameless lack of idealism, chivalry, magnanimity and courage . . . for ignoring the invasion of Belgium and the violations of the Conventions of The Hague, and then springing into the international arena with a protest relating exclusively to matters of trade." The assertion was made that "if President Wilson had protested against the violations of treaties and the principles of civilized warfare he could have protested with vastly greater effect against the arbitrary and possible indefensible intereference with American cargoes."

Bell explained that "Europeans, profoundly misunderstanding the Americans, as nearly every nation misunderstands every other, always have referred to the people of the United States as 'dollar chasers.' " Moreover, "the policy of President Wilson in the present war has crystallized the pervasive impression into a sharp and universal postulate." Pointing out that those outbursts of the Allies did not arise specifically from resentment against the American note of December 26, Bell found German sentiment toward America to be of a similar nature: "They accuse us of cringing to England, of enduring its 'arrogant monopoly of the sea,' of tolerating British control of cables, largely owned by Americans, and otherwise of showing ourselves small."

There was no doubt in Bell's mind that "as matters stand . . . when peace comes the United States will have no hand in making it." But more important, he feared the peril which America would face after the war: "its isolation, at all events so far as Europe is concerned, will be nearly complete and . . . the maintenance of not only its own traditional policies in the western hemisphere but its own national security will require the utmost naval and military strength of which it is capable."

This cable dispatch aroused considerable comment. An editorial in the *Chicago Daily News* regretted that the world as a whole would not admire a nation seeking to maintain a neutral position while a large part of the globe was locked in conflict. In London Bell's cable was favorably received by the *Morning Post* and the *Daily Chronicle.* The latter republished the article in full. In addition, Bell received more than 150 letters subscribing wholeheartedly to the contents of his dispatch. Among the writers of these letters were prominent persons such as Harry Brittain, John St. Loe Strachey, H. Gordon Selfridge, Gilbert Parker, and Francis Grierson. A group at the Savage Club sent a delegate to thank Bell for his words; Albert Grey, Fourth Earl of Grey, who had formerly been Governor General of Canada, requested Bell to come to his home to discuss the cable with him.[5]

Unfortunately, the account of the appearance of Bell's article cabled to London by the Washington correspondent of the London *Times* cast a different light on the original statement. Taking his information from the Anglophobe *Washington Post,* the correspondent described the dispatch as "explaining how Englishmen . . . really think that the United States is a selfish and cynical country ready to grumble at the first sign that trade is suffering, but quite unready to protest against violations of international law like rape in Belgium."

Bell protested to the editor of *The Times,* Geoffrey Robinson, that he had been made to appear as "blowing hot and cold" toward the Allied cause. When Robinson inferred that the grievance was against the *Washington Post,* Bell assured him that his interests were "not in Washington but in London." On the following day, the Washington cable of *The Times* recounted how the original cable had been widely reproduced particularly in the "less friendly portions" of the American press as an example of English enmity toward America. The correspondent continued: "I only repeat it for the opportunity of setting right and apologizing for a misapprehension that my message has raised as to the impartiality of Mr. Bell. . . . Mr. Bell's telegram is obviously fair and obviously prompted . . . by nothing but a desire to tell the American people the unadorned truth."[6]

One of the letters commending Bell's analysis of Allied opinion gave rise to an even stronger expression of British disappointment in American commercial interests being placed over moral issues. Recalling the American Civil War, John St. Loe Strachey, editor and owner of the London *Spectator,* drew a parallel showing how the North, to its surprise, had faced an England not sure that it would oppose slavery at any price. Strachey pointed out that the English urban population initially had sided with the South only because it wanted cotton and trade with the South and found that the North interferred with its profits. Even so, most important was the fact that the Lancashire cotton workers ultimately acquiesced in their own starvation and ruin rather than see slavery victorious.

Not questioning this oversimplified version of Anglo-American relations during the Civil War, Bell accepted the statement at face value and cabled it to Chicago for publication. He assured Strachey the article would do "nothing but good, however valiantly some Germans may strive to make capital out of it. . . . It is high time Wilson and all America were shocked out of their somnambulistic promenade towards the precipice."

The reception of the article was mixed. Fred Pitney, then in London for the New York *Tribune,* wrote Strachey that the article was so obviously written by one who was inspired by "a venomous hatred" for the American people that he could never again speak to him. He asked Strachey not to send him further invitations to the weekly tea parties he hosted at which newsmen and English writers and leaders informally met. Bell was amazed at this reaction and felt that Pitney would eventually be "remorseful." He told Strachey again that he had absolutely no reason to believe the statement had done anything but good in America.[7]

The incident of the *Dacia,* which sailed for Germany on January 23 with a cargo of cotton, did not ease Anglo-American tension. The ship was formerly a German vessel transferred to American registry.[8] An article in the London *Daily Mail,* which indicated that if the British seized the *Dacia* "hell would break loose in the United States," prompted Bell to write Robert Donald, editor of the London *Daily Chronicle.* He asked if he could reply to this assertion and deal with several relating points in the columns of Donald's newspaper. The editor agreed, and on January 27 Bell's retort appeared.[9]

After criticizing the *Daily Mail* article for its misleading statements, the London correspondent explained his views concerning the American position in the complications caused by the *Dacia.* The British feared that a precedent would be established for the purchase by Americans of German ships interned in American ports. These vessels might be used to ship cargo to Germany. To complicate the situation further, there was pending before Congress the Ship Purchase bill which would set up a government-owned corporation authorized, among other things, to buy foreign-built vessels and operate them.[10] Bell laid down the following broad assumptions:

> 1. That America will not attempt to liberate the interned German ships without an arrangement agreeable to England.
> 2. That America will do its utmost to fortify itself against the charge of facilitating in any way the conveyance of contraband to Germany or Austria.
> 3. That America means to hold tenaciously to its neutrality — a policy that debars it from countenancing any novel doctrine on the rights or duties of neutrals that would hamper England in the full use of its naval strength in its fight for life.
> 4. That America — in every drop of its non-foreign blood, and in much of the latter — believes that autocratic and militarist Germany is the aggressor in this war; and that, if right and the best political and moral heritage of history is to survive, autocratic and militarist Germany must be reduced to permanent and self-realized impotence.

And, allowing that the *Dacia* might be seized, his thesis held that the "peace between England and America is safe" for both countries were dedicated to the principle of arbitration.

Bell also attempted to answer a question in the minds of most Englishmen — why America did not officially protest against the German invasion of Belgium. He pointed out that "protest has been voiced in America, voiced by lip and pen, vehemently, brilliantly, again and again, from ocean to ocean." An official protest from Washington, however, was a very different matter. He explained, "Gentlemen in the highest official positions in all countries usually deem themselves bound to behave with extreme circumspection." Still, Bell admitted that it was an opportunity lost; he would have had the American government register a protest, at least to get the record straight.

His remarks ended with an eloquent appeal for Anglo-American friendship: "To Englishmen and to Americans I say, keep the slurs off your lips! Keep the slurs out of the headlines! Just remember that slurs, execrable in themselves, belong to the multitudinous family of ignorance!"[11]

The article evoked warm congratulations from Albert Grey, Fourth Earl of Grey. Stanley Buckmaster, the Solicitor-General of Great Britain, thanked Bell for his "clear and sensible expression of opinion at a moment when clear thinking and good sense are of unusual value to all of us." Henry Gordon Selfridge, the American department store tycoon who had transferred his merchandising abilities to London, informed the newspaperman that he had sent two hundred copies of the *Daily Chronicle* to his Chicago friends. Walter Hines Page, American ambassador at London, tried to be noncommittal when Bell sent him a copy of the article: he confessed, though, that he had read "with interest" other things by Bell and urged the writer to visit him.[12]

But it was Frederick R. Martin of the Associated Press London bureau who placed the article in its proper category: "It is vigorous and trenchant. Of course, it is not neutral but as I understand you, you are tired of neutrality." Indeed, Bell had later misgivings concerning the article he had written. To his publisher and editor in Chicago, Victor Lawson, he explained:

> I wrote the article for British consumption — I mean it was such an article as could do good only here. I write you with reference to it for fear you might object to the name of The Chicago Daily News appearing in connection with such sentiments as I express. For my own part I am not afraid of the Germans hurting me. Indeed, I should be quite willing to be hurt for my convictions in this matter. But I should be awfully sorry to have done anything that might injure the paper, especially anything that your greater penetration and wisdom might perceive lacked discretion and real intelligence.
>
> These are trying times here. Men's minds are strained. The war blood of the country is up. Even the greatest men are uneasy. . . . I wrote exactly what my mind and heart dictated, and I wrote it because I thought it would act as a sedative [*i.e.* for the pending Anglo-American crisis]. It did so act — very powerfully too. Steps have been taken to see that it reaches every center of opinion in the United Kingdom.[13]

In reply, Lawson characterized the *Dacia* article as "very strong and exceedingly well done," but from the Chicago viewpoint "some questions of expediency" did present themselves. He continued:

> However, I am disposed to the view that your action must be judged in the light of your opportunities and duties — the latter in a broad sense — as in London and not in Chicago. In other words, I am disposed to believe that your statement was justified as "a sedative," as you say.
>
> I believe that in the large view of things you have done a good piece of work, and have made a distinct contribution to safe relations between England and America.[14]

The influence of Bell's public utterance upon English and American opinion cannot be effectively measured. Nevertheless, as he had predicted, there was a considerable lack of interest surrounding the ultimate seizure of the *Dacia* by a French cruiser.[15]

Only a few weeks later, in March, Bell's reportorial acumen produced an exclusive interview bearing in part on Anglo-American relations, which was reprinted in most leading newspapers of the world. Toward the end of February, Bell addressed Prime Minister Asquith with a request for a formal interview. Because of the pressing duties of his office, Asquith declined but offered to arrange an interview with Viscount Haldane. Bell was pleased by the turn of events, for at that time Haldane was Lord High

Chancellor of Great Britain and one of the chief policy makers of the British government.

On Sunday, March 7, 1915, he went to Haldane's home:

> Lord Haldane conducted me into his study and suggested that I take notes. I told him I could make a better job of it without taking notes. Obviously he was puzzled and not a little perturbed by this statement, but he said nothing further. We talked for an hour and a half and I did not have a pencil or a bit of paper in my hands. I went away feeling that Lord Haldane was in some agony as to what I should make of it all, for we had ranged over many difficult and delicate questions. From his big dispatch box covered with red morocco, he took his secret state papers and read to me the whole of his confidential report to the British government on his interview with Bethman-Hollweg. . . . Anxious as the Lord Chancellor must have been as to what I should write, he found complete relief when the MS reached his hands. From beginning to end, I had not got a single thing wrong — not even a name or a date. How surprised Lord Haldane was you will be able to gather from his letter.[16]

Indeed, after reading the manuscript of the interview and having it approved by Foreign Secretary Sir Edward Grey, Haldane wrote Bell, "I think your words, written without a note taken at the time, are a marvelously skilful reproduction of the substance of our talk. It is wonderful what you have made of this."[17]

The interview, sent to Chicago by mail, was published on March 30. It covered slightly less than four columns. In essence, Haldane's statement was a masterly affirmation of Britain's case against Germany: this was primarily a war of democracy against militarism. Part of the interview was directed toward America. Haldane asked forbearance on the part of America while England engaged in a life or death struggle, which occasionally encroached upon neutral rights. In addition, he quashed the reported British claim that America should throw her weight onto the Allied side of the scale.

Although no one apparently realized it at the time, the importance of the article, as Haldane informed Bell, was that "it discloses for the first time what passed at Berlin in 1912." He was referring to the Haldane Mission which sought unsuccessfully to reach an Anglo-German accommodation regarding the expanding German naval building program. Haldane's words assume even greater significance when it is remembered that a few months after the war began, a violent agitation lead by the *Daily Express* was raised against Haldane, accusing him of pro-German sympathies.

When the liberal government was reconstituted in May, 1915, as a coalition under Asquith, Haldane was dropped from the cabinet. The authoritative accounts of Haldane's life as well as his autobiography make no mention of Bell's interview, and maintain that during this time Haldane "bore the often absurd attacks made on him with great dignity and absolute silence." This assertion seems inexplicable in the light of Bell's interview. The article was not presented in the form of a defensive statement on the part of Haldane; but, while admitting his spiritual affinity with Germany, certainly it leaves no question of his staunch allegiance to Great Britain particularly in reference to his mission to Germany in 1912.[18]

The interview received amazing publicity. Various American and Canadian newspapers printed it either in whole or in part; in England the pronouncement created a sensation. When it first appeared on April 1, the interview dominated the news scene. It was placarded in the streets and discussed editorially. The *Daily Chronicle* called the article an "epoch-making utterance," while the *Westminster Gazette* referred to it as a "great exposition" of the Allied cause. Even the German wireless took pains to deny Haldane's assertion that in 1912 he had warned Germany against a breach of Belgian neutrality.[19]

The interview was republished so frequently, Bell wrote Lawson a month later that "From the point of view of world publicity, The Chicago Daily News, by the Haldane interview, made its greatest score not only in this war, but in the whole history of our foreign service." The numerous clippings did not belie his words. Moreover, the *Daily Chronicle* issued one-half million copies of the interview in pamphlet form. Almost six months after the statement first appeared, Bell noted:

> It was not only reproduced in all the principal languages of the world at the time of its publication, but keeps bobbing up almost from week to week. It is permanently incorporated in the body of British political discussion. It profoundly affects the political posi-

> tion of Lord Haldane. Some hold that it killed him; others hold that it has given him a higher place in the esteem of the nation than he had before.[20]

An interesting consequence of the Haldane interview was the beginning of a series of letters between Bell and Samuel Insull, the English-born Chicago utilities executive. Insull's congratulations intimated that more of this type of material would be advisable from the Allied point of view. As a result there followed a number of letters to Bell in which Insull suggested persons from whom statements should be sought. He also wrote letters to several outstanding Englishmen, urging them to keep America informed. Most important, Insull was able to exert influence in helping Bell obtain an interview with the British Foreign Secretary, Sir Edward Grey. The broader aspects of this correspondence exhibit the close community of spirit which existed between many important Americans and Englishmen.[21]

The sinking of the *Lusitania* by a German submarine on May 7 inflamed American indignation against German methods of warfare. Bell cabled that "Dismay and anger almost baffling speech prevail throughout the American colony in London." Leading Americans there proposed holding a great mass meeting and passing resolutions calling upon the American government to protect its citizens traveling by sea. In an interview which he granted Bell, Henry Gordon Selfridge stated: "Even now I wish it were possible to think that we could get over the Lusitania horror without war, but how can we?" The London correspondent, however, skirted the question of whether or not the United States should go to war against Germany on the specific issue of the *Lusitania,* although he was greatly disturbed by the disaster. He did likewise with respect to subsequent crises resulting from submarine sinkings.[22]

There was, however, no question as to where his personal sentiments lay. To Dr. Edwin G. Cooley, Educational Adviser of the Commercial Club of Chicago, Bell wrote the following:

> As regards the war, there is just one thing I wish to see accomplished: the thorough licking that, in my judgment, Germany so richly and incontestably deserves. She has been asking for this ever since I have been in Europe.

> Of course, England is stopping some of our ships. I imagine if we were in her position we should be following a similar line. I'll tell you another thing I think: I think if England had been one-tenth part as insolent to us as Germany has been we should have gone to war with her long before now. And why, I cannot help wondering, should we be more tolerant of Germany's outrages and insults that we should be of like aggression on the part of England?
>
> However, I presume I should not talk like this — being an American and America being neutral. But personally I cannot entertain any neutrality that I conceive to be treason to civilization.[23]

During the summer of 1915 Bell maintained his running commentary on the English scene. Occasionally he spoke out against the British handling of American affairs. Concerning the effect of this activity on the American journalist, he pointed to the British cutting of political cables and to their killing of messages concerning the American shipping controversy. One of his cables attacked the British delay in dealing with suspicious American cargoes brought into port.[24] On the other hand Bell never grappled with several important issues which thread their way through the entire period from 1914 to 1917. Among these were the proposals in America to curb the sale of munitions and to ban loans and credits to the Allies. Neither did he analyze the discussions pertaining to the alteration of the rules regarding armed merchantmen.

Lawson respected Bell's objectivity in writing, but in August the editor cautioned him against quoting extreme individual opinion anonymously. Although he did not question the truth of his correspondent's stories, Lawson sent to him an "intemperate and unfair" letter, which he had received, simply to illustrate "a phase of public sentiment that it is wise to take into account." This reader had construed the anonymous statement as representing Bell's own opinion. Lawson set forth his views:

> The situation is difficult to define in terms of definite rule of treatment. The one thing is to try in a general way to put on all reports the impress of the correspondent's own unprejudice and impartial state of mind, so that the average reader will accept the correspondent's statement as a true *reflection* of the sentiment and opinion he is reporting, but not himself either approving or condemning.[25]

Bell replied that this was the fourth letter of its kind he had received, whereas the number of letters approving his cables was nearing five hundred. He unhesitatingly told Lawson that he felt it his duty to make three things clear to the American public through his dispatches:

> 1. That Germany thinks we are making war on her and that she is holding it up against us.
> 2. That our neutrality, of necessity, leaves popular world-sentiment cold toward us.
> 3. That, therefore, we ought to be in a strong posture of defense — not because we have done anything wrong; simply because we have kept out of the war and fought for our neutral rights.
>
> In a word, I have tried to throw up boldly the fact that THE AMERICAN POINT OF VIEW OUGHT TO BE ARMED.[26]

With this conviction Lawson could not quarrel.

On October 29, after some weeks of groundwork, Bell secured his second exclusive interview with an English cabinet member. Walter Runciman, President of the Board of Trade, discussed in detail the financial soundness of the British government and its allies. Conversely, he pointed out the weaknesses in the German method of financing war effort. No spectacular revelations were made. The high official's statement was designed mainly to inspire confidence in the Allied cause.

The interview was featured by most of the London press; Bell estimated that the story filled 200 newspaper columns on the day it was cabled back to England. It was also widely republished on the Continent. However, his success in interviewing cabinet ministers caused the correspondents representing New York newspapers to complain loudly against the government. A few weeks later these papers were temporarily outrivaling the *Chicago Daily News* in securing interviews and munition stories.[27]

Censorship, of course, plagued the American correspondents from the very beginning of the war. Bell, too, had frequently sparred with the British Press Bureau; but he did not publicly voice his views until late October 1915. Asserting that censorship had been administered with "inconceivable folly and fatheadedness," he claimed in his cable story that the greatest damage done by British censorship was against its own people. In his opinion, the Allied side was not being properly presented either to the British Empire abroad or to "all those whose interests are adversely affected by disaster to British prestige." As for the *Chicago Daily News,* the censorship had destroyed "tens of thousands of words . . . that had no right to be slaughtered." But most irksome was the killing of dispatches which had been passed by the censors of Britain's allies.[28]

Bell's exasperation culminated in a speech which he delivered on November 19 before the American Luncheon Club at the Savoy Hotel. In a good-natured but pointed manner, he proceeded to criticize the British censorship thoroughly on the basis of his views as expressed in October.

He said, "a strict military censorship is perfectly compatible with a censorship that permits enormous masses of news and of feature matter to reach the public." The correspondents, he continued, simply desired an opportunity to tell "Britain's world-struggle for her heritage and her life."

Of equal importance was his plea that the foreign correspondent in England be given greater privileges. Specifically, he proposed that American journalists be given the same press rights in Great Britain as British journalists enjoyed in America. Parliament and the London Guildhall, to mention only the most outstanding examples, were still closed to foreign correspondents. Bell reminded the British, "America's good opinion, if it is worth having, is more likely to be gained and kept by courage and candour than by any conceivable skill in the art of excision or suppression." Neither should the good will of other countries be endangered. At no point could Britain "neglect any measure calculated to prevent neutral opinion anywhere from becoming hostile opinion."[29]

The audience enthusiastically approved the speech. Home Secretary Sir John Simon, head of the British Press Bureau, which exercised censorship over the press, agreed with much that Bell had said. Lord Haldane referred to the address as an "excellent speech, which I have read with a good deal of sympathy." Incomprehensible as the workings of the Press Bureau were, Bell reported to Chicago on December 30 that an appreciable improvement in the censorship was noticeable.[30]

To further Anglo-American understanding, Bell deemed it his duty not only to keep English opinion of America amicable, but also to remind America that it must maintain a similar attitude toward England. By the fall of 1915 American prestige abroad had deteriorated to a new low point, particularly because of the American note of October 21, protesting British interference with neutral rights.[31]

Greatly disturbed by the antagonism between Britain and the United States, Bell acted on his convictions and cabled to the *Chicago Daily News* an open letter addressed to President Wilson. He wrote the President, "Our prestige abroad has sunk to the lowest depths it ever has reached." This sentiment was not caused by American unwillingness to enter the war on the Allied side:

> We Americans here, with good opportunities to learn the truth, believe that the low opinion held of us in England is due to our failure to give expression to our outraged conscience and sensibilities when Belgium was laid waste, and to our long suffering in the presence of repeated frightful crimes against our own and other non-combatants on the seas. As for our strong effort to maintain our neutral trade rights afloat, I do not think it would have been resented in England if we had thrown our moral weight into the scale against the invasion of Belgium, and against every other form of outrage that has made this war the most cruel in history.

Bell pointed out that not only England, but her allies and the European neutral countries held the same views toward America. As for Germany and Austria, "Their hatred of us is probably greater than is their hatred for any of their foes in the field." Germany believed that America was making war on her by supplying the Allies under the guise of neutrality with the sole purpose of glutting itself with wealth.

> All this, Mr. President, though you have declared, in a remarkable state paper, that America unhesitatingly assumed the task of championing neutral rights. This particular remark, by the way, was used not in a note protesting against attacks upon human life at sea, but in a note protesting against attacks upon neutral trading rights at sea. Every vigilant observer in Europe noted this circumstance, and we suffered further moral harm from it.

Without offering an answer to America's predicament, Bell left the President with the conundrum of why his high purposes had failed to attract world respect for America.[32]

Not waiting to learn of the disposition of the "open letter," Bell wrote Lawson, "I simply felt compelled to send it." He explained, "I cabled after an hour's close confidential talk with [American Ambassador Walter Hines] Page, following on innumerable talks with other persons. Page and his whole secretarial staff had had a conference on the subject and unanimously agreed that the facts are as represented in my cable."

When the "open letter" cable arrived in Chicago, Lawson immediately informed Bell that he thought it unwise to publish such a statement. Bell acknowledged Lawson's judgment; but, in so doing, he presented his views on the only way in which international accord could be secured:

> My effort in the Wilson cable was to make Americans understand how Europeans feel about them. My conviction is that the Americans should know what the Europeans think and that the Europeans should know what the Americans think. Unless there can be more frankness among peoples than there has been in the past, I do not see how, even in the course of centuries, the nations are to have the mutual understanding which is necessary to mutual sympathy and consequently, as I see it, to settled international peace. The problem seems to me to be how to make everything clear without stirring up animosities and provoking the recriminations which breed only blind passion.[33]

Lawson's reply explaining his reason for not publishing the "open letter" reached Bell more than a month later. Only after confirming his views with his close friend and legal counselor, John P. Wilson, had Lawson decided against publishing the letter.

He forwarded several reasons for his action. In the first place, he explained, "Usually an open letter advocates some definite thing or policy." If this letter had any purpose at all, he felt that it would exert an adverse influence on President Wilson's policy of maintaining the free exportation of war munitions to any and all buyers. Furthermore, Lawson found he could not get overwrought concerning the widespread criticism of American neutrality: "Every nation in Europe, neutral as well as belligerent, is deeply, keenly vitally interested in the war — necessarily and inevitably so — and therefore cannot be expected to exercise a dispassionate judgment respecting the views and policies different from its own."

Concerning American failure to enter a national protest against the invasion of Belgium, Lawson pointed out that the Hague convention, which America had signed, did not obligate the United States to go to war on behalf of Belgium — "and a mere protest, without military action, would, under existing conditions, involve a distinct *possibility* of our being involved sooner or later, in actual war with Germany."

Lastly, Lawson's "all-embracing and sufficient" reply to European criticism was:

> that under the unprecedented conditions of almost world-wide war the United States is charged with a world-wide responsibility, such as has never before come to any nation, to maintain such a position of neutrality of *expressed sentiment,* as well as of action, as will insure, when the time comes for the ending of war and the re-establishment of the normal conditions of world peace, that there shall be one nation of world-wide influence whose good offices *may* be invoked, should they be needed and desired, toward the accomplishment of universal peace — and is it too much to hope, of an *unending* world peace.[34]

Despite Lawson's reasoning, Bell felt a strong anxiety over American relations with the world. On March 7, he forwarded a copy of the "open letter" to President Wilson. A letter of transmittal explained briefly the fate of the original communication and Bell's conviction that it should be brought to the President's attention. In addition, Bell pointed out the course he thought America should take:

> I have read your books, particularly your historical writing. They give me hope, if I may say so without offense, that you understand the enormity of Germany's crime against humanity and civilization, and that you are alive to the unspeakable menace to ourselves involved in a German triumph over the Allies. So long as Britain's fleet holds the seas, and so long as we can avoid serious trouble with Britain and her associates in the war, we are safe. I do hope our preparations will be rushed forward with all possible speed, while we can prepare under the egis of a friendly fleet.[35]

Meanwhile Bell did not neglect any opportunities for exclusive news stories. In January he visited an unidentified British naval base. Observing British troops in action, however, was pretty well out of the question because of the official attitude. When the opportunity did arise for six representatives of the American press to go to the front, the choice of the six was left among the correspondents themselves. A combination of New York newspaper correspondents voted to exclude not only the *Chicago Daily News,* but the Associated Press, the United Press, the Hearst newspapers, and the *Philadelphia Public Ledger* as well. Not to be outdone, Bell engaged the services of the Scandinavian press representative who was making the trip to the British front. Bell's complaint to the Foreign Office about this matter netted him a visit to the British North Sea Fleet, and in mid-April he was allowed a trip to the British front.[36]

On the London news scene, Bell obtained an exclusive interview with Rear Admiral Ernest Troubridge of the British navy early in March. The Admiral recounted his recent experiences as "defender of the Danube" and described the heartbreaking Serbian retreat. After reading the reporter's manuscript, he wrote, "I only wish I had the gift of so graphic and condensed description. It really brings the tears to my eyes when my thoughts and your article meet."[37]

Bell secured another exclusive statement when Lawson sent a radiogram to the London, Paris, and Berlin bureaus. He instructed that copies be furnished the belligerent governments and the leading newspapers. For the purposes of assisting in a correct understanding abroad of American views as well as of evoking from the belligerants a statement of their position, the message set forth the American government's attitude in the controversy with Germany and Britain over neutral rights. These opinions represented the results of an inquiry conducted among high government officials by the Washington bureau of the *Chicago Daily News.*

In essence, the message declared that there was little distinction between the position of the two warring sides with respect to neutral nations: both contended that new methods of warfare had so radically changed conditions as to make a blockade under the old international rules no longer possible. Thus, if America conceded anything to one side, she would likewise have to satisfy the other. One distinction, however, was noted; while German submarine activities had affected both American lives and property, British measures had so far affected property only. The message concluded that, under these circumstances, America had no alternative other than to cling to its neutral rights against both sides. A solution would be forthcoming only when the warring nations mutually agreed on modifications of the rules of war.[38]

Charles H. Dennis, Managing Editor of the *Chicago Daily News,* later informed Bell that the statement was really designed for presentation to the German government and the German press; in fact, the whole idea originated in an appeal from the *Chicago Daily News'* Berlin correspondent Raymond Swing who asked the home office to send such a statement for general circulation in Germany. For unknown reasons, Swing and the *Chicago Daily News'* Paris correspondent Paul Scott Mowrer did not reply to the message.[39] Bell, upon informing Sir Edward Grey, the British Secretary of State for Foreign Affairs, of the message, was granted an interview by Lord Thomas Newton, Assistant Under Secretary to Grey.

Newton clearly pointed out that the claims of the belligerents were not identical. Whereas Germany held that its revolutionary submarine warfare had not been envisaged by the law of nations and that legislators should formulate a new international code, the Allies held that, with reference to the blockade, it was necessary only to apply the established principles. From this premise, Newton exhibited how empty the German claims were. The German assertion that it was illegal for the Allies to interfere with the food supply of the German noncombatant population was not borne out by the German attempt to cut off England from the outside. The German claim that the Allies had no right to interfere with their trade was disproved by Newton as being contrary to the established rights of belligerants.[40]

Soon afterward Bell achieved his most notable interview of the war period. Since the beginning of the conflict, he had been trying to make an appointment with Sir Edward Grey. A meeting, lasting an hour and a half, was finally granted on April 10 at the Secretary of State's temporary London home. As usual, Bell took no notes and was able to produce a remarkably accurate statement.[41]

Grey's words concerned mainly the war aims of Great Britain, with some reference to the type of peace he envisaged after the war:

> What we and our Allies are fighting for is a free Europe. We want a Europe free, not only from the domination of one nationality by another, but from hectoring diplomacy and the peril of war, free from the constant rattling of the sword in the scabbard, from perpetual talk of shining armour and warlords. In fact, we feel we are fighting for equal rights; for law, justice, peace; for civilization, throughout the world, as against brute force which knows no restraint and no mercy.

More specifically, Grey pledged that the restoration of Belgium and

Serbia would be carried out and that Britain would make peace only in concert with her Allies.

Looking into the future, the statesman spoke of a lasting peace — "not a wobbly peace, not a peace vulnerable to political and militarist intrigue and ambition, but a peace secured by the unified and armed purpose of civilization." Many years before the war Grey had hoped for "a league of nations that would be united, quick and instant, to prevent, and, if need be, to punish violation of international treaties, of public right, of national independence, and would say to nations that come forward with grievances and claims, 'Put them before an impartial tribunal.' "

Grey asserted that above all, "free men and free nations will rather die than submit" to Prussian tyranny — "there can be no end to war till it is defeated and renounced."[42]

The *Chicago Daily News* considered the interview "the most important expression on the subject of the war that thus far has been given to the public." Journalistically, it was most exceptional: this was the first interview Grey had granted in his eleven years as Secretary of State. Bell and others believed that Grey was the first British Foreign Secretary ever to be interviewed. As for the statement itself, Bell thought it would be "enormously valuable in the direction of better Anglo-American relations." In his mind, it clearly established "the essential identity of British and American ideals with reference to the future of mankind."[43]

Letters of praise poured into the London office. Newspapers there and in Paris, as well as in America and Canada, handled the interview as a leading feature. On the Continent the statement was widely reprinted. The German press, of course, denounced Grey's words. Some time later, the *Chicago Daily News'* Tokyo correspondent wrote Bell that the two English dailies there had reproduced the interview in full, while the Japanese papers had commented on it.[44]

Bell's work even caused repercussions in the British Parliament. A few days after the interview appeared in the London newspapers, Grey was criticized in the House of Commons by two pacifist members. They accused him of showing a lack of respect for Parliament and the people of Britain in adopting "the platform of the American press" for his utterance. As reported by the London *Times* parliamentary correspondent,

Grey's reply, made "amid a constant roll of approving cheers," swept aside the complaint against the interview as "pedantry." In reference to his public assertions, he asked, "if, while the German statesmen month by month . . . lauded their own morality and lied about Britain, British statesmen were to be denied the privilege of defending their policy and their nation against these defamations[?]"[45]

Throughout the remainder of 1916, Bell produced various feature stories. He described the growth of the British Royal Flying Corps, and the feverish activities of the shipbuilding industry. On one occasion he took a daring flight with an English aviator, and wrote an account of the first "battle-drill" flight to be experienced by any correspondent. Later the Admiralty permitted him a seaplane trip. Whenever Bell chanced to write about the shortcomings of the Allies, he never failed to urge American preparedness and universal military training. [46]

Of the several exclusive interviews he accomplished during these months, one deserves particular notice. Late in December, the Commander in Chief of the British Home Forces, Field Marshal John French, expressed the fear that Germany's small neighbors faced the danger of subjugation from this overwhelming Teutonic power. His words, widely republished on the Continent, caused some alarm among the smaller nations.[47]

During the last days of December, 1916, Bell rose to his greatest height in another effort to preserve Anglo-American accord. In a series of six noteworthy letters to the London *Times,* he not only did his utmost to interpret President Wilson and the American people to the British, but he also foreshadowed American entrance into the war.

When Wilson's peace note of December 18, 1916, bluntly declared that "the objects which the statesmen of the belligerents on both sides have in mind in this war are virtually the same," as stated by them, Bell felt it was his duty to explain this remark which the English considered quite offensive.[48] In his first letter to *The Times,* Bell explained that Wilson had been "thoroughly and deplorably misunderstood." The President was simply referring to the outward affirmations of the warring nations. What Wilson really sought through his note was a true statement of the purposes of both sides which would reveal Germany's "brigand soul." With these aims fully unveiled, Bell explained,

> I have not a doubt that President Wilson would be inexpressibly happy to see America fighting with the Allies against the Central Powers in this war. I believe if he would induce Germany, formally and officially, to state that she was fighting to subjugate Belgium, to take a slice of territory away from France, to extinguish Serbia, in a word to realize any of the aims of her scheme of world conquest — if he could do this, I believe he would appeal to the American people to join the Allies in defeating this monstrous project. In other words, I believe that President Wilson wants to go to war; I believe he wants to fight Germany; and I believe he wants Germany to commit herself to a programme that would warrant him in asking the American people to enter the conflict.[49]

Bell's words received considerable ridicule, but he remained steady in his convictions.[50] On December 27, his second letter to *The Times* appeared. He again urged, in even stronger terms, that Britain make no hesitation in precisely stating its war aims. A prompt enunciation could well be the turning point of the future.

> America cannot keep out of this war — unless Germany gives way. The time may come very soon when President Wilson will be under the necessity of making his appeal to the American nation. The Allies have done things that have been very painful to us. They have committed acts that we regard as forcible invasions of our sovereignty. But the Germans have done worse. They not only have invaded our sovereign rights, but have slaughtered and drowned our citizens in outrage of all law and of the first rudiments of humanity. The Allies have done us *some* harm, but they are fighting for what we cherish; the Germans have done us infinitely *more* harm, and they are fighting for what we execrate. For whom, then, will we be likely to fight, when we must fight?

Germany refused to state its terms for peace, but agreed to meet the Entente powers in conference to discuss possible terms of peace; the Allies replied to the American government with a joint statement of objectives on December 29 indicating among other things that "they wanted only a peace based upon principles of justice and liberty."[51] Bell's third letter was published two days later. Short and pointed, it stated, "America never will support any peace except a peace that vindicates liberty and justice, and promises the deliverance of the world from war." In view of these terms, Bell conceived that America could uphold only an Allied peace.

A few days afterward, Lord Northcliffe, owner of *The Times,* cabled Lawson: "Bell's letters to London Times did much to prevent violent public opinion here consequent on ambiguous phrasing portion of [President Wilson's] peace proposition." Ambassador Page also approved of the letters.[52]

Wilson's "peace without victory" address of January 22 was interpreted in a fourth letter as directed "solely to inform the world of what America stands for, and what he is willing to ask America if need be, to fight for."[53]

On Washington's birthday, after America had severed relations with Germany, Bell wrote his fifth letter in which he approved of the diplomatic break. This time his whole reputation was staked on his words: "I will risk the view that we are on the edge of great things in America — things worthy of Washington and Lincoln. America, I feel, is about to fructify internationally — about to make her real contribution to humanity and history." *The Times* itself declared that Bell's "sagacious and racy letter deserves careful consideration by all who are trying to understand the situation in Washington."[54]

Five days later, shortly after Wilson addressed Congress asking the right to arm American merchantmen, the last letter explained America's delay in coming to grips with Germany: "If, and when, our country takes the fateful step, Wilson wants a public temper so hot throughout America that it instantly will burn to ash any revolutionary unrest, or any opposition by pacifist die-hards."[55]

In the ensuing weeks Bell made no further statement either on the crises resulting from American ships being destroyed by German submarines, or on the need for America taking up arms at that particular time. War came to America on April 6. Bell's cables then carried the identifying phrase, "with the British Army between Ancre and the Somne." On April 20, Lord Northcliffe, also owner of the London *Daily Mail,* directed Bell's old friend and former colleague, Frederic W. Wile, to write a feature story for the *Daily Mail* on the sextet of letters addressed to *The Times.* In this article Bell was referred to as the "Man Who Knew."[56]

## *NOTES*

1. See Frank L. Mott, *American Journalism* (3d ed., New York, 1962), 615-618.
2. For the origin of *Chicago Daily News* Foreign News Service, see Benedict K. Zobrist, "How Victor Lawson's Newspapers Covered the Cuban War of 1898," *Journalism Quarterly,* XXXVIII (Summer, 1961), 323-331.
3. With the death of Isaac N. Ford in 1912, Bell became the senior American foreign correspondent in length of service. Bell to Charles H. Dennis, June, 1911, Edward Price Bell Papers, Newberry Library, Chicago. See also *Who Was Who in America,* I (Chicago, 1942), 412.
4. See Arthur S. Link, *Wilson, the Struggle for Neutrality, 1914-1915* (Princeton, 1960), 171-175.
5. Brittain to Bell, Jan. 15, 1915; J. Strachey to Bell, Jan. 16, 1915; Selfridge to Bell, Jan. 14, 1915; Parker to Bell, Jan. 18, 1915; Bell to Donald, Jan. 25, 1915, Bell Papers; *Chicago Daily News,* Jan. 13, and Jan. 22, 1915; *Morning Post* (London), Jan. 13, 1915; and *Daily Chronicle* (London), Jan. 14, 1915.
6. Robinson to Bell, Jan. 14, 1915; Bell to Robinson, Jan. 15, 1915, Bell Papers; *The Times* (London), Jan. 13, and Jan. 16, 1915.
7. J. Strachey to Bell, Jan. 16, Jan. 22, and Feb. 8, 1915; Bell to Strachey, Jan. 22, and Feb. 9, 1915, Bell Papers; and *Chicago Daily News,* Jan. 22, 1915.
8. Burton J. Hendrick, *The Life and Letters of Walter H. Page,* I (Garden City, N. Y., 1922), 392-396.
9. Bell to Donald, Jan. 25, 1915; and Donald to Bell, Jan. 25, 1915, Bell Papers.
10. Link, *Wilson, the Struggle for Neutrality,* 86-91, 138, and 143-158.
11. This article was reprinted with Bell's permission in *Sixty American Opinions on the War* (London, [1915]), 24-29. See T. Fisher Unwin to Bell, Feb. 19, and Feb. 24, 1915, Bell Papers.
12. Albert Grey to Bell, Jan. 27, 1915; Buckmaster to Bell, Jan. 28, 1915; Selfridge to Bell, Jan. 27, 1915; and Page to Bell, Jan. 28, 1915, Bell Papers.
13. Martin to Bell, Jan. 28, 1915; and Bell to Lawson, Jan. 29, 1915, Bell Papers.
14. Lawson to Bell, Feb. 11, 1915, Victor Fremont Lawson Papers, Newberry Library, Chicago.
15. Link, *Wilson, the Struggle for Neutrality,* 187.
16. M. Bonham Carter to Bell, March 3, and March 5, 1915; and Bell to Dennis, March 19, 1915, Bell Papers.
17. Richard B. Haldane to Bell, March 17, 1915, Bell Papers.
18. Haldane to Bell, April 3, 1915, Bell Papers; *The Dictionary of National Biography,* Fourth sup., 383; Frederick B. Maurice, *Haldane,* I (London, 1937), 357-364; and Richard B. Haldane, *Richard Burdon Haldane, An Autobiography* (London, 1929) 285-286.
19. Bell to News Chicago, April 1, and April 5, 1915, Bell Papers; Lawson to Bell, June 4, 1915, Lawson Papers; and *The Times* (London), April 5, 1915.
20. Bell to Dennis, April 30, and Sept. 20, 1915, Bell Papers.

21. Bell to Insull, May 5, and Aug. 2, 1915, and Feb. 22, 1916; Insull to Bell, May 17, June 24, Nov. 10, 1915, Feb. 3, and May 16, 1916, Bell Papers; and Lawson to Insull, May 17, 1916, Lawson Papers.
22. *Chicago Daily News,* May 8, 1915.
23. June 1, 1915, Bell Papers.
24. *Chicago Daily News,* July 17, and July 20, 1915.
25. Lawson to Bell, Aug. 31, 1915, Bell Papers.
26. Bell to Lawson, Sept. 15, 1915, Bell Papers.
27. Bell to News Chicago, Oct. 29, 1915; Bell to Lawson, Nov. 1, 1915; Bell to Dennis, Nov. 24, Nov. 26, and Dec. 2, 1915, Bell Papers; and *Chicago Daily News,* Oct. 30, 1915.
28. *Chicago Daily News,* July 17, and Oct. 27, 1915.
29. Original manuscript in Bell Papers. Speech later published in pamphlet form by the American Luncheon Club: Edward Price Bell, *The British Censorship* (London, 1916).
30. Bell to Dennis, Nov. 27, 1915; Haldane to Bell, Dec. 1, 1915; and Bell to News Chicago, Dec. 30, 1915, Bell Papers.
31. See Link, *Wilson, the Struggle for Neutrality,* 682-693; and Arthur S. Link, *Wilson, Confusions and Crises, 1915-1916* (Princeton, 1964), 142.
32. Bell to News Chicago, Jan. 5, 1916, Bell Papers.
33. Bell to Lawson, Jan. 10, and Jan. 12, 1916, Bell Papers; and Lawson to Epinglage London, Jan. 10, 1916, Lawson Papers.
34. Lawson to Bell, Feb. 5, 1916, Lawson Papers.
35. Bell to Woodrow Wilson, March 7, 1916, Bell Papers.
36. Bell to Guy Lecock, Feb. 1, 1916; Bell to Edward Grey, Feb. 3, 1916; Bell to News Chicago, March 3, 1916; Bell to Lawson, March 4, 1916; Bell to Dennis, April 13, and May 1, 1916, Bell Papers; and *Chicago Daily News,* Jan. 10, Feb. 11, May 30, June 2, June 17, and June 24, 1916.
37. Bell to Dennis, March 10, 1916, Bell Papers; and *Chicago Daily News,* April 24, 1916.
38. Bell to Edward Grey, March 13, 1916, Bell Papers.
39. Dennis to Bell, March 24, 1916; and Bell to Dennis, April 13, 1916, Bell Papers.
40. *Chicago Daily News,* March 25, 1916.
41. Bell to Dennis, May 1, 1916, Bell Papers.
42. *Chicago Daily News,* May 13, 1916. This interview was republished in pamphlet form: Edward Price Bell, *A Free Europe* (London, 1916).
43. Bell to Lawson, May 9, 1916, Bell Papers; and *Chicago Daily News,* May 15, 1916.
44. Selfridge to Bell, May 15, 1916; Noel to Bell, May 16, 1916; Dennis to Bell, May 16, 1916; Atter to Bell, May 17, 1916; E. W. Clement to Bell, July 10, 1916, Bell Papers; Lawson to Bell, July 21, 1916, Lawson Papers; and *Chicago Daily News,* May 17, and May 19, 1916.
45. *Chicago Daily News,* May 25, 1916; and *The Times* (London), May 25, 1916.
46. Bell to Dennis, July 19, 1916; Bell to Lawson, Sept. 19, 1916, Bell Papers; and *Chicago Daily News,* March 18, April 12, Aug. 12, Aug. 15, Aug. 17, Oct. 18, and Nov. 5, 1916.

47. Daily News to Epinglage London, Dec. 28, 1916, Bell Papers; and *Chicago Daily News,* Dec. 30, 1916, and Jan. 3, 1917.
48. United States Department of State, *Papers Relating to the Foreign Relations of the United States. Supplements. The World War, 1916* (Washington, 1929), 98; and Arthur S. Link, *Wilson, Campaigns for Progressivism and Peace, 1916-1917* (Princeton, 1965), 214-219.
49. Dec. 23, 1916.
50. Bell to Donald, Jan. 4, 1917, Bell Papers. See "Germany, the United States, and Peace," *Quarterly Review,* CCXXVII (1917), 291-292.
51. Link, *Wilson, Campaigns for Progressivism and Peace,* 220-239.
52. Northcliffe to Chicago News, Jan. 8, 1917; and Bell to Lawson, Jan. 10, 1917, Bell Papers.
53. *The Times* (London), Jan. 26, 1917.
54. *Ibid.,* Feb. 23, 1917.
55. *Ibid.,* Feb. 28, 1917.
56. *Chicago Daily News,* April 20, 1917.

# *Wilson and Gladstone*
# *Perils and Parallels in Leadership*

JAMES IVERNE DOWIE

The lives of William Gladstone and Woodrow Wilson span the historical epoch from Waterloo in 1815 to the Munich Beer Hall Putsch in 1923. At the beginning of the epoch stood Napoleon Bonaparte, and at its close came Adolph Hitler and a host of totalitarian leaders. Along the way Otto von Bismarck had used *realpolitik* with dramatic success, while Benjamin Disraeli in England and Theodore Roosevelt in the United States tentatively consented to the Machiavellian stance in international diplomacy. From some points of view Gladstone and Wilson were out of touch with their own environment when they insisted upon approaching politics and diplomacy in moralistic dimensions. In a larger sense, however, both men were caught up in a tradition which has permeated Western thought since Plato and Christ. This tradition has revolved around the mystical theme linking the City of God with the City of Man. Naive although it may appear to a disenchanted age like our own, both Gladstone and Wilson drew from the ancient wells of faith that God is active in history.

Very likely they were the last of the great statesmen seriously committed to a transcendent view of history. There are disturbing parallels in the leadership of these two men whose ideas, arising out of their heritage in the Atlantic community, were often complementary. They both came near to greatness while experiencing egregious failure. They were uncritical captives of the superficialities of their milieu which held out lavish promises and extravagant hopes. Everywhere they encountered these expectations — in the romanticized historiography which they read, the sermons which they heard, and the democratic idealism which they embraced. In their failures are some of the grandeur and much of the tragedy implicit in a culture undergoing a traumatic mutation. Carl Becker has observed how quickly and completely our own age detached itself from a time when history "could still be regarded as a transcendent idea realizing itself in the actual." Today's historian "who should surreptitiously introduce the gloss of a transcendent interpretation into the human story would deserve to be called a philosopher and straightway lose his reputation as a scholar."[1]

Critics have looked for personality defects to explain the failures of Wilson and Gladstone. Queen Victoria, herself a child of the same faith which nourished the spirit of Gladstone, opined that with Gladstone "the will and purpose of God were identified with the interest and policy of the Liberal Party."[2] Returning in anger from the Versailles Peace Conference in 1919, John Maynard Keynes, the British economist, condemned the peace settlement and its makers, particularly President Wilson whose "thoughts and feelings" were trapped "in a theological mould." Keynes had no patience for the "blind and deaf Don Quixote" who was so insensitive to his environment: He "could have preached a stately sermon . . . or have addressed a stately prayer to the Almighty, . . . but he could not frame their [Fourteen Points] concrete application to the actual state of Europe."[3] Theodore Roosevelt, who was a little insane on the subject of Wilson, called the President "a coward and a fraud." Benjamin Disraeli, Roosevelt's counterpart in Victorian politics, was equally direct in damning Gladstone:

> Posterity will do justice to the unprincipled maniac, Gladstone — extraordinary mixture of envy, vindictiveness, hypocrisy, and superstition; and with one commanding characteristic — whether preaching, praying, speechifying, or scribbling — never a gentleman![4]

Gladstone was the common enemy who strengthened the rapport

between Victoria and Disraeli. The Queen and her favorite Prime Minister shared many a delicious moment in agonizing over the foibles and shortcomings of the Liberal Party and its leader. On the other hand, the Queen who thrived on the flattery of Disraeli withered in the company of Gladstone: "The trouble with Mr. Gladstone is that he always addresses me as if I were a public meeting."[5] For his part, Gladstone was sometimes equally uncomfortable, "The Queen alone is enough to kill any man."[6] Mrs. Gladstone sought to ease the tension by suggesting that her husband should "pet the Queen a little."[7] But the arts of blandishment were alien to Gladstone's nature. Like Wilson, he was too highminded to be sensitive to the exigencies of his environment.

It is not easy to be charitable in the City of Man when one is in service to the City of God. As Gladstone might put it, good ends can only be achieved through "a righteous passion."[8] In his inaugural address on March 4, 1913, Wilson revealed his own righteous passion: "Our duty is to cleanse, to reconsider, to restore, to correct the evil without impairing the good . . ."[9] Earlier Wilson had eschewed the give-and-take of political life by a didactic affirmation that government is too serious a matter to admit of meaningless courtesies.

If such a stiff-necked approach to life kept Gladstone from being on amiable terms with Victoria, it may also account for the disasterous rift between President Wilson and his Republican opposition. The issue of the 1918 election he could raise to a cause of "righteous passion" at the risk of a major political reverse. Likewise he could pass over the political necessity of including a responsible voice from the Republican Party in the peace delegation to Paris in 1919. Because they so easily identified their political opposition with the forces of mischief, it became a matter of high principle for Gladstone and Wilson to hold aloof from the little games which ordinary men must play in order to live and to let live. Besides, Wilson never had a sense of playfulness among men, so he saw no occasion for playfulness in politics.[10] He preferred to spend his leisure time singing and chatting with the female members of his White House family. Here he found more pleasure than at the card table or in the club with other politicos. When away from Parliament and the hustings, Gladstone was no man about the London clubs fraternizing with fellow politicians.

Rather he retreated to his estate at Hawarden where, ax in hand, he continued his crusade against oak trees. Evidently to chop down a giant oak provided release from the trauma of political life, and the Prime Minister became famous from one end of England to the other for his skill as a woodsman.

Aridity of spirit instead of compassion at times faulted the leadership of the British Prime Minister and the American President. Both were attuned to nineteenth-century liberalism and evangelism. Too often the gospel of individualism — whether preached in religion or economics — did not generate social concern for human beings. Wilson's New Freedom embodied in banking, tariff, and trust reforms kept his administration alert to the needs of the American entrepreneurial class. Its needs were clear to a president whose economic thought was anchored in nineteenth-century political economy. But this same president did not respond so quickly to the needs of children at work in American industry, and his economic conservatism found convenient support in a correct constitutional stance when child-labor legislation was first proposed in Congress.

Similar contradictions were present in the career of Gladstone. Out of conscience and religious scruple he moved during his first ministry (1868-1874) to free Irish Catholics from the burdens of an alien Anglican Church, to work for land reform in Ireland, and to remove religious restrictions at Oxford and Cambridge. But when it came to problems closer to home, the need for expanded public education and social welfare, Gladstone was remiss to the point of disinterest and silence. Squalor, disease, and ignorance in the English slums had to look elsewhere for amelioration. Social problems became the special concern of the "radicals" in the Liberal Party under the aegis of men like Joseph Chamberlain.

Not all men maturing in the nineteenth century sustained fixed positions prescribed by the commitment of their age to liberalism. John Stuart Mill for one came to critical terms with liberalism and the negative liberal state. By the end of the century many Englishmen were turning away from liberalism and responding to the new collectivism. In the United States the social gospel muted some of the harsher features of the gospel of wealth, and even before Wilson's presidency the way was opening for the expanded role of the positive liberal state. Theodore Roosevelt at times understood more clearly than Woodrow Wilson the limitations of nineteenth-century liberalism in the industrial-urbanized world of the twentieth century, and his New Nationalism was something of an advance toward the welfare state.

But Mill and Roosevelt were men of lesser faith than Gladstone and Wilson. Adam Smith, Jeremy Bentham and Robert Peel had converted Gladstone, and he amplified their vision of the City of Man by his attachment to the City of God. More than most men of his time or since, Gladstone could see "the invisible hand" of God at work to shape the world of enlightened self interest. He once wrote to his sister, Helen Gladstone:

> The welfare of my fellow creatures is more than ever at stake, but not within the walls of Parliament. The battle is to be fought in the region of thought, and the issue is belief or disbelief in the unseen world, and in its Guardian, the Creator-Lord and Deliverer of man.[11]

Thomas Jefferson and Abraham Lincoln were mentors to Woodrow Wilson. Both had an almost mystical view of the people, and Wilson incorporated this romanticized abstraction of popular will into his own intimations of the City of God. In one of his Lincoln Day addresses Wilson conveyed his transcendent interpretation of the people: "The fundamental faith of democracy is that out of a mass of uncatalogued men you can always count on genius asserting itself, genius suited to mankind, genius suited to the task." Again, how had the birth of freedom in the modern world come about? "It was the conception that every man stood naked and individual in his responsibility before his God and Maker."[12]

Wilson was the historian and statesman framing the human experience in faith. Capsulizing the unbelief of our own age, another historian (perhaps just as uncritical in his response to current thought as Wilson was to his own age) has advanced the counter theme: "Man is but a foundling in the cosmos."[13] Our world in the last half of the twentieth century is small and seared. Buchenwald and Hiroshima imprison us in our parochialism and almost convince us that the faith of another age was an absurdity and a hoax. There is a kind of masochistic relief when William Hamilton tells us that "God is dead." The antiquarians among us may take some mild interest in the aberrations of men, not more than a century ago, who found comfort in knowing that "God's in his heaven — all's right with the world!"

The "Sea of Faith" was still at the full for many growing up before World War I. No doubt at the end of their political careers, when the remembrance of grand eloquence and thunderous applause could only intensify the ache and emptiness of lost causes, Gladstone and Wilson stood at last with Matthew Arnold on the "vast edges drear and naked." But history could be given a sanguine reading even in 1867 when Arnold published *Dover Beach.* That was the year of the Second Reform Bill which redeemed the promises of 1832 by a substantial expansion of the English electorate. Furthermore, between 1832 and 1867 the English public had responded in a marvelous way to mass education in the economics of free trade. Richard Cobden and John Bright had proved what Thomas Jefferson long before had surmised, namely that the informed masses can direct the course of history. Robert Peel understood this fact of political life well, and in 1846 he put the will of the people above the wish of his own Tory Party by repealing the corn laws. In a similar rally of public opinion the abolitionists had been mentors to the American people, and the peculiar institution of the American South was ended by four years of Civil War. The humanitarian thought of the West was even beginning to moderate the severity of serfdom in Russia.

Just as Gladstone and Wilson may have been the last great statesmen seriously to insist upon the hand of God in the affairs of men, they were equally innocent about the ambiguities inhering in the idea of progress in the Western world. They capitulated to the mystique of the Atlantic community. For the purposes of this essay the mystique may be described in its simplest parochial terms. English historiography has long pursued the theme of the *community of the realm.* Gladstone and Wilson were immersed in this historiography which created many of the myths and probabilities now so suspect in the white Anglo-Saxon Protestant version of history. The community of the realm found lodgement in the English Parliament and the common law. In evolving political thought John Locke at the end of the seventeenth century invested the community of the realm with sovereignty over government itself. These Lockean views of government fed on the quest for natural law and natural right so dear to men on both sides of the Atlantic during the eighteenth century. Americans anathematized King George III in the name of Locke. Presumably Ben Franklin and Thomas Jefferson cherished the gospel according to Locke and found it more instructive than the gospel according to St. John. In 1789 the French overthrew tyranny, and again there was the appeal to the community in the nebulous phrase of the "general will."

By the 1830s Andrew Jackson was the people's hero in the White House, and through majoritarian democracy "king numbers" was enthroned in Washington. Almost simultaneously by way of the First Reform Bill the English electorate was increased. Was there ever a century in which the sovereignty of the people was more clearly manifest?

Abraham Lincoln could rest the justice of the Union's cause upon the people who had given the earth its last best hope. Walt Whitman was writing a kind of orgiastic poetry in order to identify with the people. To catch a Biblical figure, now a cliche in textbooks, it was a time when new wine was being poured into old bottles. Obviously the old bottles could not hold the new ferment. In the United States the republic of the Founding Fathers (government in the hands of the "wise and virtuous" or natural aristocracy) was changing in response to egalitarian democracy. Across the Atlantic monarchy, aristocracy, and ancient class structure were no longer sufficient social controls over a burgeoning and boisterous people.

The antique mechanisms for social control were obsolete in an age intent upon urban industrialism, nationalism, and the popular voice at the highest level of decision-making. Most of the questions which arose with the forced abdication of the ancient managers of society are current in the twentieth century. Our own times have many more questions than answers, and here is the sharp difference between, let us say, 1967 and 1867. We are disenchanted with answers to which men once committed their lives. In the nineteenth century men busied themselves in spawning ideologies which other men were inclined to take seriously. It is hard to imagine a social panacea — from Robert Owen's communitarianism to Marxian socialism, Charles Kingsley's Christian socialism to Sidney Webb's Fabianism, Bentham's utilitarianism to Bakunin's anarchism, Joseph Smith's Mormonism to Houston Stewart Chamberlain's racism — which did not get a hearing on the public platform or through the printed page. At the center of almost every ideology stood two questions: how to recast society and how to define the role of the leader.

After the passage of the Second Reform Bill in 1867, Robert Lowe, a member of Parliament, came close to the heart of the matter, "We must educate our masters." Gladstone and Wilson spent their political lives educating "their masters." Despite their attachment to moral values, the techniques through which they dramatized the reciprocity between the people and the leader could later be appropriated by less ethical leaders for ignoble ends.

> In the bright noonday of intellectual liberalism, Gladstone had purchased the people's love with coin of the purest gold. That coinage was debased by his competitors, and in the auction which followed the currency was recklessly inflated. In the early days of that auction, Lord Randolph Churchill learned much from the arts which Gladstone practised in Midlothian; and he made a corrupt use of what he learned. Randolph Churchill reached out a hand to Lloyd George, and Lloyd George exchanged a nod with Adolph Hitler on the trail from Midlothian to Limehouse and from Limehouse to the Nuremberg Rally.[14]

In his youth Wilson was an assiduous student of the techniques of leadership. While still in college he was intensely interested in the qualities of leadership in contemporaries such as Prince Bismarck, John Bright, and William Gladstone. These early observations helped him to define his own role:

> I do not know of any one among modern statesmen whose character is worthier of the study and the imitation of the young men of a free country than is Mr. Gladstone's . . .[15]

Wilson believed that leaders could gain a "knowledge of men" through intuition as well as experience: "Great statesmen seem to direct and rule by a sort of power to put themselves in the place of the nation over whom they are set, and may thus be said to possess the souls of poets . . ."[16] Wilson was impressed by the quality of leadership which he found in Bright and Gladstone: "Both are preeminent in eloquence; both are conspicuous for the noble sincerity and high-strung morality of their character; both are engaged heart and soul in the pursuit of the highest interests of their country . . ."[17]

Skilled in the art of oratory himself, Wilson linked Gladstone's political success with this special gift. The English Prime Minister had the capacity for defining the higher impulses of the English race, and this power gave him authority "on the platform and preeminence in Parliament." It was "the grandeur of his statement which made his statesmanship grand." Gladstone understood that "Passion is the pith of eloquence."[18]

Shortly before assessing the role of Gladstone's leadership, Wilson had written a sketch of the career of Bismarck. His sympathies for English leaders as opposed to German leaders during World War I may have been induced by these early impressions. While conceding that Bismarck was "the most prominent figure in modern history," Wilson considered the role of the "iron chancellor" to be less grand and noble compared with his American and English counterparts.

> Neither those talents so necessary to the English statesman as a leader of Parliament nor those peculiar gifts always to be found in the guide of popular opinion and guard of popular institutions are necessary to the Prussian statesman. All the energies of the English or American statesman must be spent in governing great popular assemblies, in manipulating [sic] parties, in directing and controlling popular opinion. The Prussian statesman, on the other hand, must exert all his powers in rendering himself supreme in the royal closet; his power does not depend upon popular assemblies whose favor he must win and whose support he must command, but rests entirely with his royal master . . .[19]

Furthermore, with such leaders as Bismarck "intrigue was apt to demean the powers and sully the character of the Prussian statesman." Wilson discerned a moral gap between the achievements of Bismarck and the "stain which intrigue invariably brings."[20]

Authoritarian states, therefore, weakened their moral stance by placing their leaders beyond the reach of the people's will and judgment. This reasoning allowed Wilson to enthrone the precious principle of self-determination. He knew well the writings of the American historian, George Bancroft, whose interpretations reflected the optimism of the Jacksonian age, and Wilson could easily assent when Bancroft wrote: "The common judgment in taste, politics, and religion is the highest authority on earth."

Wilson would want to add that where there is reciprocity between the leader and the people there also is the highest moral authority on earth.

> A statesman was a man in whose ears the voices of the nation do not sound like the accidental and discordant notes that come from the voice of a mob, but concurrent and concordant like the united voices of a chorus, whose many meanings, spoken by melodious tongues, unite in his understanding in a single meaning and reveal to him a single vision, so that he can speak what no man else knows, the common meaning of the common voice. Such is the man who leads a great, free, democratic nation.[21]

Had Wilson read Gladstone's assessment of the political phenomenon of the people and the leader? "The nation is a power hard to rouse, but when roused harder still and more hopeless to resist . . ."[22] If the Prime Minister stood firm in his faith in the people, it was a shared faith, for they responded overwhelmingly to his impassioned appeals. Out in the hustings he was known as the "people's William." No time in English politics could quite match his famous Midlothian campaign of 1880 which launched him on his second ministry. Ironically, his long, popular leadership was a disaster to his own Liberal Party. Toward the end his physical deafness symbolized his loss of contact with political reality just as the physical collapse of Wilson after 1919 brought loss of communication which actually antedated his physical paralysis.

Wilson and Gladstone thought of themselves at the center of a great chorus, the people. Building the city of man with the design of God and the sanction of the people, Gladstone and Wilson left precious little ground where their opponents, at home and abroad, could take a stand for truth and justice. In Wilson's own words, as leader of the people he could "speak what no man else knows." Our own political sophistication and cynicism — products of twentieth-century war, totalitarianism, and the probings of modern psychology — make us uncomfortable in the presence of "truth bearers." Either they are naive or, more likely, sinister in their programs and purposes. At the very least they must conceal from themselves their own foibles through self deception. Consequently, according to current interpretations, both Gladstone and Wilson were inclined to put off realities by specious forms of deception.

This thesis is sustained at many remarkably similar points in the careers of the Prime Minister and the President. At an early age both men sensed the high calling of service to the state. At Eton Gladstone prepared calling cards prematurely designating himself a member of Parliament. Sixty years later young Wilson hurried himself into politics by a like draft upon the future. When they finally arrived in politics, they did so, not so much through the will of the people but rather through the more mundane, if less idealistic, manipulating of political bosses. The Duke of Newcastle (borough monger for the district of Newark) gave Gladstone his first seat in Parliament. The Democratic bosses of New Jersey pointed the way for Wilson from his office as president at Princeton to the governor's mansion in Trenton.

More easily than his critics, Wilson was able to resolve such moral ambiguities. He rejoiced in Gladstone's conversion from conservative Tory politics which had launched his career:

> Mr. Gladstone's career from its first chapter to its last, illustrates the breaking away of the older forms of English Conservatism and the advance of English public opinion to higher plains of principle . . .[23]

Prophetic of his own break-away from conservative principles after 1910, Wilson, thirty years before the time of his own conversion, traced the change in Gladstone:

> When once contact with the practical problems of government had begun to break away the foundations of his early ardent, air-built theories, the progress of transition was rapid and certain.[24]

Years after writing these prescient words, Wilson related his own story of his road-to-Damascus experience: "I know more than I did then; I have found some gentlemen out . . . When you get on the inside things look somewhat different from the way they looked on the outside."[25]

Even friendly critics have recognized the moral ambiguities for idealists immersed in practical political decisions. Some thorny parallels occurred in the foreign policies which both leaders inaugurated. Gladstone and Wilson were devoted to the principles of self-determination. In the late 1870s Gladstone argued for self determination for the Balkans. He thundered against the pro-Turkish policies of the then Prime Minister, Benjamin Disraeli, and held him in part responsible for the infamous

Bulgarian massacres. Without ever really understanding the complex nature of Balkan politics, Gladstone suggested a grouping of small independent Balkan states to supplant the imperial control of Turkey and the expansionist threats of Russia. Wilson wrote this same principle of self-determination into the Fourteen Points and the Versailles settlement. After World War I the so-called succession states came into being. Like Gladstone Wilson was quite oblivious to the vulnerability of small states and the political necessities of their larger neighbors, Russia and Germany.

The ominous juxtaposition between conscientious leadership and unconscionable dictatorship — both intent upon giving history directives either to achieve moral purposes or to meet ideological objectives — is implicit in Gladstone's Egyptian policy and Wilson's Mexican policy. During his second ministry Gladstone's sense of moral probity caused him to intervene militarily in Egypt. Condemning the fiscal irresponsibility of the Egyptian government, Gladstone sent British troops to occupy the country and to protect the Suez Canal. All his rhetoric and rationale about self determination counted for nothing against the exigencies of guarding the canal and guaranteeing European investments.

In the case of Mexico Wilson was caught in an awkward ambivalence. He understood well how theories could obsess men to the point of disaster to society. "Those are the men who are not to be trusted."[26] But he also was conscious of responsible leadership: "We are not put into this world to sit and know; we are put into it to act."[27] President Wilson wanted to teach Latin Americans to elect good men. He disapproved of the Victoriano Huerta regime in Mexico which had seized power through murder and chicanery. He sought to bring down the Huerta regime by a policy of nonrecognition. In the spring of 1914 an incident occurred at Tampico where the crew of the *U.S.S. Dolphin* were summarily arrested by Mexican authorities. Wilson allowed this incident to be blown into a confrontation involving the national honor of both Mexico and the United States. On April 21, 1914, President Wilson ordered the landing of marines at Vera Cruz, and there was bloodshed. Wilson was ready for open war with Mexico. If there were to be mediation, the President insisted upon two conditions, the removal of Huerta and agrarian and social reforms for Mexico.[28]

Wilson had earlier recognized the limits of pacifism:

> . . . there are times in the history of nations when they must take up the crude instruments of bloodshed in order to vindicate spiritual conceptions. . . . When men take up arms to set other men free, there is something sacred and holy in the warfare.[29]

Actual war with Mexico was averted when Argentina, Brazil and Chili offered to arbitrate. But Wilson's intemperate handling of the episode weakened his moral position. He had refused to take up the white man's burden to serve crass commercialism, but his willingness to go to war for freedom and moral principles forecast the role which he eventually defined for the United States in the First World War.

Here there is neither the space nor the need to examine extensively President Wilson's leadership in that war. The Wilson literature abounds in excellent and exhaustive writing on the subject. That he continued to insist upon ultimate justice and the moral nature of man's relationship to man, nation to nation, is clear from his war message to Congress on April 2, 1917:

> The right is more precious than peace, and we shall fight for the things which we have always carried nearest our hearts, — for democracy, for the right of those who submit to authority to have a voice in their own Governments, . . . for a universal dominion of right by such a concert of free peoples as shall bring peace and safety to all nations . . .[30]

Even as late as 1917, when the world was a holocaust and civilization itself was in the clutch of brutish force, Wilson could conjure up the vision of the City of Man rising under the aegis of God and His righteous people.

Two faults of character seem obvious in the thought processes of Gladstone and Wilson. Both had a tendency to deal in generalities. Both leaders often arrived at "truth" through intuition rather than careful collection of data. They were impatient with the grubby, grinding chores of research. For example, Gladstone could engage in passionate oratory on questions concerning Ireland (a concern which eventually caused a division in his own Liberal Party), but only once during his life did he bother to visit Ireland for a few weeks. His failure to acquaint himself properly with the facts probably best explains his debacle in the Charles

Gordon expedition and final disaster at Khartoum.

Wilson admitted that the laborious accumulation of detail was alien to his spirit.[31] Looking at World War I through moral spectacles, Wilson never brought himself to a careful examination of its origins and the hard-core problems of peace. As a consequence he was derelict in defining for the American people the true dimensions of the war which they were asked to fight.

Furthermore, both statesmen would have served their causes more judiciously if they had shown greater generosity toward other men whose opinions were at variance with theirs. Faith and hope they possessed in an over-abundance, but charity was not their forte. When John Stuart Mill died in 1872, the Prime Minister withheld his support and blessing for a public subscription to memorialize Mill because he had advocated contraceptives. The advocacy of contraception in Victorian England was political dynamite, but Gladstone was also opposed on personal grounds. Following his own wish, Benjamin Disraeli was not buried in Westminster Abbey, but in a country churchyard. Gladstone remarked gratuitiously, "As he lived, so he died — all display, without reality or genuineness."[32]

Wilson could be equally stern with his opposition. While president at Princeton he had little patience with dissent from his own views about university policies. He castigated opponents in Congress as a band of wilful men.

But it is easy to be diverted by dwelling upon the personality defects of these leaders and thus to ignore the larger questions which their careers raise. Fundamentally their careers are a comment on the totality of our Western heritage. The Atlantic world, England and America, has cherished its heritage of religion and democracy. Did Wilson and Gladstone take their heritage too seriously? In the nineteenth century both Christianity and democracy assumed a moral universe where justice and truth coexist with progress. Recently the ecumenical movement and the conception of coexistence between East and West (communism and Western-style democracy) have sought to ease the tension in religion and politics. But in the loss of tension between our own religion and political system vis-ā-vis competitive alternatives there may well come ambivalence and imprecision which will certainly modify our religious and political heritage. But the world of Wilson and Gladstone was, in many ways, still essentially Western in thought and Protestant in hope.

Looking back at a closing chapter in Western history, Alfred North Whitehead explained the need for a new direction in political and social thought in the West. "Undoubtedly," Whitehead wrote in 1933, "something has come to an end."[33] Once the unique characteristic of the Western world was that "wise men hoped, and that as yet no circumstances had arisen to throw doubt upon the grounds of such hope."[34] Unlike Gladstone, whose entire life was encompassed by the nineteenth century, Woodrow Wilson moved out of the age of "hope" into the new age of disenchantment. The Great War shredded the fabric of optimism woven out of eighteenth-century rationalism and nineteenth-century political and technological advance.

War-time presidents like Woodrow Wilson are under constant pressure to internalize the tension between the reality and the wish. To keep up courage — to block out insanity itself — there comes a compulsive search for hope to balance the blood-cost of battle. At Gettysburg Lincoln looked for words to turn desperation into hope "that these dead shall not have died in vain . . ." Many years later Wilson incorporated the idea into his last public address on war and peace. He was pleading for ratification of the Versailles settlement and America's participation in the League. The date was September 25, 1919, and the place chosen for what became his valedictory was Pueblo, Colorado:

> There is one thing that the American people always rise to and extend their hand to, and that is the truth of justice and of liberty and of peace. We have accepted that truth and we are going to be led by it, and it is going to lead us, and through us the world out into pastures of quietness and peace such as the world never dreamed of before.

*NOTES*

1. Carl L. Becker, *The Heavenly City of the Eighteenth-Century Philosophers* (New Haven, 1932), 18.
2. Philip Magnus, *Gladstone* (New York, 1954), 207.
3. John Maynard Keynes, *The Economic Consequences of the Peace* (New York, 1920), 41-43.
4. Magnus, 245.
5. Walter L. Arnstein, *Britain Yesterday and Today* (Boston, 1966), 122.

6. Magnus, 308.
7. Arnstein, 122.
8. Magnus, 241.
9. *The Messages and Papers of Woodrow Wilson,* ed. by Albert Shaw, I (New York, 1917), 2.
10. John Morton Blum, *Woodrow Wilson and the Politics of Morality* (Boston, 1956), 111.
11. Magnus, 219.
12. *The Public Papers of Woodrow Wilson, College and State,* ed. by Ray Stannard Baker and William E. Dodd, II (New York, 1925), 390-391.
13. Becker, 15.
14. Magnus, 328.
15. *The Papers of Woodrow Wilson,* ed. by Arthur S. Link, I (Princeton, 1966), 626.
16. *Ibid.,* 628.
17. *Ibid.,* 632.
18. *Ibid.,* 636.
19. *Public Papers of Wilson, College and State,* I, 5-6.
20. *Ibid.,* 6.
21. *Ibid.,* 95.
22. Magnus, 270.
23. *Papers of Wilson,* I, 627.
24. *Ibid.,* 629.
25. *Public Papers of Wilson, College and State,* II, 393.
26. *Ibid.,* 91.
27. *Ibid.,* I, 461.
28. Blum, 91.
29. *Public Papers of Wilson, College and State,* II, 295.
30. *War and Peace, Presidential Messages, Addresses, and Public Papers by Woodrow Wilson,* ed. by Ray Stannard Baker and William E. Dodd, I (New York, 1927), 16.
31. Ray Stannard Baker, *Woodrow Wilson, Life and Letters* (Garden City, N. Y., 1927), 228-229. Writing to Ellen Axson (the future Mrs. Wilson) on Feb. 24, 1885, Wilson declared, "I have no patience for the tedious toil of what is known as 'research'; I have a passion for interpreting great thoughts to the world; I should be complete if I could inspire a great movement of opinion . . ."
32. Magnus, 280-281.
33. Alfred North Whitehead, *Essays in Science and Philosophy* (New York, 1948), 112.
34. *Ibid.,* 114.

# *Fissures in the Melting Pot*

Carl Wittke

For many years the United States has been described as the melting pot of many ethnic groups from which eventually there would emerge a new and unique civilization hammered out on the anvil of Americanization. Immigration helped to expand the concept of American democracy into a haven of refuge for all who wanted to share in its promise of liberty, opportunity, peace and prosperity. Complete Americanization requires time and patience, and attempts to hurry the process by hot-house methods generally have been only partially successful. Lasting Americanization depends upon sincere appreciation for one's adopted country. It takes time to establish home and family in a new environment, and to learn from experience that in the free atmosphere of the American Republic one could achieve and enjoy what was unobtainable in the fatherland. More important than immediately learning a new language or the intricacies of the American Constitutional system is the development of a loyalty grounded upon the immigrant's own satisfying experiences and the realization that he has become a citizen of a nation where political unity is based upon cultural diversity.

More recently, the traditional view of the United States as "God's Crucible" in which all ingredients can be blended into a homogeneous nation has been seriously challenged. The National Origins Act of 1924 was based on the theory that there should be no further dilution of the American stock and that its earlier components must be reinforced. It also has been suggested that some religious and ethnic institutions perpetuate separatism and delay the process of amalgamation.[1]

In the long history of immigration many factors have both speeded and retarded the normal Americanization process. We are concerned here with only one aspect of the problem, the fissures which have appeared in the American melting pot whenever grave international crises in the immigrant's native land have produced strong emotional reactions in this country. In the words of Horace M. Kallen, "America is a young country with old memories." Consequently it is a natural, human reaction for a nationality group to follow, with sentimental interest, events in the homeland. Consciousness of national origins has been slow to disappear even among the older immigration.

The "wrongs of Ireland" welded three generations of American Irish into a solid, anti-British phalanx, and a minority political block among American voters which has been super-sensitive to any affront to its importance.[2] For three generations, Irish Americans, many of whom have never set foot on the "auld sod," hated England for what they claimed was for the good of the United States.

The first Irish paper in this country, *The Shamrock* of New York, on the eve of the War of 1812 called upon Irish-Americans "to exult at the possibility of doing England an essential injury."[3] During the abortive Canadian Rebellion of 1837-1838, Irishmen kept the border aflame with threats of invasion. In 1860, when the Prince of Wales visited New York, the Irish in the 69th New York regiment refused to parade for "the beardless youth" and the "golden calf of monarchy." In 1883, Irishmen threatened to blow up the Brooklyn Bridge because dedication ceremonies happened to fall on Queen Victoria's birthday, and four years later, the Boston Irish milled around Faneuil Hall where a banquet was in progress in honor of the Queen's Golden Jubilee.

The most amazing incident in United States history of dangerous activity by an immigrant group is the Fenian invasion of Canada at the close of the American Civil War. This attack upon a friendly neighbor was a foolhardy scheme of Irish-Americans to win independence for Ireland by using American soil as the base for military operations. The Fenian raids, in the words of Thomas D'Arcy McGee, a refugee of the Irish rebellion of 1848, indicated that the Irish were "still an alien population, camped but not settled in the United States."

The Fenian Brotherhood had its "circles" in the Union Army, in which many Irish served with distinction, and in a number of American cities. The grandiose plan to invade Canada would have done credit to a major field operation. A provisional government for an Irish Republic was created in the United States, and on the night of June 1, 1865, the Fenian host crossed into Canada, called upon Canadians to throw off the British yoke, and fought several skirmishes around Fort Erie, before they were forced to retreat to United States territory. William H. Seward, the American Secretary of State, waited five days before issuing a proclamation of neutrality, for in this critical period of party realignment after the Civil War, no politician could risk antagonizing Irish voters on the eve of the Congressional elections of 1866. Seward also made good use of the incident to pressure the British Government into settling the Alabama claims, an irritating aftermath of the Civil War. Prosecutions of Fenians who had been arrested when they re-crossed into the United States, were quietly dropped, and the Fenian army was permitted to return to their homes with their arms, and in many cases at government expense, — further evidence of the respect American politicians had for this important nationality block.[4]

Fenian excitement continued along the international boundary until 1871, but the whole affair must be described as a colossal fiasco which might have had serious international consequences. From it many Irish-Americans got an exaggerated notion of their political power. Another result was to bequeath to their American-born descendants a violent Anglophobia which continued to manifest itself in various ways until the Irish Free State was established in the present century. American Irish generously supported the National Irish Land League and crowds turned out in 1880 to greet Charles Stewart Parnell when he toured the United States on its behalf. "Skirmishers," armed with bullets and dynamite, went to Ireland to free Ireland by a policy of terrorism and demanded the protection of the American government when they were convicted in the British courts for their lawless acts.

American Congressmen made pro-Irish speeches for the benefit of their constituents, and in 1884 and 1886 both parties made special appeals for the Irish vote. During the Venezuela crisis of 1895, a large part of the Irish-American press hoped the boundary dispute would lead to war between the United States and Great Britain. During the Boer War, Irish-Americans sympathized with "the embattled farmers" of South Africa, carried Boer flags in their St. Patrick's Day parades, and recruited an Irish brigade to fight British imperialism in Africa.

There also was a certain amount of "Fenianism", among the German immigration of the 1850s, in the sense that prominent refugees of the German Revolution of 1848-1849, wanted to use the United States as a springboard for another uprising in the German states. These refugees become known in American history as the "Forty-eighters," although many did not reach the United States until the 1850s. Their number included graduates of the German gymnasia and universities, journalists, public officials, and other professional men who contributed a cultural leaven to the entire German immigration and provided the intellectual transfusion that accounted for the many cultural interests of the German element a century ago.[5]

In the larger American cities, patriotic meetings adopted resolutions that called for the liberation of all Europe. The German-language press appealed for men and money to support another revolution in Germany and promoted the formation of revolutionary societies in the United States. Many "Forty-eighters" looked upon their stay in the United States as but temporary and impatiently scanned the political horizons for signs of a new uprising. Louis Kossuth, the Hungarian hero, and Gottfried Kinkel, the professor whom Carl Schurz had rescued from prison and spirited to safety in England, toured the United States to plead for funds to finance another revolution, and both were welcomed by large and enthusiastic crowds. Leading "Forty-eighters" believed it was the mission of America to expand its beneficent form of government and the Monroe Doctrine to cover the world. They emphasized the irreconcilable world conflict between despotism and republicanism, and insisted that the United States was morally obligated to intervene wherever liberty was suppressed and the people were ready to revolt. Actually no new revolutions broke out in Europe, and Germany eventually was unified not along republican lines, but by Bismarck's policy of "blood and iron," under a Hohenzollern Emperor. Having failed to reform Europe, "Forty-eighters" now channeled their restless energy into reforming the United States, and finally found in the slavery controversy and the new Republican Party the moral issue which satisfied their zeal for reform.

By 1871, when Germany was unified as a result of the Franco-German War, many of the fiery radicals of 1848 had lost much of their youthful enthusiasm. Nevertheless, when it was reported that the Grant administration was selling surplus war supplies, by dubious routes, to French agents, Carl Schurz, now a Senator from Missouri, charged the President with being pro-French and demanded a Senate investigation.[6] Their earlier idealism diluted and mellowed by their generally satisfactory experience as American citizens, the "Forty-eighters," with rare exceptions, joined with the whole German immigration, to express pride in the rapid progress of the fatherland, openly rejoiced in the victories of its armies, and voiced their filial devotion to the land of their origin. In 1871, "victory celebrations" were arranged throughout the United States; financial support for Germany ran into thousands of dollars, and the German-language press, in glaring headlines, revealed the breathless excitement and the unrestrained joy which pervaded the German-American community. The romantic idealism of the 1850s had given way to boastful pride in a new Germany, which many German-Americans believed would improve their own status among their fellow Americans.

The Boer War (1899-1902) aroused the Hollanders in America from their accustomed political lethargy, to support their blood brothers in South Africa whom British imperialists were trying to rob of their homes. The valiant stand of the handful of Boers against the might of the British Empire won the sympathy of many Americans, and stirred their traditional love for the underdog, as the Dutch of the Transvaal Republic and the Orange Free State fought courageously in defense of their country. Dutch communities in Michigan, Iowa and elsewhere organized public meetings where they sang the Dutch national hymn, raised money for relief of the

Boers, and dispatched telegrams to London denouncing British atrocities and concentration camps. The Dutch language paper of Orange City, Iowa, asked how Hollanders could continue to vote the Republican ticket in view of President William McKinley's and Theodore Roosevelt's failure to protest against "British lust" in South Africa. The neutral policy of the United States came under heavy fire, and Hollanders protested vigorously against the sale of American horses and mules for use in the British army.

Ministers of Dutch churches took part in these demonstrations, and on several occasions, meetings were addressed by representatives of the Boer Republics who were touring the United States to raise money and win popular support for their cause. The Dutch press featured every report of British defeats in South Africa; merchants announced "Transvaal Days" when they would give a percentage of their receipts to the Boer relief fund; American Dutchmen wore "Oom Paul" buttons in honor of President Kruger of the Transvaal Republic, and parents named new-born babies for the heroes of the Boer War. Three years after its close an Iowa paper objected when a Hollander was about to accept a Cecil Rhodes scholarship to study at Oxford, because the "money [was] stolen from the Boers, [and] bespattered with their blood."[7]

Greek immigration reached maximum volume at a time when the Greek national spirit was at its height. When Greece twice emerged victorious from the Balkan Wars of 1912-1913, its territory was nearly doubled. In the spirit of the age, Greeks dreamed of reviving the glories of ancient Hellas and reestablishing the Byzantine Empire with its seat in Constantinople. Greek immigrants in the United States contributed to the realization of "The Great Idea" by sending money home for churches, schools, public improvements and by building up their country's military potential. During the Balkan Wars, one out of every five or six Greeks in the United States went home to fight the Turks and the Bulgarians. The majority returned to the United States.

World War I resulted in political chaos in Greece, as monarchists and liberals battled over whether their country should side with the Allies or the Central Powers. The Greek-American community was split into Liberty Clubs and Loyalty Leagues, whose members engaged in bitter debates about King Constantine, brother-in-law of the German Kaiser, and

Eleutherios Vanizelos, friendly to the Allied Powers. At the close of the war, the American "Friends of Greece" bombarded President Wilson with demands that the "unredeemed" Greeks in Asia Minor be added to the Greek national state. Lobbyists were at work in Washington to promote their cause, but got little more than a resolution of sympathy from the United States Senate. Many Greeks served in the armed forces of the United States in World War II, and the Greek-American community raised millions for relief and for the reconstruction of their homeland after the war. Their experiences in supporting the American war effort greatly hastened their Americanization.[8]

The international crises discussed hitherto seem relatively unimportant and temporary when compared with the effect of two World Wars on American nationality groups. In World War I, the large Anglo-Saxon element naturally sympathized with Britain and her allies and did what it could to help them to victory. It was equally natural for the German nationality group to sympathize with the Central Powers, and to hope for a German victory.

As far as the German-Americans were concerned, World War I came upon them with the suddenness of a thunderclap from a cloudless sky. They were well-organized, in cultural, social and benevolent societies. The National German-American Alliance, chartered by Congress in 1899, claimed a membership of 2,000,000 in 1914. The much smaller German-American Historical Society, founded in 1901, was largely the creation of a professor of German of Yankee colonial stock.[9] In none of these organizations was there much interest in the politics of Germany or the Kaiser's alleged plot to dominate the world. They trained their biggest guns on women's suffrage and the "white-ribbon hordes" of the prohibitionists who wanted to inflict "the temperance swindle" on a liberty-loving people.

When war broke out in Europe in the summer of 1914, President Wilson called for neutrality in deed and "in thought," a request that was unenforceable in a nation as heterogeneous as the United States, where many ethnic groups had not yet been sufficiently fused to withstand the shock of a European war. Certain ingredients in the melting pot began to recrystallize along with internal lines of fracture. Most Britishers were pro-British and Germans were pro-German. The lines of fracture became appreciably wider as a result of the vigorous propaganda of both belligerents to win American sympathy and support.[10]

There was no need to spend German gold to get German-Americans to sympathize with Germany in the war. The *Davenport Demokrat* of August 12, 1914, summarized the attitude of most German-Americans in the statement, "Our strength, our labor and our loyalty [belongs] to the new fatherland; our hearts to the old." In the following year the Milwaukee *Germania-Herold* compared the lot of its readers with that of a man forced to choose between his mother and his wife, but made it clear that the ultimate loyalty of the German element must be to the United States.

British propaganda increased with the progress of the war, and a large part of the American press seemed to slant the war news in favor of the Allies. It featured lurid tales of German atrocities in Belgium, and called all Germans "Huns" and "barbarians." As a result, many German-Americans became more pro-German than they might have been otherwise, and the German language press enjoyed a temporary boom in circulation, as it tried to counteract the pro-British attitude of many American newspapers by reporting the war news in a spirit of "fair play." Huge bazaars in the larger cities and other devices to raise money produced large sums for the relief of Germany's war victims, and resolutions and petitions were addressed to Congress demanding an embargo on the munitions traffic and a directive to keep Americans from traveling on the ships of the belligerents. That German-American leaders during these heated discussions were guilty of indiscretions and poor judgment which could be considered as disloyal is easy to understand, for the battle over American neutrality which raged from 1914 to 1917 was a furious one.

Most German-Americans believed the war came about because of Russian pan-Slavism, French eagerness for revenge, and British jealousy of Germany's phenomenal progress. Attacks on President Wilson's "unneutral neutrality" increased in violence, and the German language press mounted a barrage of criticism of the administration's attitude toward British interference with neutral trade, Germany's submarine warfare, the floating of Allied loans in the American money market, and the sale of war materials to the Allied powers. Into this welter of controversy, President Wilson and Theodore Roosevelt hurled the charge of "hyphenism," with its obvious connotations of disloyalty, and projected the issue of "Hyphenated Americanism" into the campaign of 1916 as a major issue. A few German-Americans, like Professor Kuno Francke of Harvard objected to all political activity which "would set Germans apart," "as a class by themselves," but their admonitions were unceremoniously brushed aside.

In 1916, both parties angled for the German and Irish vote. To judge from the tone of the German-language press, the Democrats were engaged in a hopeless task. In his keynote address to the Republican National Convention, Warren G. Harding expressed no surprise that in a life and death struggle in Europe immigrant groups showed "sympathy and partiality for the land of their nativity," and Charles W. Fairbanks, Republican vice presidential candidate, declared that "the greater danger to our country is not the man who loves two countries, but the man who loves none." Here was the answer to the charge of hyphenism. Apparently, German voters did not go to the polls in 1916 in a solid, anti-Wilson phalanx, however. St. Louis and Milwaukee gave majorities for the President; in Ohio, Cincinnati went for Hughes, but Cleveland and Columbus for Wilson, and the *New York Times* concluded that not a single electoral vote was determined by German-American voters.

In April, 1917, the United States entered the war against Germany. Last minute feverish efforts by German and Irish-Americans, pacifists and others, to "keep us out of war," proved futile. For German-Americans, the declaration of war constituted an emotional crisis that required a searching of soul. The choice between sentiment for the old country and loyalty to the new was soon made in favor of the new, and the period of emotional readjustment was relatively brief. The record of the German group, judged by the purchase of war bonds, compliance with war regulations and actual military service, met every test of loyalty and should have closed the breach between them and their fellow Americans.

Unfortunately, the war also produced an hysterical reaction to all things German, and thus aggravated the charge of hyphenism. This concomitant of war left scars which it took years to heal. While the newspapers of Germany were denouncing German-Americans for betraying the fatherland in its hour of greatest peril, the German element in the United States was crucified for its earlier pro-German activities. German music disappeared from concert halls; German books were burned in patriotic demonstrations; German was dropped from the curriculum of many schools and former teachers of German were hastily converted into instructors in American citizenship; German societies had to curtail or cease their activities; the German-language press was boycotted, and under constant attack; war bonds were often sold "with a club," street and family names were changed to hide their German origin; Bismarck herring disappeared from restaurant menus, and sauerkraut was named liberty cabbage. Nothing like this *furor Americanus* had ever been experienced in the history of the United States. "German-America," a rather amorphous community which had existed in the United States since the 1850s, collapsed during World War I and has never been successfully revived.[11]

A rapprochement between German and Irish-American organizations had been developing since the 1890s, when there were rumors of a secret Anglo-American Alliance. During the war, it developed into a firm liaison, as Irish-Americans accepted the German version of the origin of the war, and their persistent Anglophobia led them to hope that the war would produce a free and independent Ireland. German propagandists worked hard upon the American-Irish to reinforce their suspicion that President Wilson was pro-British and not interested in "genuine neutrality." The German Information Service in New York furnished news releases to the Irish press, depicting the President as "a vassal of England," and many Irish groups joined with the Germans to demand an embargo on the traffic in munitions. Sir Roger Casement received financial support from the United States for his Easter Rebellion of 1916. When the participants in this ill-fated venture were executed, even the *New York Times* described making them martyrs as "incredibly stupid."

When the United States entered the war, Irishmen did their full share to win it, although many made it clear at the outset that they were for "America First" and were not fighting for England. Like the Germans, they were embittered because the President had raised the issue of "hypenism." They discovered that as early as 1914, while dedicating a monument to John Barry, the Irish naval hero, Wilson had referred to him as one Irishman whose "heart crossed the Atlantic with him."

In 1919, Eamon de Valera, a Sinn Feiner involved in the Easter

Rebellion, escaped to the United States, to collect American dollars for the support of an Irish Republic. Three Irish-Americans went to the Paris Peace Conference to plead for self-determination for Ireland, much to the embarrassment of President Wilson who was frequently reminded of the power of the Irish vote in the United States. In the presidential campaign of 1920, many Irish leaders and most of the Irish-American press supported Warren G. Harding, the Republican candidate, in revenge for Wilson's alleged betrayal of the Irish cause at Paris. James M. Cox, the Demorcatic candidate, ran on a Wilson platform which favored American entry into the League of Nations, a diabolical British device, according to many Irish leaders, to involve the United States in endless European crises and to pull British chestnuts out of the fire. Governor Cox recognized that he was opposed by "a militantly anti-Wilson Catholic oligarchy" and by "the professional Irish" who hated Wilson.[12]

In 1932, the Irish Free State was born. Thereafter, although Ireland was not yet completely united, the Irish question faded into the background as far as Irish-Americans were concerned. Ireland's destiny now was in her own hands, and the Irish in America and the Irish in Ireland began to drift apart. The American amalgam was not likely to be affected again by "the wrongs of Ireland." St. Patrick's Day still is something of a national American holiday, and the Irish have gone native.[13]

Several smaller immigrant groups also were affected by the first World War. Swedish-Americans generally sympathized with Germany, although their major concern was to keep the United States out of the war. Influential papers like the *Minnesota Stats Tidning* voiced the Swedes' historic hatred of Russia, but the Swedish language press was about equally divided between its support of the Allied and Central Powers. Swedish Lutheran pastors believed Germany somehow was championing Protestantism and Teutonic culture against pan-Slavism and Catholicism, and there was much criticism of President Wilson's "flabby" foreign policy, but also considerable condemnation of Germany's resort to submarine warfare.

In 1916, the Republican campaign committee advertised in the Swedish press and accused the Democratic administration of unneutral conduct, especially in its failure to stop British interference with Swedish commerce and mail, and insisted that an early embargo on munitions would have ended the war. Charles Evans Hughes was described as a wise statesman who would enforce strict neutrality and keep the United States out of the war.

The bulk of the Swedish-American press remained true to its traditional allegiance to the Republican party. Many readers, however, seem to have switched their votes into the Democratic column because they believed President Wilson could be trusted to keep the United States at peace. Minnesota, for example, remained Republican in 1916 only because voters in several German counties left the Democratic party to vote Republican. With the exception of a small, Socialist minority, Swedes and their press supported the war on Germany in 1917 with undivided loyalty, although some Lutheran pastors denounced attacks on the foreign language press and church services conducted in a foreign tongue, and denied their pulpits to "four minute men" engaged in selling war bonds. Others resented the demands of their fellow Americans that they give positive proof of their loyalty to the United States.[14]

President Wilson's enunciation of the right of self-determination for the suppressed nationalities of Europe had an immediate effect upon several smaller American immigrant groups. In a sense, Czecho-Slovakia was "made in America." Czechs and Slovaks in the United States began early to raise funds to support national movements which would enable their European blood brothers to break away from the old Austro-Hungarian Empire. In September, 1918, representatives of the oppressed nationalities of the Hapsburg Empire staged a demonstration in Carnegie Hall, New York, and from this and similar meetings there developed a Mid-European Democratic Union. Spokesmen for each group signed resolutions for the independence of their respective countries at a ceremony in Independence Hall, Philadelphia, and in June, 1918, Czechs and Slovaks signed a convention in Pittsburg which promised the Slovaks autonomy in a new Czecho-Slovak state. The Czech National Alliance and the Slovak League successfully appealed for funds, and under the guidance of Thomas G. Masaryk, who had many friends in the United States, were able to realize their objective of an independent Czecho-Slovakia.[15]

As early as 1915, Polish-Americans began the propaganda for an independent Poland and recruited volunteers for the Polish army in France.

In 1918, Poles met in Detroit in a national convention, created a Polish Central Relief Committee with Ignaz Paderewski, artist turned statesman, as honorary president, and raised hundreds of thousands of dollars for the liberation of Poland. The war emphasized the group consciousness of the suppressed nationalities, but their activities raised no problems for the United States since their objectives coincided with the war aims of the American government.

The 1930s saw the rise of a dictatorship in Germany under Adolf Hitler and a new threat to world peace. Nazi propaganda in the United States failed to enlist anything like the response among German-Americans which the German cause had produced in 1914. The Nazi *Bund* had members in the larger American cities, especially in the East, where they paraded in brown shirts and gave the Nazi salute, but the great majority of German-Americans had not forgotten their experiences during World War I and were not eager to be burned again. To counteract the fascists, the German-American League for Culture emphasized the liberal traditions of the German immigration. Both fascist and antifascist organizations remained small, however. Meantime, Hitler's sadistic policy toward the Jews in Germany became more and more hateful, and when war came again with Germany in 1941, German-Americans supported it without hesitation. There was no repetition of the anti-German hysteria of the first World War, and the German-born joined wholeheartedly with other Americans in patriotic demonstrations against the Japanese "Yellow Peril" on the West Coast. Because of the Hitler terror the United States again received an amazing collection of talented, refugee intellectuals, comparable in the contributions they made to the United States with refugees of the Revolution of 1848.[16]

Mussolini's rise to power in Italy split the Italian-American community into two camps, whose differences became so violent that they produced disgraceful riots in some cities. The Italian language press repeatedly pleaded for an end to such disorders. Many Italians expressed pride in the achievements of Il Duce, and like many other Americans, were impressed because Mussolini had the trains running on time and the beggars off the streets. A Fascist League was started in the United States in 1925 and through this and other channels like the lodges of the Sons of

Italy, Mussolini fed his propaganda to Italian-American communities. Parades of black-shirted fascists sometimes ended in fisticuffs between pro and anti-fascists. When Mussolini invaded Ethiopia, Italian-Americans collected funds to support Italy's war effort. President Roosevelt was bitterly attacked for his attitude toward Mussolini's African war, and like the Germans in 1914, Italian-Americans clamored for "strict neutrality" and accused the administration of being pro-British. The United States also received a number of Italian refugees, including such distinguished intellectuals as Max Ascoli, Count Carlo Sforza and Gaetano Salvemini, the historian, and under their leadership such societies as the Friends of Italian Freedom and the Mazzini Society tried to counteract fascist propaganda among their Italian countrymen. When the United States became a belligerent, these cleavages quickly disappeared, and Italian-Americans closed ranks to prove that their first loyalty was to the United States.

It was during the Hitler period that American Jewry developed a new group consciousness that had some of the earmarks of a religious revival. Jews who had been completely Americanized, who lived in suburbia and had changed their names and seldom attended synagogue or temple, suddenly felt a new commitment to their faith and to their suffering brethren abroad. The threat to European Jewry created a more homogeneous Jewry in the United States, and Zionism, in which the majority of American Jews became interested, provided a close tie with the state of Israel, which was generously supported by American Jews. The fight against Nazism and the revival of Zionism provided a common objective for Reformed, Orthodox and Conservative Jews. There was a revival of the study of Hebrew; Jewish parochial schools multiplied; books were published on the role of the Jews in world history and in the United States; and in various other ways, the Jewish renaissance manifested itself. The international disaster which had befallen the Jews reinvigorated the American Jewish community with a new "feeling of Jewishness." Thus far no situation has arisen to affect the financial and spiritual commitment of American Jewry to Israel, whose position in the Middle East remains precarious. Whether an attack on Israel would mobilize a "Jewish vote" in the United States and a concerted effort to influence American foreign policy, fortunately, is still only a hypothetical question.

The incidents discussed in this essay are examples of the persistence of the consciousness of nationality even among well-established American immigrant groups. Emotional reaction to crises in their homelands revived or reinforced their identity with blood brothers in the fatherland and had an effect upon the Americanization of the foreign-born. The controversies over the Treaty of Versailles, the League of Nations, the World Court, Soviet-American relations, the Hungarian Revolution and the pro-Cyprus campaign of the Greek-American community, as well as the treatment of Japanese-Americans during World War II, are other examples of the same phenomenon which cannot be discussed here for lack of space.

American diplomacy and American politics reveal the fact that the United States still is an amalgam of many ethnic groups whose special interests get special attention. In all cases which involved the hazards of actual warfare, however, fissures in the American melting pot were closed in the fiery furnace of international conflict. The foreign-born insist upon being heard on public issues of special concern to them, but their ultimate loyalty has been to their adopted country, despite emotional conflicts which many of their fellow Americans often failed to understand.

*NOTES*

1. See, e.g., Nathan Glazer and Daniel Patrick Moynihan, *Beyond The Melting Pot, the Negroes, Puerto Ricans, Italians and Irish in New York City* (Cambridge, Mass., 1963), Preface.
2. Thomas N. Brown, "The Origins and Character of Irish-American Nationalism," *Review of Politics* (Notre Dame), XVIII (July, 1956), 320-350.
3. Jan. 18, 1812.
4. William D. D'Arcy, *The Fenian Movement in the United States, 1858-1886* (Washington, 1947).
5. See especially chap. viii in Carl Wittke, *Refugees of Revolution, The German Forty-eighters in America* (Philadelphia, 1952) and *The Forty-Eighters, Political Refugees of the German Revolution of 1848,* ed. by A. E. Zucker (New York, 1950).
6. W. B. Hesseltine, *Ulysses S. Grant, Politician* (New York, 1935), 265-266.
7. See Jacob Van Der Zee, *The Hollanders of Iowa* (Iowa City, 1912), 349-362, and Henry S. Lucas, *Netherlanders in America* (Ann Arbor, 1953).
8. Theodore Saloutos, *The Greeks in the United States* (Cambridge, Mass., 1964), and "The Greeks in the United States," *The South Atlantic Quarterly,* XLIV (Jan., 1945), 67-81.
9. See John J. Appel, "Marion Dexter Learned and the German-American

Historical Society," *The Pennsylvania Magazine of History and Biography,* LXXXVI, No. 3 (July, 1962), 287-317.

10. H. C. Peterson, *Propaganda for War* (Norman, Okla., 1939).
11. See Clifton J. Child, *The German-Americans in Politics, 1914-1917* (Madison, 1939) and Carl Wittke, *German-Americans in the World War* (Columbus, 1936).
12. James M. Cox, *Journey through My Years* (New York, 1946), 273-274.
13. For more detail, see Carl Wittke, *The Irish in America* (Baton Rouge, 1956), especially chaps. xv, xxv, and xxvi.
14. George M. Stephenson, "The Attitude of Swedish-Americans toward the World War," *Proceedings of the Mississippi Valley Historical Association,* X, Pt. I (1918-1919), 79-94.
15. Thomas G. Masaryk, *The Making of a State* (New York, 1927), 207-263.
16. See Donald P. Kent, *The Refugee Intellectual, The Americanization of the Immigrants of 1933-1941* (New York, 1953).

# *Sweden in the American Social Mind of the 1930s*

MERLE CURTI

Given the increasing role of Swedish-Americans in public life during the Progressive period and the occasional recognition at that time of the world-wide aspects of social reform, one might expect that Swedish achievements would have played some part in American discussion. But if English-language books and periodicals were indicative, interest in Swedish social welfare achievements was slight during the first decades of the twentieth century. To be sure, an occasional article in the Progressive era and in the 1920s called attention to housing, child welfare, workers education, public health and to the constructive role of the government in recovery from the depression that followed the Great War.[1] Woodrow Wilson's Minister to Sweden, Ira Nelson Morris, reached a somewhat wider audience in calling attention to the vitality of her social democracy and to her skill in joining progressive social measures to an old civilization.[2] But insofar as popular attention focused at all on the Northern countries, Americans looked to Denmark's democratic and successful involvement of a great part of her population in the cooperative movement.[3]

After the depression of 1929, however, conditions were such that Swedish achievements, popularized by Marquis W. Childs as "the middle way," played an important part in American political and economic debate. Although, as we shall see, it would be going too far to hold that there was no positive influence of Swedish experience on the New Deal, the main significance of "the middle way" was in the psychological functions it served. Bewildered by the heated controversies between the opponents and the champions of the New Deal and, in the liberal camp, by the disillusionment of many admirers of the Soviet Union, Americans, needing to buttress their own faith in some middle ground, found in the enthusiastic presentation of Sweden a symbol of democratic success in economic as well as in political matters. The will to believe that it was possible to cope with the problems of modern industrialism in a democratic way through sustained and determined effort was given articulation and force by reference to Sweden.[4]

In the 1930s the first thing to attract attention to Sweden was the tempo of her recovery from the initial thrust of the Great Depression. The interest in foreign countries in Sweden's recovery was, in the opinion of one of her leading economists, less because of outstanding success than because her policy, first in currency matters and later in public finance, had been "a little more determined or explicit than policy in other countries."[5] Swedish recovery measures included the unorthodox resort to long-term borrowing during a severe depression, the distinction between capital budget and current budgets, the latter not being balanced in lean years, but over-balanced in good years, and government supported public works. But the currency experiment attracted early and special interest.[6] The lively debate on this involved experts and laymen, businessmen and social critics, Swedish-Americans and Americans who visited Sweden. Both the international and the American history of the idea of managed currency was already long, complex and controversial.[7] By the 1920s American economists were interested in the "advanced" character of the thinking of several Swedish economists on monetary policy; one of the best known, Professor Gustav Cassel, testified in 1928 at a Congressional hearing on a bill designed to alter monetary policy.[8] By the time of Franklin Roosevelt's inauguration the steps Sweden had taken toward managing its currency had attracted a good deal of attention among economists close to the new administration.[9]

A popular exposition of Sweden's experiments which appeared in *The Forum* in the early autumn of 1933 may serve as an introduction to what was to become a fairly widespread discussion of the question. The author of the article, Charles T. Hallinan, an American living in London and engaged in buying and selling securities, contended that in the preceding twenty months the Swedish government, taking its cue from lines laid down by "modern economists," had with almost complete success fought the world-wide decline in prices by "managing" the supply of credit and currency. According to Hallinan the use of a newly devised sensitive weekly index of "Swedish buying power" had effectively stabilized prices independently of the gold standard which Sweden had abandoned. Hallinan urged Americans to imitate the Swedish "moderation" in managing relationships between savings, investments, and a controlled price level.[10]

In the following year, 1934, Professor Irving Fisher of Yale, long known as an exponent of managed currency, published *Stable Money.* This discussed the Swedish experiment with reference to the history of the idea as well as the immediate setting. Fisher, while admitting that the extent to which the Riksbank's policy had accomplished the stability of the consumption index was controversial in Sweden itself, nevertheless held that however much the effect of stabilization were deprecated on either side of the Atlantic, "the simple fact remained that Sweden *did* stabilize the internal purchasing power of her krona according to the official measure set up for that purpose." Moreover, Fisher argued that if Sweden, a small country largely dependent on foreign trade, had been able to maintain her chosen index numbers almost unchanged, the same result was *economically* possible elsewhere; and in Fisher's opinion the avowed Roosevelt policy was the goal the Swedish experiment had achieved.[11]

In a more specialized study published in the same year a Swedish-American economist, Erik T. H. Kjellstrom, came to different conclusions. He held that nothing in the Swedish experience proved any close dependence of recovery on banking policy, that the efficacy of currency management had been greatly overemphasized, that the stabilization of an index of representation prices had not prevented heavy fluctuations in production and employment, that no matter how well defined a monetary system might be, it was incapable of controlling all other economic factors; in short, that it was untenable to regard a central bank with powers to manage currency as "an earthly paradise." While admitting that some of the fundamental principles useful in one country might be applied elsewhere if the transplantation was "intelligent," Kjellstrom insisted that, contrary to the contention that other governments might successfully adopt what some regarded as a "success," such a policy, however successful, could not be indiscriminately imposed where banking habits, trade conditions and other variables differed materially. In his foreword to the book Professor H. Parker Willis of Columbia University, an authority on banking, went somewhat further in maintaining that academic and other adherents of the view that prices could be moved about almost at will by merely shifting the quantity of credit "released" by a central bank, were in effect propagating a "superstition" to "demonstrate" their own preconceived ideas. Thus Professor Willis regarded Kjellstrom's book as a "valuable sedative for the excited minds which are now evolving new and strange monetary theories which they (on hearsay) ascribe to Sweden as the originating source of the experimentation."[12]

The general reception of Kjellstrom's book in the professional guild was favorable.[13] The consensus was summed up in the notice in the *American Economic Review* which held that the author had given a competent report on Sweden's policy, a report which should prove useful both to "enthusiastic 'money-managers' and to 'readers-at-large.' "[14]

Studies which appeared after Kjellstrom's book differed in regard to the success of Sweden's managed currency policy. One of Fisher's students, Richard Lester, in a thorough study published in 1939, concluded (contrary to Fisher) that from many points of view conditions in Sweden had been ideal for monetary management but, even when allowance were made for conflicting purpose, difficult choices and practical problems, the Swedes had not made the most of their opportunities. But there was, he went on, a real possibility for improving economic conditions through a rational monetary policy, and it was to be hoped that in the near future Sweden might more fully realize that opportunity.[15] While other competent economists, including Brinley Thomas of the London School of Economics, arrived at similar conclusions,[16] Arthur Montgomery of the Stockholm Institute for Economic History, after emphasizing the complex variables in the situation, concluded that it was "pretty generally recognized that the country's monetary policy played a very important part in combatting the depression."[17]

Throughout 1934 and the following year Swedish economic recovery continued to be discussed on both the popular and specialized levels. In midsummer of 1934 *Business Week* noted that the key industries of iron, steel and paper showed more activity than in 1929 and that living costs had decreased. The editorial offered as an explanation of the recovery the retooling of foreign plants, the flow of foreign investment into the country because of pessimism about conditions elsewhere and optimism about Sweden, and Sweden's own extensive construction program.[18]

Other writers emphasized, in addition to the managed currency policy, the effect of public works programs in reducing unemployment to one percent of the labor force. The new motor roads, airports, electrified railways and public buildings not only employed workers but promoted recovery by increasing mass purchasing power. The principal academic discussion of this issue, that of Dr. C. J. Ratzlaff, professor of economics at Lafayette College, stressed the significance of the fact that relief through public works was accepted as a continuous government function. But Ratzlaff insisted that the unemployment problem was closely related to other social questions. He felt that some discussions of the achievements made more of unemployment insurance than the facts warranted — he argued that it played a restricted role in relief programs.[19] Success in collective labor bargaining, cooperative merchandising, building and manufacturing, as well as low tariffs, also seemed to several commentators pertinent factors in Swedish recovery.[20] In a flattering account of housing problems an American writing in the *New York Times* reported that Sweden had proved to her own satisfaction that a successful slum clearance program required a technique reaching far beyond traditional concepts. The country had "discovered that decent homes for the poor are economic assets of the highest order, decreasing crime and restoring to men and women self-respect and giving them a new outlook on life."[21]

Of special note was the long-range perspective through which Swedish achievements in the depression were occasionally seen: the more than century-old period of peace, the positive way in which the Swedish government and people faced the problems of industrialization from 1870 to

1930, including the elimination of slums, sweatshops and child labor, state support of insurance for every person from birth to death, the continuous performance of the National Unemployment Commission since its appointment in 1914, and the quarter century experience with public works as a government alleviation of unemployment. Although several writers took cognizance of the fact that Sweden had not waited until an acute depression struck before attacking the problems of industrial dislocation, no one put the matter as clearly as Per Wijkman, the commercial counselor at the Swedish Legation in Washington. "The changes brought about in the economic structure of our country," he wrote in 1935, "are tremendously far-reaching, even more so than is generally recognized. Labor has passed the fighting period and has loyally taken its share of the responsibility for the management of public affairs. Consumers have joined in an organization of great influence. Social welfare has been regulated in accordance with a new standard of public obligation." But, Wijkman concluded "these changes have been made gradually, in accordance with Swedish traditions, in line with democratic ideas and within the framework of a well established system of representative government."[22]

Not all writers accepted the idea of Sweden as a "middle way" between pre-1929 American capitalism and pre-Stalin Russian socialism, but several made the point that the Swedish economy differed from both in important ways. Thanks to long process of education, capitalists in certain instances supported the cooperative movement.[23] Henry Goddard Leach explained "happy Sweden" in terms of a "triple set-up of business, part conducted by the state, part by private capital, and part by cooperative societies."[24] Others also had a mixed economy in mind in noting on the one hand the accumulation and investment of capital within the frame of individual initiative and, on the other, enterprise with cooperative association and government action in promoting a high standard of living and the welfare of workers both through some control of business and some participation in economic life.[25]

Comparisons between what Sweden had done and what the New Deal was trying to do were of course inevitable. A Swedish writer in the financial section of the *New York Times* in June, 1935, held that Sweden had, in a small way and under simpler conditions, anticipated the New

Deal by making "relief by work" the motto of unemployment policy all through the post-war years and by promoting a program of economic expansion.[26] Sweden, declared the widely travelled Henry A. Phillips, had by 1934 offered the best example of the Roosevelt ideals.[27] While noting several similarities between the Swedish record and the New Deal, especially in the sphere of economic regulation and consumer activity, Henry Goddard Leach, writing in 1934, contrasted the American emphasis on subsidies to business enterprise with the Swedish emphasis on self-help (the cooperatives, for example, had for thirty-five years refused help both from the government and from private capital); he also contrasted the Swedish effort to lower, rather than to raise consumer prices.[28] Another writer, after contrasting the two experiments by insisting that what was a New Deal to the United States was the ordinary course of matters in Sweden, stressed the well-established Swedish enlistment of economic experts and the general American suspicion of "brain-trusters."[29] Finally, a good deal was made of the difference between the voluntary cooperation of the several sectors of the Swedish economy and the opposition of a considerable part of the American business community to the Roosevelt innovations, including collective bargaining, which the Swedes had long taken for granted.[30]

Before considering the expressed interest of New Dealers in the Swedish experience some account is in order of the most widely read American exposition of what had taken place in Sweden. This, of course, is Marquis W. Childs' *Sweden the Middle Way,* published in January, 1936. The reception of this book can be understood in the context of the considerable body of writing that had appeared before 1936, to which Childs himself had contributed a notable article in the early stages of the discussion, and of the intensity of American feeling in the mid-1930s about economic and social values and programs.

An interest in Sweden on the part of Childs, who had been influenced by LaFollette "progressivism" in his student days at the University of Wisconsin, was initially aroused by Victor Praetz and Tage Palm, who had done much in Chicago and New York to bring the attention of Americans to Swedish industrial art. His interest was confirmed when, as a member of the staff of the *St. Louis Post-Dispatch,* Childs visited Sweden in 1930 to attend a housing exposition. The interest deepened, partly because Naboth

Hedlin of the American-Swedish News Exchange supplied him with a good deal of material and partly because of his experiences when he returned to Sweden in 1932 for a two-year stay.[31]

Childs' admiration of Sweden was first communicated in articles on the cooperatives which appeared in the *Post-Dispatch* in the summer of 1933. His national audience resulted from an article in the November, 1933, issue of *Harpers Magazine* to which he gave the arresting title "Sweden: Where Capitalism is Controlled."[32] Later published as a John Day pamphlet, the article argued that Sweden, because of its advanced industrialization and its emphasis on a high standard of living, was more relevant to American needs than the other Scandinavian countries. In brief, Childs added to the emerging discussion of various aspects of Swedish experience the central idea that Sweden's prosperity in the midst of depression could be understood because of its "planned domestic economy." This concentrated on the consumer and on a high living standard with the effect of preventing the "ravages of the depression" from becoming as serious as elsewhere. The planned economy also involved an appreciable participation, through ownership and operation, of government in the economy — even in 1929 government investment in "businesses" exceeded $663,000,000. This government participation in production, particularly of electrical power, had driven inefficient competition out of the field. The planned economy also involved the recognition of cooperative unions and leagues. Childs argued that the state and consumers cooperatives had been responsible for controlling "the capitalist in his operations within the country; in the domestic market it had been impossible to exploit the consumer to the ultimate limit of his capacity to pay." Although the depression retarded the socialization of such major export industries as paper, the orderly evolution toward socialism was still the goal of the dominant Social Democratic party. The government program of unemployment relief along Keynesian lines was to be regarded not only as a device for restoring purchasing power but also as giving "a breathing space" until the gradual transition to a socialistic type of economic organization could be resumed. In other words, Sweden was to be regarded as standing midway between capitalism and socialism. Over a thirty-year period it had achieved control of capitalism with the result that even leading industrialists and bankers "cooperated" with the evolutionary movement: in part, at least, this was to be explained by the extraordinary program of adult education and in part by the "national character."

The response to the *Harpers* article was mixed. While C. J. Ratzlaff disagreed with Childs in regarding Sweden as standing midway between "the uncontrolled capitalism of America before the crash and the arbitrary Marxian communism of Russia," he agreed that the Swedish education, broadly defined, had led many Swedish industrialists and bankers to "strengthen the domestic economy along cooperative lines."[33] On the other hand, Dean Lloyd Garrison of the University of Wisconsin Law School, Paul Douglas, professor of economics at the University of Chicago, and others hailed the article as opening new and significant vistas for Americans concerned with the depression and government responses to it. Understandably Henry Goddard Leach of the *American Scandinavian Review* and Oscar Cooley, editor of the *Cooperator,* welcomed Childs as a valuable recruit.[34]

Taking care in his book,[35] which elaborated the main points in the article, to state that he did not believe Sweden had achieved "an approximation to Utopia," Childs nevertheless often seemed to reflect such a judgment.[36] When he learned that to many Swedes the account seemed unduly favorable in overstressing the "lights" and underplaying the "shadows," he replied that he could not help admiring the order, reason and calm intelligence with which the Swedes had met their economic and social problems and that when he was shown poverty he "could not recognize it for poverty because it was so well ordered and so clearly understood."[37] Childs did indeed take into account such favorable circumstances as relative geographical isolation, a small, homogeneous population, able leadership, and "national character," but his main emphasis was on the success of a forty-year struggle in which the country had come "closer to achieving an economic democracy as well as a political democracy than any other country." In his view, three social checks or "brakes" had controlled "unbridled capitalism" — the cooperative movement, state ownership of such utilities as telephones, railways, electric power and other semi-public monopolies, and the trade union movement's contributions through political action to the gradual evolution of the welfare state. The book, admittedly a popular exposition, was clearly and forcefully written.

On the popular level *Sweden the Middle Way* was an immediate success. Herschell Brickel gave it a fine send-off in the *New York Evening Post* — "an intelligent volume that might well be read with pleasure and profit by all thinking people."[38] Lewis Gannett devoted his column in the *New York Herald Tribune* to it, finding nothing in the book itself to criticize, and much to commend. Reviews in the *New York Times,* the New York *World-Telegram,* the *Washington Post* and the *Chicago Daily News* offered little or no criticism either of the book itself or of the Swedish policies and programs it praised. In the *Saturday Review of Books* Agnes Rothery, whose popular and delightful *Sweden the Land and the People* (1934) had been widely read, hailed the Childs book for its "well assembled and authentic" indications of how Sweden managed its currency, stabilized its prices, lowered its taxes and eliminated its slums and illiteracy.[39] To the *Christian Century* the book was an enthusiastic but sane and fully documented account of the triumph of social welfare over corrupt politicians and popular ignorance. Contrary to some opinions the reviewer praised Childs for not representing Sweden as "a fully achieved Utopia" and for not even "retouching the shadows."[40] Approval went on and on: the *Atlantic Monthly, Scribners, Harpers, Management Review, Railway Clerk* and the *Journal of Home Economics.*[41] The advisory committee of *Current History* chose it as one of the ten best books of the year[42] while *The Forum* thought it "probably the season's most useful book."[43]

Although not without appreciation for what Childs had done a few critics in the journals of opinion had some reservations about what he had left out or failed to stress or overemphasized. Childs' enthusiasm for the "middle way" seemed unwarranted to the corporative-state oriented and "humanistic" *American Review.* Its critic held that Childs had failed to see that the Swedes had only superficially touched the basic ailments of modern society — the moral relationships of man to man and the loss of liberties for which capitalism and communism were equally responsible.[44] Writing in the *New Republic* Sidney Hertzberg felt that Childs should have given a more extensive treatment of the trades unions. Nor did he believe that the "middle way" could in the end be a lasting solution of the problems of modern industrial economy.[45] In somewhat the same vein Norman Thomas, while finding much to praise in the treatment of its subject, thought that it would have been a better book had it analyzed the dynamics of the changes it described. Childs was on sound ground, the Socialist leader continued, in emphasizing so much that was reassuring and even inspiring in the Swedish record. But he seemed, in his enthusiasm for the cooperatives and in his overpraise for what had been achieved through social security legislation, to have failed to realize that more than these, more even than the good sense, shrewdness and democracy of the Swedish people were needed to "solve the problems of plenty, peace and freedom in a troubled world."[46]

On the whole the specialized and professional journals, whose reviewers spoke with presumed competence, found much to approve. The *American Scandinavian Review* declared that none of the articles and books that had discussed Sweden covered the whole problem so well.[47] Professor C. J. Ratzlaff of Lafayette College, an authority on the Scandinavian unemployment relief problem, reported in the *American Swedish Monthly* that the book, which added considerably to our knowledge of "the peculiar nature of Sweden's social structure," deserved to be seriously considered by professional economists and statesmen as well as by the general reader.[48] The *American Economic Review's* notice regarded the book as "an excellent and informative study" but took exception to Childs' failure to see that much that Sweden had accomplished was to be explained by the fact that it had escaped Calvinistic individualism in its social-economic relationships which derived rather from traditional Germanic cooperative customs in everyday life.[49] Professor Walter Thompson, who had written approvingly on Sweden's liquor control, and who assessed Childs' book for the *American Political Science Review,* thought that the author had presented "an able and up-to-date discussion of cooperation, cooperative housing, the state power system, state railways" and all the rest. To be sure, portions of the work showed haste and if one read with an eye for fault-finding he could uncover inaccuracies both as to fact and conclusion. But these minor errors, Thompson concluded, did not "seriously mar the excellence of the work which obviously was intended to be popular and panoramic rather than 'meticulously exact.' "[50] The London *Economist,* which many American scholars and executives read, recommended Childs' "instructive and thoughtful book" to anyone interested in Sweden's" remarkable economic and social achievements."[51]

Yet not everyone writing with some authority shared in the generally favorable reactions to the book. Carle C. Zimmerman of Harvard criticized the claims made for Sweden's "balance between collectivism and individualism" and was not convinced, on putting the book down, that the Americanism and capitalism of the pre-1930 variety were fundamentally less sound for the United States than the Swedish system; he was even ready to argue that the American way might work better for Sweden itself.[52] To be taken more seriously was the comment of a distinguished Swedish authority which reached a wide American audience through *The Rotarian.* Its author, Dr. Bertil Ohlin, one of Sweden's leading economists who knew the United States and who generally supported the social and economic programs about which Childs was so keen, held that it simply was not true that his country had found "a *safe middle way,"* that Sweden was on the contrary faced by serious and even urgent problems. He rejected the claim for a superior Swedish standard of living and denied that the problem of industrial strife had been entirely solved. On the other hand he admitted that an advanced social policy had helped to preserve human resources and create a feeling of cooperation and confidence among workers and employees. Most impressive of all, Ohlin concluded, was the fact that Sweden's progress from real poverty had been unusually rapid.[53] The balanced position taken in *The Rotarian* article informed most of the scholarly articles in the special issue of the *Annals of the American Academy of Political and Social Sciences* which Ohlin edited in 1938 on the occasion of the Swedish-American tercentenary.

No careful or complete study has been made of reactions in Sweden to Childs' book. Not unexpectedly the liberal newspaper *Dagens Nyhyter* wrote about it in a sympathetic tone while the conservative *Svenska Dagbladet* was critical.[54] Much evidence suggests that many Swedes did not like the book. One distinguished economist expressed surprise that a leading American university press published such a journalistic account.[55] Richard A. Lester, a young Yale-trained economist who was studying monetary policy in Sweden, reported that the Swedes who had talked to him and to other Americans criticized the book on the grounds of taste, interpretations and inaccuracy. The inaccuracy that gave the most trouble was Childs' account of the great financial and industrial family, the Wallenbergs, who, according to him, had thwarted the cooperative movement.[56] Albin Johannson of the prestigious Kooperativo Forbundet took special exception to Childs' misstatements and the Wallenbergs themselves were offended.[57] Childs expressed regret and the matter was more or less patched up.[58]

An interesting and perhaps representative evaluation was that of Thorsten Odhe of *Kooperaton* who, while commending the book as one likely to stimulate further study of and interest in America in Swedish achievements, felt that the author had permitted himself certain improvisations with resulting distortions and even erroneous impressions. In any case this authority on the cooperative movement held that it was in actuality much less comprehensive than Childs had claimed.[59]

Other evidence also points to Swedish reservations about Childs' account. On returning from the States, Professor Eli Heckscher reported that Americans were far too romantic about the country and deplored the "current myth that Sweden is some sort of Utopia."[60] During a stay in the United States in 1937 Professor Bertil Ohlin reportedly tried to correct the impression that Sweden was "a fortunate land," an effort commended by the pro-American newspaper *Aftonbladet*.[61] Other Swedish writers and Americans with some first-hand knowledge also reported Swedish reservations and misgivings. On a visit to Sweden H. B. Elliston found that many Swedes were "somewhat irritated" by the fashion in American writing of paving "the road to utopia with Swedish panaceas."[62] Commenting on Childs' book a few years later, an American authority observed that if readers had the impression that Sweden had solved the problems of economic stability and security, the Swedes themselves did not hold any such opinion.[63] After spending some time in America, traveling widely and speaking at several universities, Nils Herlitz, professor of public law at the University of Stockholm, observed that just as many of his countrymen had, during the great exodus, looked on America as a wonderland, so many Americans had come to see Sweden. In view, however, of the country's many faults and unsolved problems Herlitz asked the reader "who may be struck by the lights of the picture always to remember that there are shadows too."[64] Finally, Childs himself, after revisiting Sweden, reported that its spokesmen seemed to feel he had been overly enthusiastic about what had been done and expressed perplexity at the American applause for his writing.[65]

Whatever reservations Swedish readers had, there is no doubt about the popular appeal of the book at home. Thanks to advance publicity and the first enthusiastic reviews in the metropolitan newspapers a thousand copies were disposed of in the first three days after publication. The Yale University Press was delighted at the book's "great success." It quickly made the best-seller list. Advertisements in leading newspapers and magazines and the wide distribution of "a flock of circulars" quoting the favorable comments of John Chamberlain, Harry Elmer Barnes, Sterling North, Hershell Brickell and others pushed up the sales as did the attention given it by such columnists as Dorothy Thompson, David Mallon and Harry Hansen.[66] *Sweden the Middle Way* was reprinted and reprinted again. By the end of the year it reached the ninth printing and a sale of 25,000 copies.[67]

Nor is the evidence of popularity confined to reviews and sales. The Carnegie Endowment increased the book's prestige by buying 760 copies.[68] A Swedish visitor, Johan Hansson, heard it talked about from New York to San Francisco.[69] The number of American tourists in Sweden, eager to see the cooperatives and other wonders at first hand, doubled in two years.[70] The popularity of the book and the ideas it conveyed owed something to favorable references in the speeches of Colonel Theodore Roosevelt[71] and to the enthusiasm Philip LaFollette and Mr. Justice Brandeis expressed.[72] Childs himself received many invitations to speak about the Middle Way from cooperatives, students and religious groups.[73] Interest in Sweden and its achievements was also furthered by the tercentenary of the first Swedish settlements on the Delaware. Distinguished visitors who came for the occasion included Crown Prince Gustav who, on receiving a degree from Harvard, caused a ripple of laughter when he said that Swedish cooperatives were better known in America than in Sweden itself and who several times modestly but engagingly interpreted the Swedish way.[74].

On revisiting Sweden in 1937 Childs reported his impressions in an article in the *Yale Review*.[75] While noting continued gains in the cooperative movement and in the development of electric power under government auspices, the essay stressed the complexity of the forces explaining Sweden's prosperity and the danger of overstating the country's "inner harmony." Childs emphasized the important role of the "brilliant organization" of industry over the past two decades as a factor in the national well-being and quoted leading Social Democrats to the effect that the reforms had largely been carried through in a time of prosperity, that the next steps were bound to be hard ones, and that progress must be related to gains yet to be made. Gunnar Myrdall was quoted as saying that the emphasis on success encouraged others to emphasize failures in order to discredit socialism. Childs also discussed Swedish concern over recent revelations of poverty and even undernourishment in the northern district and other evidence of a declining population growth which admittedly explained, at least in part, achievements in housing. At the same time he praised the Report of the Population Commission for its intended effort to jar complacency and for the first time, in any country, facing squarely declining birthrate.[76] Nor was the low-keyed picture brightened any by the dark shadows of a threatening European war and the issues this was bound to raise for Sweden's economic and social democracy.[77]

With the great success of *Sweden the Middle Way* in mind the Yale University Press encouraged Childs to write a new book with the title of the article in the *Yale Review*. But he felt that the first success could not be repeated and the decision was made to bring out a new edition with errors corrected, statistics updated, and the "utopian" character of the first edition played down.[78] While neither the Press nor Childs expected the new edition would approximate the unexpected success of the first, it sold well and reached its fifth printing in 1944.[79]

But Childs was not yet done with Sweden.[80] He continued to discuss it in several articles that appeared in the late 1930s. One interpreted Swedish success with company towns, which he laid largely at the door of effective pressure of the trades unions and of public opinion for the maintenance of reasonable rates and high standards.[81] Another was concerned with aspects of the trade union movement only touched on earlier and with farmer-labor relations as well as with efforts to find a way out of the "nightmare dilemma of scarcity in plenty."[82] In 1938 Yale published *This is Democracy: Collective Bargaining in Scandinavia.* Safeguarding himself against criticisms by announcing it as a largely journalistic account, Childs made much of the atmosphere in Sweden of tolerance and mutual respect in management-labor relations and of the trades unions' encouragement of the formation of employers' organizations and company towns. Though the book was widely and in general favorably reviewed as a useful and sober report of an important achievement with lessons for the United States,[83] it was not widely read if the disappointing sales record were a measure.[84] As in the case of Childs' earlier work, this popular exposition was followed by scholarly studies from other writers. In these the implications for America of the Swedish record, including the labor courts, were more fully probed.[85]

But many, like Childs himself, at least in his first book, hesitated to draw explicit lessons from Swedish experience because of the great differences between the two countries in size and complexity of the population and in traditions and national character. Yet it was common to hold that whatever the differences, a young nation could learn much from an older one if, like Sweden, it had achieved "a well-tempered modernity."[86] On a more specific level, it is noteworthy that commentators on the New Deal, from "right" to "left," used the Swedish example in quite different and even contradictory ways.

Thus conservatives praised Sweden for its respect for constitutional procedures in contrast with what was taken to be the authoritarian and regimented methods of the New Deal: Swedish respect for property rights and for the businesslike character of the cooperatives; also the regard of its people for order and discipline in labor-management as in other relationships, in contrast with American propensity toward violence.[87]

Moderates and liberals on the other hand stressed the point that Sweden had overcome the depression, not as the New Deal tried to do, by curtailing production, but by increasing it, not by holding in check prices and wages, but by raising them.[88] Above all moderates and liberals never tired of contrasting the bitterness of American contests over policy with the Swedish refusal to let realities and needs be obscured by dogma and ideology, of American conservatives' adamant opposition to change, with Swedish readiness to give and take, to compromise.[89] Also in contrast with what seemed to be the indifference of most Americans toward decision-making was the Swedish involvement of everyone in organizations in such a way as to exalt citizenship through the increased sense of ultimate responsibility: a Swede was certain that "he owns his country and controls its destiny to a degree not true . . . of the average American."[90] In the judgment of liberal and radical critics of the New Deal the fresh ideas and vistas that Sweden provided included proof that a democracy might engage successfully in economic planning without jeopardizing democracy. Several contrasted America's feeble and hesitant moves toward social security with its fuller fruits in Sweden.[91] All but avowed socialists insisted that the greatest lesson Sweden had to teach was the falsity of the view that America was compelled, in the throes of its economic breakdown, to choose between traditional capitalism or an undemocratic collectivism.[92]

The major importance of the discussion of Sweden in relation to the New Deal lay, then, in the uses made of it by its supporters and critics. Yet it would be going too far to claim that there was no positive influence of the Swedish experience on those who planned and executed the New Deal. Several in a position of influence were either intimately associated with Childs — Harry Hopkins is an example[93] — or explicitly indicated their conviction of the importance for America of Swedish precedents and experiences. "Your book on Sweden has made a good deal of intellectual history in these parts," Adolph Berle Jr. wrote to Childs from Washington.[94] Thurman Arnold's comments on the bearings of Swedish experience on American conditions, even with the qualifications made, are nevertheless impressive.[95] Henry Wallace was especially struck by what Sweden had done in the field of conservation.[96] Members of Congress introduced into the *Congressional Record* several speeches commending the Swedish record and pointing to its relevance for America — only one such insertion, that of Harold Knutson, repudiated the "new" Swedish philosophy.[97]

It is not entirely clear why President Roosevelt decided, in June, 1936, to send a commission to Sweden and other countries to study cooperatives in the fields of production and marketing, credit operations, insurance, banking and electrical production, and to report on the effectiveness of cooperatives in obtaining a wider distribution of wealth and promoting economic stabilization. The public response to Childs' book, two copies of which were in his library and which he was understood to have read, was certainly one factor. At the press conference of June 23, 1936, at which the President announced the appointment of the commission, he spoke of *The Middle Way* and of his own "tremendous" interest in the Swedish cooperatives.[98] An exchange of letters between Childs and Roosevelt lends some support to the assumption that the book had something to do with the appointment of the commission.[99] No doubt other factors, too, influenced the decision. In the preceding spring Axel Werner-Gren, president of Electrolux, had discussed cooperatives with the president.[100] He must also have been aware of the bill which Representative Bryon H. Scott of California had introduced into Congress proposing a Cooperative Bank and a Consumers Administration.[101] It is not unlikely that Roosevelt also felt that an official recognition of the Administration's interest in cooperatives might take some of the wind from the sails of William Lemke who was launching a third party during the election campaign and was pledging government support for cooperatives.[102]

The commission took its assignment seriously. Its chairman, Jacob Baker, had been Assistant Administrator of the Federal Relief Administration and was currently attached to the WPA. The other original members were Leland Olds, economist on the staff of the National Labor Board and secretary of the New York State Power Authority, and Charles E. Stuart, a member of a New York engineering corporation who had served with the National War Industries Board. When leading figures in the cooperative movement complained that it was in no sense represented, additional members from its ranks were appointed — Robin Hood, Clifford Gregory and Emily Bates.[103] The reception in Sweden was cordial: members of the commission conferred at length with important figures in the government, including the Prime Minister and the Under Secretary of State to the Treasury (Dag Hammarskjöld), leaders in industry, finance, labor and the university world. Albin Johannson, president of the Cooperative Union, gave a large dinner for the commission, which also visited cooperatives and gathered and read reports. In the discussions importance was attached to the role of the cooperatives in providing a price yardstick and in making price-fixing by private monopolies impossible, in providing stability for the economy, in promoting efficiency in private retailing by taking the lead in modernization, and in making adult study circles functional and realistic.[104]

Before the commission returned in the late autumn of 1936 the Administration had been made aware of the uneasiness of small businesses which feared that government support of the cooperatives might be forthcoming to the detriment of small business. Officials of the United States Chamber of Commerce reportedly spread the rumor that the government might, as a result of the commissions' recommendations, provide low interest loans to the cooperatives for instruction in business management.[105] When a Democratic county chairman expressed concern at what might issue from the commission's recommendations, he was told that the significance of the inquiry was "exceedingly slight" and that no extension of government activity was contemplated.[106]

The report, while containing some interpretive material, was mainly factual. It recommended that a survey of consumer and service cooperatives in the United States be made, that some government agency be designated to give advice to cooperatives comparable to that extended to farmers' cooperatives and business enterprises, and that steps be taken to assure consumer cooperatives credit parity.[107] After much rumor about divisions within the commission, the inexplicable loss of the report after it had been given to the President, and much uncertainty within the administration as to what should be done with it, the advice of Secretary of Agriculture Wallace to publish most of the report, without the recommendations, was followed.[108] Issued by the Government Printing Office,[109] it had been sent to 8800 persons or agencies by midsummer.[110] Contemporary as well as later comment suggests that the report was, as far as the American cooperative movement went, a helpful if limited gesture.[111]

This was not the only commission sent to Sweden. In 1938, when interest in the Wagner Act was keen, Roosevelt appointed another commission, headed by Gerard Swope, former president of General Electric, to study labor-management relations in Sweden and Britain. The published report, prefaced by the President's appreciative comment, paid tribute to Swedish achievements in this field. Swope spoke of these as "a new high in voluntary agreements between employers and workers" and implied that the achievements were not without import for the United States.[112] Such also was the judgment of scholars writing later about the matter.[113]

The interest in the 1930s in Sweden was part of a widespread effort to discover how other countries were dealing with the social and economic problems that were troubling Americans. It also reflected an awareness on the part of Roosevelt and other leaders that much more needed to be done, particularly in attacking poverty, and an uncertainty of just what should be done. Hence the commissions of inquiry such as those that were sent to Sweden and other countries.

Interest in Sweden's welfare state did not disappear either on the official level [114] or on that of general discussion.[115] But the extensive and vigorous interest receded as other issues, particularly the outbreak of the Second World War, dominated thought and action. Nevertheless the relatively brief preoccupation of so many Americans with the Swedish record was of intellectual as well as emotional importance in the troubled, creative America of the 1930s and thus occasioned an episode of significance in the long history of the transatlantic community.

## *NOTES*

1. Mary Rankin Cranston, "How Sweden Selects and Adapts to her Own Needs the Results of the World Wide Social Experiment," *The Craftsman,* X (Aug., 1906), 570-578; Gabrielle Reval, "Sweden, Land of Democracy," *Living Age,* CCCXV (June 27, 1925), 670-671; and "What the War Did for Sweden," *Literary Digest,* CIV (Jan. 11, 1930), 20.
2. Ira Nelson Morris, *From an American Legation* (New York, 1923); "Sweden's Position in the New World of Today," *Saturday Evening Post,* CXCII (May 29, 1920), 22-23 and 73-75; and "Hard Times in Scandinavia," *ibid.,* CXCIV (June 10, 1922), 25 ff. and 69 ff.
3. Frederic C. Howe, *Denmark: A Cooperative Commonwealth* (New York, 1921). Howe, an old-time "progressive" reformer, presented Denmark as a model to nations in this widely read and discussed book.
4. This interpretation was suggested by Marquis W. Childs in typescripts for articles and addresses, particularly those entitled "There is No Utopia" and "Sweden the Tragic Dilemma," in the Marquis W. Childs Manuscript Collection, Wisconsin State Historical Society, Box 5.
5. Bertil Ohlin, "Economic Recovery and Labour Market Problems in Sweden," *International Labour Review,* XXXI (April, 1935), 498. See also Ohlin's *The Problem of Employment Stabilization* (New York, 1949).

6. See Erik T. H. Kjellstrom, *Price Control. The War against Inflation* (New Brunswick, N. J., 1942), 10 ff.
7. See, for example, Irving Fisher, *Stable Money. A History of the Movement* (New York, 1934); and Donald Winch, "The Keynesian Revolution in Sweden," *Journal of Political Economy,* LXXIV (April, 1966), 168-176, a recent discussion of the controversy over the relative importance of the contributions of British and Swedish economists.
8. Fisher, *Stable Money,* 182.
9. For the generally sympathetic attitude toward the Swedish experiments of two of the chief early economic advisers to the Roosevelt administration, George Frederick Warren of Cornell and James Harvey Rogers of Yale, see Arthur W. Crawford, *Monetary Management under the New Deal* (Washington, 1940); Norman Lombard, *Monetary Statesmanship* (New York, 1934); James Harvey Rogers, *America Weighs Her Gold* (New Haven, 1931) and *Capitalism in Crisis* (New Haven, 1938); and Edgar S. Furness and W. W. Rostow, *James Harvey Rogers 1886-1933* (Privately printed).
10. Charles T. Hallinan, "Sweden's Managed Currency," *Forum and Century,* XC (Sept., 1933), 159-163.
11. Fisher, *Stable Money,* 330 ff., 399-400, and 408-409. For Fisher's relations with Roosevelt see Irving Norton Fisher, *My Father Irving Fisher* (New York, 1956).
12. Erik T. H. Kjellstrom, *Managed Money, the Experience of Sweden* (New York, 1934), vii-xi and 5.
13. *New York Times,* April 29, 1934, 19; and *Annals of the American Academy of Political and Social Science,* CLXXVI (Nov., 1934), 237.
14. *American Economic Review,* XXIV (Sept., 1934), 532.
15. Richard A. Lester, *Monetary Experiments. Early American and Recent Scandinavian* (Princeton, 1939), 282-283.
16. Brinley Thomas, *Monetary Policy and Crisis. A Study of Swedish Experience* (London, 1936), xx and 232-233.
17. Arthur Montgomery, *How Sweden Overcame the Depression 1930-1933* (Stockholm, 1938), 5.
18. "Better than 1929," *Business Week* (July 27, 1935), 24.
19. C. J. Ratzlaff, *The Scandinavian Unemployment Relief Program* (Philadelphia, 1934), 117, 137 ff., and 156. Ratzlaff made a point of the importance of centralized administration and decentralized supervision.
20. Roger L. Simons, "The Garden of Sweden," *North American Review,* CCXXXVIII (Nov., 1934), 414-420; Per Wijkman, "Recovery in Sweden," *American Swedish Monthly,* XXIX (Feb., 1935), 34; Robert Hessby, "Why Sweden Has Recovered," *ibid.* (June, 1935), 19; and Vilgot Hammarling, "World Watching Sweden's Rally," *New York Times,* July 20, 1936, 3, July 21, 1936, 16.
21. Mabel B. Lee, "Sweden Offers Us a Lesson in Housing," *New York Times,* June 9, 1935.
22. Wijkman, "Recovery in Sweden," 34.
23. Ratzlaff, *Scandinavian Unemployment Relief,* 156.
24. Henry Goddard Leach, "Where Consumers Produce," *The Forum,* XCII (Sept., 1934), 162 ff.

25. Wijkman, "Recovery in Sweden," 34; and Ebha Dahlin, "My First Impressions of Swedish Social Democracy," *American Swedish Monthly,* XXIX (Dec., 1935), 6 and 42.
26. *New York Times,* June 2, 1935, Sec. III, 1.
27. Henry A. Phillips, "Sweden as a Rooseveltian Model," *Literary Digest,* CXVIII (Sept. 15, 1934), 15.
28. Leach, "Where Consumers Produce," 165.
29. "Social Democracy Bids Farewell to Depression," *Christian Century,* LII (Feb. 6, 1935), 166.
30. Phillips, "Sweden as a Rooseveltian Model," 15.
31. John Griffith, "Marquis W. Childs, Foe of Extremes," *Detroit Free Press Sunday Magazine,* May 29, 1949, in Childs Collection, Box 6; and an unsigned letter, dated Feb. 6, 1946, to Thomas L. Stix, Box 1.
32. Marquis W. Childs, "Sweden: Where Capitalism Is Controlled," *Harpers Magazine,* CLXVII (Nov., 1933), 750-758.
34. Lloyd K. Garrison to Childs, Nov. 6, 1933; Paul Douglas to Childs, Jan. 24, 1934; Naboth Hedin to Childs, April 30, 1934; and Oscar Cooley to Childs, Jan. 24, 1934, Childs Collection, Box 1.
35. When the John Day Company decided that a full length book might not sell sufficiently to be justified, the Yale University Press agreed to publication. Childs to Critchell Remington, n.d.; Rimington to Childs, Jan. 23, Jan. 26, 1934; and Eugene A. Davidson of the Yale University Press to Childs, Feb. 19, 1934, Childs Collection, Box 1.
36. Davidson to Childs, Sept. 20, 1935, Childs Collection, Box 1.
37. Marquis W. Childs, *I Write from Washington* (New York, 1942), 307.
38. Norman V. Donaldson to Childs, Jan. 20, 1936, Childs Collection, Box 1.
39. Quotations from an advertising brochure in Childs Collection, Box 5; *New York Herald Tribune,* Jan. 29, 1936; *New York Times,* Jan. 30, Feb. 2, 1936; and *Saturday Review of Literature,* XIII (Feb. 15, 1936).
40. *Christian Century,* LIII (March 4, 1936), 364.
41. *Harpers Magazine,* CLXXIII (Nov., 1936), 632-633; *Scribners Magazine,* C (Sept., 1936), 133; *Journal of Home Economics,* XXVIII (Sept., 1936); *Railway Clerk,* XXXV (Sept., 1936), 358; and *Management Review,* XXV (Sept., 1936), 295.
42. John Chamberlain in *Current History,* XLIV (April, 1936), vi; and George P. Day to Childs, Dec. 9, 1936, Childs Collection, Box 1.
43. *The Forum,* XCV (April, 1936), vi.
44. H. M. Lowes in *American Review,* VII (Summer, 1936), 319-322.
45. *New Republic,* LXXXII (May 27, 1936), 82.
46. *The Nation,* CXLII (March 18, 1936), 358-359; and Norman Thomas to Childs, Sept. 9, 1936, Childs Collection, Box 1. "Your book on Sweden is, I think," Thomas wrote, "doing a lot of good all over the country. Certainly I enjoyed it and I am much honored that you liked the review. I did want to call attention to what irritates me, perhaps unduly; namely, the tendency of people in America who do nothing to build up the cooperative movement to say to me, 'See, all you need is cooperation as in Sweden.' "
47. Neilson Abeel, review of *Sweden the Middle Way* in the *American-Scandinavian Review,* XXIV (March, 1936), 85.

48. *American Swedish Monthly,* XXX (Feb., 1936), 28-29.
49. *American Economic Review,* XXVI (June, 1936), 27.
50. *American Political Science Review,* XXX (June, 1936), 603.
51. *The Economist,* CXXIV (Sept. 19, 1936), 520.
52. *Annals of the American Academy of Political and Social Science,* CXXVI (July, 1936), 266.
53. Bertil Ohlin, "Sweden Still Has Problems," *The Rotarian,* LI (Dec., 1937), 12-13 and 56-58. See also Ohlin, *The Problem of Employment Stabilization* (New York, 1949).
54. Naboth Hedin to Childs, April 28, 1936, Childs Collection, Box 1.
55. Prof. Richard A. Lester to Merle Curti, Feb. 14, 1967.
56. Richard A. Lester to Yale University Press, July 29, 1936, Childs Collection, Box 1.
57. Naboth Hedin to Childs, May 5, May 16, 1936; Norman Donaldson to Childs, Aug. 10, 1936; Mrs. Childs to Donaldson, Aug. 11, 1936; Childs to Albin Johannson, Oct. 11 ,1936; and Childs to Ira Nelson Morris, Oct. 11, 1936, Childs Collection, Box 1.
58. Childs to Johannson, Oct. 11, 1936; and Childs to Marcus Wallenberg, Oct. 11, 1936, Childs Collection, Box 1.
59. Thorsten Odhe, review in English typescript of *Sweden the Middle Way,* in *Kooperaton,* No. 10, Childs Collection, Box 4.
60. *New York Times,* June 5, 1938, Sec. IV, 5.
61. Marquis W. Childs, "Sweden Revisited," *Yale Review,* XXVII (Sept., 1937), 32.
62. H. B. Elliston, "Unflattered Sweden," *Atlantic Monthly,* CLX (Dec., 1937), 766.
63. Leonard Silk, *Sweden Plans for Better Housing* (Durham, N. C., 1948), 59.
64. Nils Herlitz, *Sweden, a Modern Democracy on Ancient Foundations* (Minneapolis, 1939), xi.
65. Childs, *I Write from Washington,* 307.
66. Norman Donaldson to Childs, Jan. 30, Feb. 1, March 23, March 27, April 20, May 15, July 1, July 7, 1936, Childs Collection, Box 1.
67. Donaldson to Childs, Sept. 10, 1937, Childs Collection, Box 1.
68. Davidson to Childs, July 7, 1936, Childs Collection, Box 1.
69. Naboth Hedin to Childs, May 16, 1936, Childs Collection, Box 1.
70. Childs, "Sweden Revisited," 33.
71. Donaldson to Childs, April 21, 1936; and Theodore Roosevelt to Childs, May 6, 1936, Childs Collection, Box 1.
72. Donaldson to Childs, Feb. 4, 1936, Childs Collection, Box 1.
73. For example, Hilda Loveman to Childs, Oct. 14, 1936; and Rabbi Leon Frain to Childs, Dec. 3, 1936, Childs Collection, Box 1.
74. *New York Times,* July 7, July 11, and July 12, 1936.
75. Childs, "Sweden Revisited," 31-44.
76. Childs to Davidson, Sept. 2, 1937, Childs Collection, Box 1.
77. Childs developed his concern over the implications of a general war in several typescripts for lectures or radio talks, Childs Collection, Box 5, and in an article in *Current History,* LI (April, 1940), 60.

78. Davidson to Childs, Nov. 22, 1937; Childs to Davidson, Nov. 25, 1937; Donaldson to Childs, Dec. 9, 1937; Davidson to Childs, June 22, June 29, 1938, Childs Collection, Box 1.
79. Donaldson to Childs, Aug. 25, 1938; Davidson to Childs, Nov. 17, 1938; Childs to Donaldson, March 21, 1939; and Donaldson to Childs, Sept. 22, 1944, Childs Collection, Box 1.
80. A new, revised, and enlarged edition of *Sweden the Middle Way,* bringing the discussion of developments to date, appeared in May, 1947.
81. *The Forum,* C (Nov., 1938), 260.
82. *Yale Review,* XXVIII (Sept., 1938), 62-63.
83. *New York Times,* Sept. 28, and Oct. 16, 1938, Sec. VI; *Saturday Review of Literature,* XVIII (Oct. 8, 1938), 10; *Management Review,* XXVIII (Jan., 1939), 34; *Yale Review,* VIII (March, 1939), 615-616; *Christian Century,* LV (Nov. 2, 1938), 1331-1332; *American-Scandinavian Review,* XXVI (Dec., 1938), 369-377; and *The Nation,* CXLVII (Oct. 15, 1938), 383.
84. Donaldson to Childs, March 14, 1939, Childs Collection, Box 1.
85. Paul H. Norgren, *Swedish Collective Bargaining System* (Cambridge, Mass., 1941), 296 ff., together with the foreword by Sumner H. Slichter and James Jacobs Robbins in *Government of Labor Relations in Sweden* (Chapel Hill, N. C., 1942).
86. John Daniel, "An Old Land with New Ideas," *American Swedish Monthly,* XXXI (April, 1937), 15.
87. Isaac F. Marcosson, "The Swedish Recovery," *Saturday Evening Post,* CCVIII (Feb. 22, 1936), 23 and 66-70.
88. John Chamberlain, "The World in Books," *Current History,* XLIV (April, 1936), vi. In his *New York Times* review of *Sweden the Middle Way* (Jan. 30, 1936), Chamberlain argued that the New Deal was an experiment in "the socialization of losses," tending to push capitalism further along the road to monopoly, whereas Swedes had been careful to prevent capitalism from reaching the monopoly stage.
89. Simeon Strunsky, in a review of *Sweden the Middle Way, New York Times,* Feb. 2, 1936; Nelson Abeel, in a review of the same book in *American-Scandinavian Review,* XXIV (March, 1936), 85.
90. Hubert Herring, "The Incredible Swedes," *Harpers Magazine,* CLXXIII (Nov., 1936), 632 ff. and 643.
91. N. H. Hedin, "New Steps toward More Social Security in Sweden," *American Swedish Monthly,* XXXI (June, 1937), 23.
92. Ernest K. Lindley, "If This Be Despotism," *Scribners Magagine,* C (Sept., 1936), 133; Ludwig Love, "Scandinavia's New Democracy," *The Nation,* XXLV (Sept. 25, 1936), 315; *The Forum,* XCVIII (Oct., 1937), 183; and *Atlantic Monthly,* CLX (Dec., 1937), 770.
93. Robert E. Sherwood, *Roosevelt and Hopkins. An Intimate History* (New York, 1950), 835.
94. Berle to Childs, Aug. 26, 1938, Childs Collection, Box 1.
95. Thurman W. Arnold, *The Folklore of Capitalism* (New Haven, 1937), 9, 12, and 333; and *The Bottlenecks of Business* (New York, 1940), 14-15 and 240.
96. Henry Wallace, *The American Choice* (New York, 1940), 86; and *Democracy Reborn* (New York, 1944), 114.

97. *Congressional Record,* 74th Congress, 2d Sess., LXXX, Part 10, June 19, 1936; 75th Congress, 1st Sess., LXXXI, Part 10, July 29, 1937 and Appendix LXXXIV, Part 13, 2928. Knutson's speech, given at Manchester, New Hampshire, on May 22, 1938, is in *Congressional Record,* 75th Congress, 3d Sess., LXXXIII, Part 10, 1938.
98. I am indebted to Dr. Elizabeth Drewey, Director of the Franklin D. Roosevelt Library, for this reference and for making available microfilm copy of Documents Relating to the President's Commission of Inquiry on Cooperative Enterprise in Europe, hereafter cited as Documents on Cooperative Enterprise.
99. Childs to Roosevelt, Aug. 4, 1936; and Roosevelt to Childs, Aug. 12, 1936, Roosevelt Library.
100. Jacob Baker to Col. Marion McIntyre, Aug. 10, 1936, Documents on Cooperative Enterprise.
101. Memo, July 22, 1936, indicating reply of McIntyre to Dr. Walter Turner, Documents on Cooperative Enterprise.
102. *New York Times,* June 24 and July 12, 1936; and letter from Howard A. Cowden to Leroy Peterson, June 25, 1936, Documents on Cooperative Enterprise.
103. Rexford Tugwell to Roosevelt, July 1, 1936; Cordell Hull to Roosevelt, July 9, 1936; and Howard Cowden to Leroy Peterson, June 25, 1936, Documents on Cooperative Enterprise.
104. The Place of Cooperatives in the Economic Life of Scandinavia, Baker to President Roosevelt, Sept. 22, and Dec. 28, 1936, Documents on Cooperative Enterprise.
105. Dr. Walter Turner to Roosevelt, July 22, 1936; McIntyre to Turner, July 30, 1936; Ben Glasgow to Roosevelt, Aug. 22, 1936; and McIntyre to Glasgow, Aug. 25, 1936, Documents on Cooperative Enterprise.
106. L. E. Linnan to Roosevelt, Aug. 12, 1936; and memo for reply, Documents on Cooperative Enterprise.
107. Baker to Roosevelt, Dec. 28, 1936; and Baker to Steven Early, Mar. 2, 1937, Documents on Cooperative Enterprise.
108. *New York Herald Tribune,* Feb. 28, 1937; Baker to Roosevelt, Feb. 23, 1937; Charles E. Stuart to McIntyre, March 9, 1937; and Wallace to McIntyre, March 10, 1937, Documents on Cooperative Enterprise.
109. *Report of the Inquiry on Cooperative Enterprise in Europe in 1937* (Washington, 1937). The report on Sweden's cooperatives does not appear anywhere but in an Appendix.
110. Memo for Roosevelt, July 12, 1937, Documents on Cooperative Enterprise.
111. *New York Times,* June 24, 1936, 12; June 27, 1936, 16; June 28, 1936, Sec. IV, 1-2; *Printers Ink,* CLXXX (Aug. 19, 1937), 58-67; and Henning Friis, *Scandinavia between East and West* (Ithaca, N. Y., 1950), 340.
112. *Commission on Industrial Relations in Sweden, Report of the Commission on Industrial Relations in Sweden* (Washington, 1938), v. See also *New York Times,* May 21, 1939, Sec. IV, 8; and June 8, 1939, Sec. IV, 9.

113. Paul H. Morgren, *The Swedish Collective Bargaining System* (Cambridge, Mass., 1941), 293 ff.; Robbins, *Government of Labor Relations in Sweden. Some Comparisons with American Experience* (Cambridge, Mass., 1951), 112.

114. For example, the long memorandum entitled "The Creation of a Budget for the United States Treasury According to Swedish Budgetary Procedure" in the Harry Dexter White Papers, Princeton University, for a xerox copy of which I am indebted to the Manuscript Division of the Princeton University Library.

115. For example, David Hinshaw, *Sweden, Champion of Peace* (New York, 1949); Wilfred Fleisher, *Sweden, the Welfare State* (New York, 1956); and the excellent study by Franklin Scott, *The United States and Scandinavia* (Cambridge, Mass., 1950).

# *Recollections of a Childhood and Youth*

O. Fritiof Ander

Adapted from *Augustana Swedish Institute,*
Yearbook 1963-1964

When I arrived in America a few years after World War I, I had never heard of Augustana College. There were no good reasons why I should have. I had lived much in a world of my own in which it was difficult to separate fantasy from reality.

I was born in Gendalen, about forty-five English miles from Gothenburg. Gendalen was not a large village, but it was my world, and the only world which counted. My roots were deep in the village and I loved its narrow, winding and hilly roads and paths. It seemed as if I knew all the rocks, pebbles, and straws of grass of the small village, not to mention its birds. I loved Gendalen for these; but the village had a history, too, one which had become essentially a legend. Gendalen had once been known as Geneved and as such it rivaled Värnamo as a medieval fair to which people, peddlers, and merchants from many parts of Sweden came annually to sell and barter their wares.

Once on the fair grounds there had been a church and a burial ground around which the fairs had been held. But there was no vestige left of the church. The beginning of the twentieth century called for better roads and the heights of the old fairground contained essential gravel for the improvement of roads. I recall how the gravel pit grew until one day the pit was closed as skulls and skeletons had been uncovered. The gravel pit apparently violated a place once hallowed, the cemetery of the old church. There was no wonder, therefore, that horses traveling the road at night past the gravel pit had shied. Near the gravel pit stood an old blacksmith shop. I cannot recall ever seeing the blacksmith, but the people had held him in awe and fear. He saw visions and he could heal. Everyone knew that he had contacts with another world, but which one no one knew. Across the road from the blacksmith shop was a large boulder for which I developed a great respect. It was said that someone had shot himself at the place. No one knew when and why or who it was. Again and again conversation would turn to ghosts and to dreams and the meaning of all these things.

A child listened attentively without understanding and gave full reign to a lively imagination. The literature of children also drew heavily upon the world of giants, trolls, and fairies with the result that it was, indeed, difficult to distinguish between fantasy and reality. In the world of Hans Christian Andersen, the home gave a sense of security in which the parents, brothers, sisters, and servants played an important role. This was a tangible world, something to which to hold fast, and I wanted it to last forever. But little by little it fell apart and as it did, I left Sweden for America and found my way to Augustana College.

It is difficult to say how a child's world crumbles. The mere process of growing up does its part, but some things seem more perceptible in review. I thought that I could never be happy anywhere other than Gendalen. I recall how I talked to the grass and the little stones or pebbles in our park-like garden in which our large home was situated, assuring them of my deep love. Although my brothers and sisters and I were soon sent away to "realskola" in Gothenburg, I dreamed about the coming of vacations and the reunion with all those who were so important in my life. There outside of Gothenburg one could walk barefooted at times, go swimming in the old creek and fish — it seemed like all day — and play Indians and various games. There were two boys in particular with whom I liked to play. Sometimes my playmates must have tired me, but there were two essential escapes. One was day-dreaming, which seldom if ever took me away from Gendalen. Another was reading.

My father was a merchant, living on the estate of his father which he had purchased. Neither my father nor my grandfather gave any attention to farming. Both became successful merchants. My father had attended a secondary school at Vänersborg, and he was interested in promoting education. My brothers, sisters, and I had unusual opportunities for learning. Tutors prepared us for direct entry into "realskola." They bceame a part of the household.

My father also sponsored book auctions, seeking to encourage reading among the farmers. He probably purchased some of the books himself, and they included a wide variety of literature, part of which had to be stored in the attic. When I was bored I found my way into the attic where my young mind was unable to distinguish between good and bad literature. I would place myself on my stomach and proceed to read. At first illustrations or covers, titles of books, pictures or drawings directed my reading. The sagas had a great appeal to me, and I soon began to wonder why my forefathers had ever deserted the worship of the old gods. My own name (Fritiof) seemed to indicate that my father had become fascinated by the ideas and the ideals of the Gothic school of literature which flourished in Sweden during the first part of the nineteenth century. Esaias Tegner and Gustaf Geijer became favorites as they stressed manly virtues of courage and valor. To go from Tegner and Geijer to Zane Grey might seem ridiculous to a scholar, but in the attic of Gendalen, it was an easy matter. In the attic were old journals with pictures describing the Japanese-Russian War, and these also began to interest me. Some of the journals had funnies, two of which I recall, namely, "Life with Father," and "Buster Brown." I believe that it was possible for me to identify myself with the latter. He was not actually a "bad" boy, but he did get himself into trouble, and I marveled at how he succeeded in getting out of it.

There was an unbelievable freedom in Gendalen. The household was a large one and we were many children, accounting for the fact that we were left much to ourselves. My mother had been brought up in a deeply religious home. Her parents were pietists but still staunch supporters of the State Church. My father had respect for her religion and wanted his household to attend church service when feasible. We did not go often since Gendalen was situated nearly four miles from the parish church at Stora Mellby. I think that I recall his reading from a "postilla" by Fredrik

Hammarsten one Sunday, but this did not become a practice. On Sunday we were dressed in our best clothes. Mother, who was the kindest person in the world, did not wish us to treat Sunday as any other day. To her it was a holy day. To me it became most often a boring day with nothing to do. Once I was caught by my mother in the woodshed whittling away with a knife on a stick. My mother said, "Fritiof, do you not believe that God will see you even in this woodshed?" Perhaps because of my mother many of the stories in the Bible appealed to me. Moses and Joseph seemed to have wrestled with problems which were also mine. We said grace faithfully before and after our meals, and evening prayers were seldom forgotten. But there seemed to be little or no compulsion in these matters. In Gothenburg there were Sunday schools, but our "kind of people" did not attend these. We held pietists and particularly sectarians in low esteem.

The tutors certainly did much to guide our education, stressing the 3 R's and German. There was endless drill in grammar in spelling. The tutors gave their entire time to us children, and their major interest was to make it possible for us to enter the second class in the "realskola." This type of education was deadening. It was far more pleasant to sneak away into the attic and join the vikings of old in brave contests, share the many experiences of the ancient gods, and especially Thor in his war against the giants. Hans Christian Andersen was usually read with fullest approval of the parents, I am sure, and these, too, would not have objected to the *Eddas* and works of Tegner and Geijer. Fritiof's Saga had been the source for my own name. But the attic yielded other treasures, which were not for young boys, namely, Boccaccio's *Decameroné* and Balzac's *Droll Stories*. These made deep impressions upon my mind. Immorality was amusing and sensual, but gullibility became an unpardonable sin. How much Boccaccio and Balzac contributed toward the crumbling of Gendalen, the world of ideal and fantasy, I do not know. This world was not destroyed by any single blow.

In order to educate the children, my parents moved to Gothenburg, and Gendalen became a summer home. Christmas was always celebrated in Gendalen. My father established a branch of his business in Gothenburg, but World War I destroyed his cheese sales. Cheese was no longer to be had. Food became very scarce and was rationed. Mother died in 1916.

Poor health and business worries would bring on my father's death three years later. These were the most serious blows to a world of fantasy. The central characters of that world were being removed.

Meanwhile my literary interests were expanding and seemed perfectly natural in their development. From Esaias Tegner and Gustaf Geijer the literary adventures went to John Runeberg and Zacharias Topelius; courage and valor as well as patriotism were nourished. In the years before World War I there was a widespread scare in Sweden of the Russian bear, and many tramps, peddlers or "saw and knife sharpeners" were thought to be spies. Newspapers capitalized upon an awakened nationalism. Runeberg kept alive the memories of the war with Russia in 1809 when Sweden lost Finland. Topelius fostered images of great kings and courageous men when religious prejudices were deep. Russians and Catholics were to be feared indeed.

It is not clear exactly how Sweden's poets of the late nineteenth century fit into the picture, but a few of these also left their imprint upon me. Perhaps to strengthen the fortress around my world, I developed a passion for Swedish novels of the late nineteenth century, particularly Emilie Flygare-Carlén's works. In these the courage and valor of the past were transplanted into the contemporary world as modern man struggled with other forces than giants and trolls. But a more sophisticated young adolescent craved other lands. A period of illness provided ample time to read fairly extensively from the works of Victor Hugo and Alexander Dumas. Gallantry as a new vision appeared important. There had been gallantry in the Wild West stories, but never more magnificent than in the adventures of *The Three Musketeers* or the *Count of Monte Christo.* Someone else in the household must have become interested in Jack London and for a short time London's stories seemed to be true, for few children liked dogs better than I did. My older brother developed a taste for detective stories, and Sherlock Holmes and Arséne Lupin adventures were avidly read. Somewhere I became acquainted with August Strindberg. Mother had died and the walls of the fortress of fantasy and ideals had developed serious cracks, which I had failed to notice. Now the walls tumbled. I read *The Red Room* and I believe most of the works of Strindberg, including his history of Sweden. My mind was not prepared to repair the damage done by Strindberg, and I became an unhappy, restless young man.

I looked for adventures on the sea as World War I ended, and these brought me to ports in North and South America. The life of a sailor was very different indeed from life in Gendalen. John Steinbeck is undoubtedly correct in *Travels with Charlie* when he compares truck drivers upon our main American highways with sailors. They travel over a great deal of country without seeing anything. I was eager to terminate my experiences, and upon the ship's return to Gothenburg, I hurried to Gendalen. I wished to recapture something which was lost. But Gendalen was only a shell, it seemed to me, of what it had been.

Shortly after my arrival in Gendalen my father came home from an extended "rest" at a resort. He was a sick man, soon to die. One day he called me into his room. It was a most memorable meeting. I did not know my father very well, since he had always seemed so busy. People held him in high regard. He was respected, perhaps a little feared. He knew how to command and he expected to be obeyed. Yet, he loved to watch the smaller children play. This time he was kindness itself. If I had thought that I would be reprimanded, my fears were groundless. He wanted to talk to me about my future, and the most amazing thing was that he made no demands upon me. I was free to do anything that I wished.

My wish was to join the office staff of my father's company. However, after my father's death I served in the Swedish army. Reading, movies, and camaraderie could only temporarily relieve a general feeling of aimlessness, and one day while talking to a friend over the telephone, I said: "I am bored to death. I think that I will go to America." No thought could have been further away from my mind. I do not know why I said it, but I had. My friend replied: "If you go to America, I will go along." So it happened that in 1922 a young man, who still wanted to feel very much at home in Gendalen, exchanged his world of make-believe for America. A little later at Augustana College, the most challenging task became to recreate a new world, an inner meaningful world.

What thought I might have had as I waved good-bye to my relatives, I do not know. One does not say good-bye to Gendalen. Chance or accident had played an important role already in my young life. I found no work to my liking in Chicago, my American destination. Rather than to idle my time away, I was advised to attend Augustana College and I did so perhaps just in order to do something. A significant religious experience caused me to give thought to an education in preparation for the ministry. This gave me direction.

Augustana seemed to me, at first glance, to be an unsophisticated place, but I soon learned to love its teachers and my loyalties for the college grew day by day. But it was a gradual process of which I could hardly have been conscious during the first two years. As I did not meet the requirements for entrance into the college, I was permitted to enroll in the academy where the education was very similar to what I had experienced in Sweden. Thus I had no difficulties and found my academic program very light. This must have become apparent to the principal of the academy, Professor August W. Kjellstrand, who was to play an important role in guiding my education. Kjellstrand encouraged me to do a great deal of reading during the summer of 1923 in order to meet the requirements for graduation from the academy. Among the recommended readings were works by Walter Scott and Richard D. Blackmore, namely, *Ivanhoe* and *Lorna Doone*. Scott and *Ivanhoe* were no strangers to me, but it was important for me to read and think in the English language. Neither Scott nor Blackmore did anything to assist me in the task which was mine, namely, to recreate a new image of the world.

At one stage I grew impatient and restless but was prevented by Kjellstrand from withdrawing from the college. He arranged for me to be invited to the home of the president, Dr. Gustaf Andreen, who treated me with coffee and cookies in a "Swedish manner." Kjellstrand was there, too, and we conversed cheerfully in Swedish after I had been given a chance to air my complaints. Next to Kjellstrand, Andreen came to play the most important part in my life, directing it back to Augustana upon the completion of my graduate work at Illinois.

My own love and affection for Augustana grew as I did my graduate work. Though I have never seemed more happy and content than when I was a graduate student, Augustana took on new dimensions; it was more and more replacing my old world of fantasy, my Gendalen. I believe that it is important for a person to have such a dream by which to live. Thus I was most happy to leave the University of Illinois and come to Augustana as a teacher. I had never dared to entertain such a dream. The Augustana of 1930 to which I returned was a very different place in many ways. The faculty had been enlarged and the standards had become higher. College courses and majors had increased.

Many times since 1930 I have sought to recapture a part of Gendalen, my childhood. This is perhaps no uncommon experience for an immigrant. I have done so with a clear intent, and with careful plans. I felt it was so much a part of myself that I could not lose it. In company with my wife I have visited and revisited Sweden. I have gone to Gendalen to relive old experiences. I have, with my oldest brother, gone to the old swimming hole. It was no longer there. The hills in which we rode bravely and swiftly down on our sleighs had shrunk. I walked along the creek together with a nephew, fishing pole in hand, knowing full well that there were no fish in the creek. Visiting the grave of my parents and sitting in the pew of the parish church provided no Aladdin's lamp. The doors to Gendalen were closed forever, but new ones had opened at Augustana.

In an effort to analyze my childhood world, I see many characters moving about — parents, brothers, sisters, all in the setting of my home, Gendalen. They move, they talk, they love, they laugh, and they are happy. I, the creator of the characters, remain in the background although I must have been in the very center of things as I made them move and react as they did. It was my world, a world of my making. But Gendalen had no permanence. The characters died or grew older. Gendalen simply could not be saved. No one of the family wanted it. Gendalen was sold. Its park-like garden with its numerous grottos has fallen into decay. Now it is only a place which once was or was thought to be.

The world which replaced it seems more permanent. It is true that here, too, certain characters, the old venerable teachers, have played their part. There is much of the past in the dream of Augustana, just as in that of Gendalen. But while Gendalen is like a book from which many chapters have been permanently lost, Augustana is like a book which is yet to be completed. Gendalen grew musty, staled by time; Augustana lives. As it lives, new characters move in to replace the old, and generation upon generation of new students enter its halls, making and expanding the dream and hope for Augustana.

# *One Does Not Say Goodbye to Gendalen*

Betsey Brodahl

The man whose world once was Gendalen may write of it as a world which crumbled, died, and is no more, but many of us who are his students have seen it alive and continue to see it in the man who is Fritiof Ander.

As his narrative "Recollections of a Childhood and Youth" ends, Fritiof Ander has moved from Gendalen and found place and purpose as a student and teacher in America. The place was Augustana which he describes as his new world. From the two worlds — Sweden (Gendalen) and America (Augustana) — came the central interests of his life — the immigrant, the Sweden from which so many came, and the America which the immigrants helped to shape.

This interest led him from Augustana to the University of Illinois to do graduate study and assist in the History Department. In 1927, the year he earned his Master's degree, Fritiof Ander taught at Trinity Junior College in Round Rock, Texas. After the one year he returned to the University of Illinois to complete the degree of Doctor of Philosophy in 1931 and to take up an Associate Professorship in the History Department at Augustana. This was to be his work — the teacher-scholar — and this was the place — Augustana. He became full professor, Head of the Department of History and Chairman of the Division of Social Studies.

From time to time he left the campus. There were two Guggenheim

Fellowships awarded to Dr. Ander (1938, 1940) which allowed him to do research in Sweden in preparation for *The Building of Modern Sweden: The Reign of Gustaf V*. Other awards for research and writing came from the American Council of Learned Societies, the Social Science Research Council, the American Philosophical Society, as well as from Fullbright funds. Usually Dr. Ander did his work in Sweden, writing not only historical studies of Sweden and the immigrant, but preparing guides to the use of Swedish sources in the United States and Sweden for the encouragement of other scholars. The king of Sweden recognized the importance of his scholarship and conferred upon him the Order of the North Star, and Uppsala University bestowed upon him the Doctor of Theology degree.

As a teacher Dr. Ander was visiting professor at the University of Minnesota and the University of Illinois. Under the sponsorship of the State Department he lectured at Swedish universities. Each time he returned to take up his work with continuing confidence in the opportunity that was his with Augustana students. Choosing the small campus as his place of work and giving it his life-time effort, he nonetheless maintained personal as well as professional association with the main stream of scholars in history. Always politic, he took students with him to professional meetings, introduced them to leading historians, maintained close connection with the graduate schools, and brought to his own campus to lecture and lead seminars the scholars whose works his students read.

Fritiof Ander always took his work seriously. He commanded in the classroom, went to battle in the faculty meeting, goaded in the administrative office. This same man consoled when a student's best effort failed, acknowledged his own error with grace, and was ever ready with encouragement and praise for what he thought worthy. Grand in manner and dramatic in speech, he was saved from the pompous by a remarkable ability to laugh at himself.

With him in these ventures was Ruth Johnson whom he married while a student at Augustana and who has shared in an unusually complete way the work of the teacher, the life of the campus, the association with students and scholars. Theirs was a home of warmth, welcome and hospitality. Their 34th Street, just off the Augustana Campus, was no Gendalen; but Fritiof Ander would stride about it as though it were his estate. He extended the Ander hospitality and concern to encompass its people as the family of the manor.

The boy whose mind and imagination were fired with the wonder of the books at Gendalen has lived always among books, has made books and their resources come alive for the student, has written his own books, and has made the development of libraries a major interest in his life.

The world of Gendalen is not lost. This is no ordinary man, Fritiof Ander. He knew Gendalen and it made a difference.

# *Bibliography of the Published Writings of Dr. O. Fritiof Ander*

Compiled by ERNEST M. ESPELIE

Dr. O. Fritiof Ander's stimulating personality and scholarly interests have influenced many generations of Augustana students. His first published work was his doctoral thesis treating the pioneer Swedish-American theologian, T. N. Hasselquist, the second president of Augustana College. Professor Ander's published writings, spanning nearly forty years, have stamped him as one of the foremost scholars in America treating the history of the Swedish immigrant.

It is appropriate that Professor Ander should be honored at this time when his native land is awakening to the importance of the study of Swedish emigration to America. During the mid-1960's two new institutes to study the causes of the exodus of a million and a quarter Swedes to the Americas have been established in Sweden, one at the University of Uppsala and the other at Växjö.

Not all of Professor Ander's work is included in this bibliography. There are dozens of book reviews in professional journals as well as many speeches which are not included. A quick scanning of the list of books and articles will reveal that he has always been busy. There is hardly a year that he did not have something published, and more often than not two or three projects were undertaken concurrently. Not only has he constantly been engaged in research, but he has been the stimulus for hundreds of Augustana students. Some of these students are contributors to this volume.

## BIBLIOGRAPHY OF THE PUBLISHED WRITINGS OF DR. O. FRITIOF ANDER

### *BOOKS and PAMPHLETS*

*T. N. Hasselquist: The Career and Influence of a Swedish-American Clergyman, Journalist and Educator* . . . [Rock Island, 1931] 260 pp. 2 ports. (Augustana Library Publications, no. 14)

Issued also by the Augustana Historical Society as its Publication no. 1, and as Dr. Ander's Ph.D. thesis (Univ. of Illinois).

*Some Letters Pertaining to the Proposed Minnesota Synod.* (Rock Island, 1933) 31 pp.

"Translated and edited by O. F. Ander."

*Guide to the Material on Swedish History in the Augustana College Library.* (Rock Island, 1934) 75 pp. [Augustana Historical Society Publication, vol. 4, pt. 2]

Alternate pages left blank.

*Augustana Historical Society Publications,* vol. V. (Rock Island, 1935) 160 pp.

Dr. Ander was the editor of this volume.

*Swedish-American Political Newspapers* . . . (Stockholm-Uppsala, 1936) 28 pp.

"A guide to the collections in the Royal Library, Stockholm, and the Augustana College Library, Rock Island."

*The American Origin of the Augustana Synod; from Contemporary Lutheran Periodicals, 1851-1860.* (Rock Island, 1942) 192 pp. (Augustana Historical Society Publications, vol. 9)

"A collection of source material, gathered and edited by O. Fritiof Ander and Oscar L. Nordstrom."

*Illinois, a Bibliography.* [Springfield, Illinois State Library, 1948] v.p.

Mimeographed.

"Compiled by O. Fritiof Ander, 1948."

Also in *Illinois Libraries,* 30:386-408, Oct. 1948.

*This is Illinois.* A pictorial history, by Jay Monaghan. (Univ. of Chicago Press, [1949]) 211 pp. plates.

"Fiftieth anniversary publication of the Illinois State Historical Society."

"Committee to help select pictures: John H. Hauberg, O. Fritiof Ander."

*Mores and American Presidential Elections* . . . (Malung, Sweden, Malungs Accidenstryckeri, 1952) 16 pp.

"An address delivered before the Swedish-American Association of Borås on November 27, 1952, and dedicated to Alex Angblom . . ."

*The John H. Hauberg Historical Essays.* Compiled and edited by O. Fritiof Ander. [Rock Island, 1954] 70 pp. ports., plates. (Augustana Library Publications, no. 26)

*The Cultural Heritage of the Swedish Immigrant; Selected References.* [Rock Island, 1956] 191 pp. (Augustana Library Publications, no. 27)

An invaluable bibliography of the Swedish immigrant in America.

*The Building of Modern Sweden; The Reign of Gustav V, 1907-1950.* [Rock Island, 1958] 271 pp. (Augustana Library Publications, no. 28)

*Lincoln Images: Augustana College Centennial Essays* . . . Edited by O. Fritiof Ander. (Rock Island, 1960) 161 pp. ports. (Augustana Library Publications, no. 29)

"Dedicated to Carl Sandburg, a son of Swedish immigration."

*In the Trek of the Immigrants: Essays Presented to Carl Wittke.* Edited by O. Fritiof Ander. (Rock Island, 1964) 325 pp. port. (Augustana Library Publications, no. 31)

Also:

Co-founder of *Illinois Junior Historian* (Oct. 1947) and co-editor of vols. 1 and 2 (1947-49). *Illinois History* since Jan., 1957.

Co-founder of *American Heritage* (1947)

*ARTICLES*

"Swedish-American Newspapers and the Republican Party," *Augustana Historical Society Publications,* no. 2, pp. 64-78, Rock Island, 1932.

"Some Factors in the Americanization of the Swedish Immigrant, 1850-1890," *Journal of the Illinois State Historical Society,* 26:136-50, April-July, 1933.

"The Immigrant Church and the Patrons of Husbandry," *Agricultural History,* 8:155-68, Oct., 1934.
Also reprinted.

"Possibilities of Historical Research at Augustana College," *Faculty Viewpoints: A Seventy-fifth Anniversary Publication,* by Augustana College, Rock Island, 1935. pp. 7-10.

"The Swedish-American Press and the Election of 1892," *The Mississippi Valley Historical Review,* 23:533-54, March, 1937.

"The Swedish-American Press and the American Protective Association," *Church History,* 6:165-79, June, 1937.

"The Thirty-fourth Annual Meeting of the Mississippi Valley Historical Association," *The Mississippi Valley Historical Review,* 28:207-18, Sept. 1941.

"The Effects of the Immigration Law of 1924 upon a Minority Immigrant Group," American Historical Association, *Annual Report for 1942,* vol. 3, pp. 343-52.
Also in reprint form (Washington, 1944)

"The Agricultural Revolution and Swedish Emigration," American Swedish Historical Museum. *Yearbook,* 1945. Philadelphia, 1945. pp. 48-54.

"The New Augustana Plan and an American Studies Major," *The Mississippi Valley Historical Review,* 32:95-100, June, 1945.

"What about Teaching the History of Illinois in Our Public Schools?" *Journal of the Illinois State Historical Society,* 39:196-207, June, 1946.

"State Historical Societies and the Teaching of History," by O. F. Ander and Hazel Phillips. *Social Education,* 11:22-23, Jan., 1947.

"An Experiment in Education in Rock Island County, Illinois," *Illinois Libraries,* 29:150-55, April 1947.

"Our Aims and Plans for Teaching State and Local History in Rock Island County," *Educational Press Bulletin,* 38:18-22, May, 1947.

"A Functional Major in the Social Studies for Future Teachers," *The School Review: a Journal of Secondary Education,* 58:541-47, Dec., 1950.

"The Church Libraries," *Illinois Libraries,* 34:69-75, March, 1952.

"John H. Hauberg, 'The Standing Bear'," *Journal of the Illinois State Historical Society,* 45:136-45, Summer, 1952. Port., plate.
Also reprinted (11 p.)

"Are Our Public Libraries Obligated to Collect and Preserve the Historical Records of the Community?" *Illinois Libraries,* 34:442-47, Dec. 1952.

"The Public Libraries of Scandinavia," *Illinois Libraries,* 35:191-99, May, 1953. Illus.

"A Home Crafts Collection; Unique Gift to Augustana from Swedish Woman," *The Lutheran Companion,* 98:17-18, June 24, 1953.

"Foss Tradition at Augustana: Historians Return to Views of Famous Teacher," *The Lutheran Companion,* 98:11, Oct. 14, 1953. Port.

"The Augustana College Archives," *Illinois Libraries,* 37:168-75, June, 1955; 40: 279-86, Apr., 1958.

"A New Chapter in Interlibrary Relations," *Illinois Libraries,* 40:627-29, Sept., 1958.
Quad-city area cooperation during National Library Week (1958) is detailed.

"Meet Mr. S. W. McMaster," Rock Island *Argus,* Feb. 28, March 7, 14, and 21, 1959.

"Building in a Brave New World; the Swedish Immigrants in Illinois," *Illinois History,* 12:150-52, March, 1959.

"Law and Lawlessness in Rock Island Prior to 1850," *Journal of the Illinois State Historical Society,* 52:526-43, Winter, 1959. Illus.

"Augustana-Kyrkan vid sitt Sekelskifte," *Kyrkohistorisk Årsskrift,* 60:[146]-84, 1960.
Also in pamphlet form (Stockholm, Almqvist & Wiksell, 1960)

"Lincoln and the Founders of Augustana College," *Lincoln Images: Augustana College Centennial Essays.* Rock Island, 1960. pp. 1-22.
This article also appears in *The Swedish Pioneer Historical Quarterly,* 11:45-72, April, 1960, with footnotes.

"Immigrationshistoriens utveckling i Amerika," *Historisk Tidskrift,* 81:289-304, Nov., 1961.
Also reprinted (Stockholm, P. A. Norstedt, 1961)

"Invandrarna och Amerikas Skolvasen," *Kristendomslärarnas Förenings Årsbok,* 5:59ff., Uppsala, 1961.

"Reflections on the Causes of Emigration from Sweden," *The Swedish Pioneer Historical Quarterly,* 13:143-54, Oct., 1962.

"An Immigrant Community during the Progressive Era," *The Swedish Immigrant Community in Transition: Essays in Honor of Dr. Conrad Bergendoff.* Rock Island, 1963. pp. 147-66.

"The Swedish-American Press in the Election of 1912," *The Swedish Pioneer Historical Quarterly,* 14:103-26, July, 1963.

"Four Historians of Immigration," *In the Trek of the Immigrants: Essays Presented to Carl Wittke.* Rock Island, 1964. pp. 17-32.

"Sweden," *Collier's Encyclopedia,* 21:683C-683D, 684-89. New York, 1965. Fold. col. map, illus.
This article, covering both cultural life and history, is jointly written by O. F. Ander and R. E. Lindgren.

"The Two Worlds of George Malcolm Stephenson, 1883 to 1958; the American Dream and Twentieth-Century Reality," *Kyrkohistorisk Årsskrift,* 65:[237]-57, 1965.
J. Iverne Dowie, joint author.

Also in pamphlet form (Stockholm, Almqvist & Wiksell, 1965)

# *Index*

# *A Note on Contributors*

O. Fritiof Ander was chairman of the department of history at Augustana College for many years prior to retirement. Among his many publications is *The Building of Modern Sweden.*

Conrad Bergendoff served as president of Augustana College for twenty-seven years. He combined his administrative duties with his career as professional historian. He is presently writing a history of Augustana College.

Theodore C. Blegen is emeritus dean of the graduate school of the University of Minnesota. In addition to his administrative role, Professor Blegen has devoted his career of professional historian to immigration. Since retiring from the University in 1960 Dean Blegen has been associated with the Minnesota Historical Society where he has continued his researches in Minnesota history.

Betsey Brodahl began her teaching career at Augustana College in 1947. In addition to her assignment with the history department she serves in the college administration as dean of women.

Merle Curti has had a distinguished career in American intellectual history at the University of Wisconsin. He has written extensively in his field. In 1947 he received the honor of being designated the Turner Professor at Wisconsin.

J. Iverne Dowie is professor of history at Augustana College. He has concentrated upon immigration and British history.

Ernest M. Espelie served for twenty years as librarian at the U.S. Coast Guard Academy at New London, Conn. He assumed his duties as librarian of Augustana College in 1959. He is editor of the Augustana College Library Publications.

A. Ben Jasper began his teaching in the art department at Augustana in 1963. He is presently chairman of the department, and his special interests include print making and painting.

Emory Lindquist is the author of *Smoky Valley People.* While he is at present in administration, serving as president of the University of Wichita, he has continued to pursue his professional interest in immigration history.

Ross Paulson is an associate professor of history at Augustana College and currently on leave as visiting scholar on the campus of Rice University. In 1967 he achieved distinction by winning the Frederic Jackson Turner History Prize for the best manuscript. His monograph on the Vrooman family has recently been published.

Franklin D. Scott is a distinguished historian who has been teaching at Northwestern University since 1935. Many of Professor Scott's publications fall in the field of immigration history. In 1962 he was visiting professor at Stanford University. Recently Professor Scott has spent time in Africa where he has extended his interests in African history.

C. W. Sorensen is president of Augustana College. President Sorensen is a professional geographer by training, and he continues to publish extensively in that field.

J. Thomas Tredway is a member of the Augustana history department. This past year he has been visiting professor at Waterloo University in Canada. Professor Tredway is currently researching the life and writings of John Henry Newman.

Carl Wittke was dean of the graduate school at Western Reserve University prior to his retirement in 1963. Professor Wittke has the distinction of being among the eminent pioneer immigration historians. He has written extensively on American immigrants with particular attention to German-Americans.

Benedict K. Zobrist was Command historian with U.S. Ordnance Command prior to his affiliation with Augustana College. He began to teach at Augustana in 1955. His special areas include American diplomatic and Asian history. He is chairman of the Augustana department of history.